Food Innovation and Legal Challenges

Food Innovation and Legal Challenges

Edited by

Lucia Scaffardi
Chiara Cerbone

BRILL | NIJHOFF

This publication was funded by the following project:

Project funded under the National Recovery and Resilience Plan (NRRP), Mission 4 Component 2 Investment 1.3—Call for tender No. 341 of 15 March 2022 of Italian Ministry of University and Research funded by the European Union—NextGenerationEU;
Project code PE00000003, Concession Decree No. 1550 of 11 October 2022 adopted by the Italian Ministry of University and Research, Project title 'ON Foods—Research and innovation network on food and nutrition Sustainability, Safety and Security—Working ON Foods'.

This book is available as an open access publication via https://www.degruyterbrill.com

ISBN 978-90-04-74089-1
ISBN 978-90-04-74090-7 (PDF)
DOI https://doi.org/10.1163/9789004740907

Library of Congress Control Number: 2026932145

Brill Nijhoff and Koninklijke Brill BV are part of De Gruyter Brill.
www.degruyterbrill.com

Questions about General Product Safety Regulation: productsafety@degruyterbrill.com

Contents

Preface

Innovation in the agrifood sector has always stood at the intersection of science, law, and society. Today, the challenges of ensuring sustainability, safety, and security in food systems demand not only technological progress but also thoughtful regulatory responses. This volume emerges within this dynamic context as a collective reflection on how legal frameworks can guide, accompany, and sometimes restrain the transformative power of innovation in the food chain.

The book brings together contributions developed under the Research Project *'Regulating technological innovation for a sustainable agrifood chain: from GMOs to vertical farming—INN_LEG'*, part of *Spoke 1, 'Global Sustainability—Fair food market for healthy citizens'*, within the broader project *'ON Foods—Research and innovation network on food and nutrition Sustainability, Safety and Security—Working ON Foods'*. Funded through the Italian National Recovery and Resilience Plan (Mission 4, Component 2, Investment 1.3—Call No. 341 of 15 March 2022, Ministry of University and Research) and supported by the European Union—*NextGenerationEU* (Project Code PE00000003, Concession Decree No. 1550 of 11 October 2022), ON Foods represents a major national investment in the future of food.

At the core of INN_LEG lies an exploration of how technological advances—from genetic modification and gene editing to vertical farming—reshape the legal and ethical landscape of the agrifood chain. The research, coordinated by Professor Lucia Scaffardi and carried out by three university teams (University of Parma, University of Bari 'Aldo Moro', and University of Milan), forms the conceptual foundation of this collective work. Each chapter examines, from a legal and policy perspective, how innovation can coexist with sustainability, fairness, and public trust.

The diversity of perspectives reflected in these pages mirrors the collaborative spirit that has animated the project. Scholars from various Italian universities and institutions have joined forces to offer a multidisciplinary and cross-sectoral approach. The intended readership extends far beyond the academic sphere: policymakers, public authorities, professionals in the food industry, researchers, and citizens are all invited to engage with these analyses, conceived to inform public debate, support evidence-based policymaking, and counter misinformation and ideological polarization.

This volume has benefited from the generous contributions and dedication of many individuals and institutions. The Editors express their deepest gratitude to all the authors for their insightful work and to Professor Laura Pineschi for her rigorous coordination and her expert supervision of the sections devoted to international law. Special thanks are due to Marica Mileo for her careful editorial review and steadfast collaboration, and to Kaveri Marathe for the precise and thoughtful English language revision. We are equally grateful to the BRILL editorial team for their professional guidance and enduring support throughout the publication process.

We also wish to acknowledge the scientific leadership of Professor Daniele Del Rio, Chair of the ON Foods Foundation Board of Directors and Scientific Coordinator of the Project, and to thank Professor Filippo Arfini, responsible for Spoke 1, within which the INN_LEG research was conducted. The Department of Law, Politics and International Studies of the University of Parma has provided essential institutional backing within the broader 'Food for Future' Project (Department of Excellence 2023–2027).

Lucia Scaffardi
Chiara Cerbone

Figures and Tables

Figures

Tables

Introduction

The agrifood sector is experiencing profound transformation driven by scientific breakthroughs, technological advancements, and the intensifying imperative to develop sustainable and resilient food systems. While long-standing legal concerns—such as the right to food, food security, policies to address food loss and waste, intellectual property protection, and food safety regulations—remain central to legal and policy discussions, emerging regulatory challenges are also arising from rapid innovations in food production, processing, and distribution. Cutting-edge developments in biotechnology, precision agriculture, alternative proteins, and digital farming technologies necessitate a reassessment of existing regulatory frameworks, which often struggle to keep pace with scientific progress and its social implications.

These advancements raise fundamental questions: how can legal systems balance the competing interests of innovation, consumer protection, environmental sustainability, and food security? To what extent should regulatory frameworks be harmonised internationally, and where should national and regional legislators retain autonomy? Which legal instruments best ensure that innovation in the agrifood sector is consistent with basic values, such as public health, ethics, and socio-economic justice? Answering these questions requires a multidimensional and interdisciplinary approach that extends beyond standard doctrinal legal analysis to encompass socio-economic, ethical, and political considerations.

This volume contributes to this discourse by offering a systematic and interdisciplinary analysis of the evolving legal framework on food innovation. It stems from the OnFoods project, a collaborative initiative bringing together legal scholars, economists, and policy experts from diverse backgrounds. The research team encompasses both academics with extensive expertise in agrifood law and early-career scholars whose work reflects the latest methodological and thematic advancements in the field. As the project nears completion, we are committed to disseminating its findings broadly, through an open-access publication, to maximise its impact within academic, professional, and policy-making communities.

The volume is structured into three main parts, each addressing distinct yet interconnected aspects of food innovation and their legal implications.

The first part, 'Innovation in the Agrifood Sector', opens with a chapter by Lorenza Violini, who outlines a theoretical framework by exploring the intersection of law, science, and technological progress in the agrifood domain.

Specific attention is devoted to the issue of sustainability, which emerges as a crucial element for the protection of fundamental rights. Given its economic, environmental, and social implications, sustainability calls for a strategic regulatory approach rather than a merely static planning model.

From the second chapter onwards, the focus shifts to selected aspects of the international legal framework and the regulatory approach adopted by the European Union. In particular, the chapter by Ludovica Di Lullo examines various instruments of international law—such as the Agreement on Trade-Related Aspects of Intellectual Property Rights (TRIPS), the International Treaty on Plant Genetic Resources for Food and Agriculture (ITPGRFA), and the recent World Intellectual Property Organisation Treaty on Intellectual Property, Genetic Resources and Associated Traditional Knowledge (WIPO Treaty)—highlighting how international law fosters food innovation and ensures food security through the regime of intellectual property rights. In this context, the analysis seeks to assess whether the rules on the protection of patents and plant varieties facilitate or hinder access to agricultural technologies, and whether this, in turn, may affect the enjoyment of certain human rights.

From the perspective of European Union (EU) law, Nicola Bergamaschi's contribution focuses on the EU's efforts to support research and innovation in the agrifood sector. It draws attention to the role played by EU funding mechanisms, notably, the 'Horizon Europe' research programme and the Common Agricultural Policy (CAP), in assessing the centrality of food innovation and sustainable development in EU policymaking.

A further central theme concerns the regulation of so-called Novel Foods within the EU, with specific reference to the legal and economic challenges associated with edible insects and lab-grown meat. This topic is addressed in the chapters authored, respectively, by Maria Laura Grilli and Giulia Formici, Giacomo Degli Antoni, and Marco Faillo. Maria Laura Grilli highlights the potential of Novel Foods as sustainable protein sources with high nutritional value and reflects on regulatory challenges, consumer scepticism, and fragmented national policies—factors that frequently hinder the commercialisation of such products.

The chapter by Giulia Formici, Giacomo Degli Antoni, and Marco Faillo, on the other hand, focuses on the results of a survey conducted on a diverse sample of the Italian population and investigates public awareness of the existing regulatory framework concerning cultivated meat and consumer preferences regarding how such regulations ought to be structured.

The second part, 'New Methods of Agricultural Production', examines the transformation of agricultural production systems, with a focus on innovative techniques that may challenge traditional regulatory paradigms.

The opening chapter, by Maria Giulia Corazza, explores the concept of 'Agriculture 4.0', which encompasses the digital transformation of agriculture through big data analytics, artificial intelligence, and precision farming. The adoption of such technologies raises significant legal and regulatory issues concerning data ownership, cybersecurity, liability, and competition law. Against the backdrop of the EU's broader digital strategy, the chapter investigates how regulatory frameworks can support the development of a fair and transparent digital agrifood economy, while simultaneously safeguarding the rights of farmers and the interests of consumers.

Following this line of inquiry, Simone Pitto focuses on the legal implications of vertical farming, an increasingly relevant model of urban and controlled-environment agriculture. This innovative method of production offers a response to the rising demand for food while also promoting sustainable models of food production and consumption. Additionally, the spread of vertical farming has a potentially positive environmental impact, due to its reduced use of water and pesticides. In this context, the chapter examines the current EU regulatory framework—which, however, does not explicitly include vertical farming within its main agricultural policies—and analyses a legislative proposal, developed by a group of young scholars, aimed at providing a subnational legal framework for vertical farming in Italy.

The following chapter, authored by Maria Chiara Errigo, turns to the legal regulation of biotechnologies in the agrifood sector, encompassing both Genetically Modified Organisms (GMOs) and New Genomic Techniques (NGTs). While such techniques and technologies may contribute to enhanced agricultural productivity and climate resilience, they remain highly controversial from a legal, ethical, and political perspective. The chapter evaluates the divergent regulatory approaches adopted in different jurisdictions and assesses the extent to which recent legislative developments within the EU facilitate—or hinder—the adoption of gene-editing techniques in agriculture.

The third and final part, 'Innovation and the Fight Against Food Loss and Waste', addresses one of the most pressing challenges facing contemporary food policy: food loss and waste (FLW). Given the scale of the phenomenon at both the production and consumption levels, reducing FLW is not only an environmental and economic imperative, but also a legal and governance challenge requiring a holistic approach. This part of the volume examines how international and national legal frameworks are evolving to address FLW; evaluates the effectiveness of existing rules and policies; and identifies areas in need of reform.

More specifically, the chapter by Luca Romano examines the role of technological innovation in reducing FLW from the perspective of international law, with a focus on the extent to which binding and non-binding legal instruments—adopted in the context of sustainable development and human rights protection—address this issue. The chapter pays special attention to soft law tools, including the UN Food and Agricultural Organisation's Voluntary Code of Conduct for Reducing Food Loss and Waste, which, while not legally binding, represents a key instrument in promoting innovation in the agrifood sector and fostering international cooperation.

The following chapter, by Chiara Cerbone, provides a comparative legal analysis of the same issue, focusing on legislative and policy measures adopted at both the supranational and national levels to combat food waste and food poverty. The chapter compares the legislative approaches adopted by Italy and France, with particular attention to an experimental measure introduced in Italy—the *reddito alimentare*—which seeks to redistribute surplus food to vulnerable, urban communities.

In a similar vein, but from an agricultural law perspective, the chapter by Laura Costantino examines preventive legal instruments for the sustainable management of agricultural production. Starting from the framework of the CAP, this chapter analyses the Italian legal system, with a special focus on the role of key actors—legislators, policymakers, public administrations, and producers—in implementing policies capable of effectively balancing production and consumption to limit food waste.

Finally, Alessia Depietri's chapter considers the 'bioeconomy strategy' as a crucial approach to addressing food waste and promoting circularity in the agrifood sector. By analysing legal instruments aimed at encouraging the use of agrifood by-products in biorefining, biomaterials, and energy production, the chapter highlights the role of law in fostering sustainable and resource-efficient food systems.

While many of the topics explored in this volume have been the subject of individual studies, its overall novelty lies in its integrated and systematic approach. By bridging multiple disciplines—including Constitutional Law, Agrifood Law, EU Law, International Law, Comparative Public Law, and Administrative Law—the volume offers a comprehensive and nuanced understanding of the complex legal issues arising from food innovation.

The interdisciplinary nature of this open-access publication is further strengthened by the diverse expertise developed within the broader OnFoods project, spanning different areas of law and economic policy. This volume also stands out for its strong commitment to early-career researchers, who play a central role in its development. Over the past year, PhD students, postdoctoral fellows, and assistant professors have actively contributed to this project through research networks, presentations at scientific conferences and workshops, and interdisciplinary training initiatives. By featuring their work alongside contributions from senior academic scholars, this volume provides a unique platform for emerging voices in the field.

In conclusion, 'Food Innovation and Legal Challenges' intends to make a groundbreaking contribution to the study of legal and regulatory issues in the agrifood sector. By combining theoretical analysis with case studies and policy-oriented recommendations, it seeks to inform the academic debate, have an impact on the legal process, and support stakeholders—including policymakers, industry leaders, and civil society organisations—in navigating the evolving landscape of food innovation.

Above all, this volume raises fundamental questions—many of which have been highlighted in this Introduction—concerning the capacity of legal systems to adapt to change, while simultaneously shaping it in accordance with the principles of human dignity and environmental protection.

Lucia Scaffardi
Chiara Cerbone
Parma, 30 July 2025

CHAPTER 1

Reconciling the Fluid and the Rigid: the Intersection of Law, Science, and Sustainability

Lorenza Violini

Summary

1 Introduction

This contribution emerges from reflections developed during my experience as scientific coordinator of the Research Centre 'Innovation for Well-being and Environment' (CRC I-WE, University of Milan), where I have been working to explore the intersections between law and science through the lens of the 'One Health' approach. This interdisciplinary framework has highlighted the urgent need for integrated strategies that address human, animal, and environmental health in a unified manner. In pursuing this research, I have come to recognize that we stand at the early stages of a crucial and ambitious scholarly path—one that demands deeper engagement with the evolving connections between legal systems, scientific knowledge, and sustainability imperatives.

The aim of this contribution is to offer an introductory analysis of the dynamic relationship between law and science, examine the emergence of sustainability as a core principle in regulatory thinking, and explore its growing relevance across European policy frameworks and sectoral applications. In particular, the discussion will focus on key challenges facing sustainability governance, recent legislative developments such as the European Green Deal, and national-level implementations. The paper will also consider the implications of sustainability for strategic regulation, especially within the food sector,

HTTPS://DOI.ORG/10.1163/9789004740907-003

as part of a broader transition toward long-term, adaptive, and interdisciplinary policymaking.

2 The Dynamic Relationship between Law and Science

Scholars and practitioners have long attempted to understand the complex relationship between law and science. At the heart of this ongoing discussion is a recognition of the distinctive nature of each field: while science is inherently dynamic, ever evolving, and based on continuous research and discovery, law has traditionally been perceived as more static, designed to provide a stable framework of rules and regulations to guide society. The central challenge that has emerged—and continues to evolve—is how to reconcile the fluidity of scientific progress with the relative rigidity of legal structures in a way that allows for both scientific innovation and legal coherence.[1]

Historically, this relationship has been explored through a variety of lenses, including jurisprudence, philosophy, administrative law, and, more recently, interdisciplinary approaches that bring together experts from both fields. These explorations have raised some fundamental questions, such as: what kind of legislation do we need to accommodate rapid scientific advances? What level of certainty must scientific evidence provide to support the creation of regulations that are not only coherent but also adaptable? Addressing these questions is essential in creating a regulatory system that can keep pace with scientific developments without sacrificing the stability and predictability that the law seeks to provide.

The intersection of law and science affects numerous legal sub-topics, from environmental law and intellectual property to criminal and administrative law. Aspects of each of these areas require legal frameworks to adapt based on evolving scientific knowledge. In environmental law, for example, regulations must respond to new research on climate change and pollution, often based on emerging data that is continuously being refined and updated. In intellectual property law, advancements in biotechnology, pharmaceuticals, and software development challenge traditional ideas of patents and copyrights, creating new demands for legal protections that accommodate rapid innovation without stifling competition or access. In criminal law, the use of forensic science has transformed how evidence is gathered, analysed, and presented in court,

---

1 Natalino Irti and Emanuele Severino, *Dialogo su diritto e tecnica* (Editori Laterza 2001).

but it also raises concerns about the reliability of certain scientific techniques and the ethical implications of their use.

One prominent example of this dynamic relationship can be seen in biotechnology, where innovations in genetics, stem cell research, and synthetic biology have created vast new fields of inquiry and, along with them, significant regulatory challenges.[2] Legal systems worldwide are still grappling with how to address issues such as genetic privacy, the patentability of genes, and the ethical implications of gene editing technologies like Clustered Regularly Interspaced Short Palindromic Repeats (CRISPR). In cases like these, the law must find a way to respond to ethical questions and ensure public safety while allowing for scientific breakthroughs that could lead to improved medical treatments and solutions to pressing health issues. Here, an adaptable regulatory framework is essential, one that can evolve with the technology rather than be rendered obsolete by technology's rapid pace.

Furthermore, the challenge of integrating science and law is also evident in the area of public health. The COVID-19 pandemic demonstrated the need for swift, science-based responses to protect public health, but it also highlighted the tension between rapidly changing scientific data and slower, more deliberate legal processes. Laws and regulations regarding mask mandates, vaccine distribution, and social distancing had to be implemented and adjusted in real-time based on evolving scientific knowledge about the virus. In such situations, policymakers faced the difficult task of balancing the public's need for both timely interventions and lawful and constitutionally sound measures.

2.1 *Reconciling Conflicts between Science and Law*

The need for a flexible, evidence-based approach to regulation is becoming increasingly clear as scientific advances continue to impact society. This means that legal systems should not only be informed by current scientific understanding but should also be designed to adapt as that understanding changes.[3] However, this is easier said than done. The legal process is often slow, partly due to the careful deliberation required to ensure that laws are fair, equitable, and enforceable. Meanwhile, science progresses quickly, with new discoveries sometimes invalidating previous ones. One potential solution is to build mechanisms into laws and regulations that allow for periodic reviews and updates based on the latest scientific evidence. This approach would

2 Sheila Jasanoff (ed), *Reframing Rights: Bioconstitutionalism in the Genetic Age* (MIT Press 2011).

3 Sofia Ranchordás, 'Innovation-Friendly Regulation: The Sunset of Regulation, the Sunrise of Innovation' (2015) 55 Jurimetrics 201.

provide a balance between stability and flexibility, ensuring that laws remain relevant without constantly overhauling the legal system.

Another promising approach to bridging the gap between law and science is to promote greater interdisciplinary collaboration between scientists and legal professionals. By fostering dialogue between these fields, policymakers can gain a more comprehensive understanding of the scientific principles behind various issues, which can inform more nuanced and effective regulation. Legal professionals, on the other hand, can help scientists understand the potential legal implications of their research, encouraging responsible innovation. This interdisciplinary approach has already proven valuable in areas such as environmental protection and health care, where science and law are inextricably linked, and it holds promise for other fields as well. The first example that comes to mind is COVID-19[4] regulation; the law decrees approved in Italy and other countries during the pandemic used an interdisciplinary approach to protect the general interests of society, while trying to preserve as much as possible all the other rights present in the constitutions.[5]

Finally, as science and technology continue to reshape society, it is vital to consider the ethical dimensions of this intersection. While scientific advancements can lead to significant societal benefits, they also raise questions about privacy, fairness, and the appropriate limits of human intervention. Legal frameworks serve as an important means of addressing these ethical concerns by providing guidelines and protections that uphold societal values. However, the ethical implications of scientific advances are often complex and evolving, requiring laws that are both principled and adaptable. In situations in which the general will of society on a certain matter is not unanimous it is particularly important the role that the law can have in balancing all the different interests at stake. One example that has been particularly relevant in Italy recently is the physician-assisted suicide that showed the role of the government in setting the principles on a very divisive matter, also the decision not to regulate a specific matter is important in this sense, it can show that the parliament and the government recognise that, even if there are technological and medical

4 Burmeister, Fabian, et al. 'Toward Architecture-Driven Interdisciplinary Research: Learnings from a Case Study of COVID-19 Contact Tracing Apps'. *Proceedings of the 2022 Symposium on Computer Science and Law*. 2022.

5 Ioanna Pervou, Mpogiatzidis Panagiotis, 'Restrictive human rights measures against the spread of COVID-19: an interdisciplinary approach between law and health-care management'. *International Journal of Human Rights in Healthcare* 17.4, 2024, 475–486.

advancements, it could be impossible to balance the positions present in order not to discriminate anyone.[6]

3 The Rise of Sustainability as a Core Principle

Sustainability has introduced a crucial third dimension to the relationship between law and science, gaining significant traction in recent decades at both the national and international levels.[7] Today, sustainability is not merely a scientific or legal concern; it has become deeply political, reflecting the global discourse of the 2020s. As sustainability takes centre stage in international policy discussions, it becomes increasingly imperative to understand its evolution, legal implications, and scientific foundations, which collectively inform regulatory strategies and governance models worldwide. The successful integration of sustainability criteria into the law requires a multidimensional approach that considers transnational frameworks, regional policies, and legal obligations while aligning with scientific advancements in climate change, resource management, and environmental preservation.

The concept of sustainability[8] has developed via two primary tracks: European and international. At the international level, the 1987 Brundtland Report and the 1992 Rio Earth Summit brought the concept of sustainable development to the global arena. These initiatives emphasized the need for a development model that extends beyond traditional economic indicators like Gross Domestic Product (GDP) and incorporates environmental and social considerations. The Brundtland Report notably defined sustainable development as 'development that meets the needs of the present without compromising the ability of future generations to meet their own needs'. The report advocated for a forward-thinking approach to resource conservation that balanced the need for economic growth with environmental protection. The Rio Earth Summit further cemented these principles, leading to the adoption

6 Luciana Riva, 'The physician-assisted suicide pathway in Italy: Ethical assessment and safe guard approaches' (2024): 21.1 Journal of Bioethical Inquiry 185–192.

7 Ewerton R Mesias and André L Cateli Rosa, 'Sustainable Economic Development: The Necessary Dialogue between Environmental Law and Economics' (2022) 4 (1) Macro Management & Public Policies 21 <https://journals.bilpubgroup.com/index.php/mmpp/article/view/4634/3665> accessed 23 June 2025.

8 Nico J Schrijver, *The evolution of sustainable development in international law: inception, meaning and status* (Martinus Nijhoff Publishers 2008).

of key international agreements, such as Agenda 21[9] and the United Nations Framework Convention on Climate Change (UNFCCC), laying the foundation for subsequent climate policies, including the Kyoto Protocol and the Paris Agreement.[10]

In parallel, at the European level sustainability considerations have been integrated more and more into legal frameworks and policy initiatives.[11] Beginning with the 1986 Single European Act, the European Union (EU) positioned itself as a global leader in sustainability policy, enacting stringent environmental regulations aimed at emissions reduction, circular economy strategies, and biodiversity conservation. The Treaty of Amsterdam (1997) formally incorporated sustainability into EU law, mandating that environmental protection be integrated into all the policies that were not directly focused on environmental topics. This commitment was further reinforced by the European Green Deal, an ambitious policy framework introduced in 2019, which aims to make Europe the first climate-neutral continent by 2050. The Green Deal encompasses wide-ranging legislative measures targeting carbon emissions, energy efficiency, sustainable finance, and green innovation, reflecting an overarching effort to align economic development with ecological responsibility.

These two integration processes—the international and European ones—illustrate the growing recognition that economic performance depends

9 Agenda 21 is a non-binding action plan adopted at the United Nations Conference on Environment and Development (UNCED), also known as the Earth Summit, held in Rio de Janeiro in 1992. It provides a comprehensive framework for sustainable development, addressing issues such as poverty eradication, environmental protection, resource management, and social development. Intended to guide policy at global, national, and local levels, Agenda 21 emphasizes the role of states, international institutions, and civil society in promoting environmentally and socially responsible growth in the 21st century.

10 The United Nations Framework Convention on Climate Change (UNFCCC) is an international treaty adopted at the United Nations Conference on Environment and Development (Earth Summit) in Rio de Janeiro in 1992 and entered into force in 1994. It establishes a global framework for intergovernmental cooperation to combat climate change by stabilizing greenhouse gas concentrations to prevent dangerous anthropogenic interference with the climate system. The Convention provides the foundation for subsequent legally binding instruments, notably the Kyoto Protocol (1997), which introduced quantified emission reduction commitments for developed countries, and the Paris Agreement (2015), which marked a shift toward a universal, bottom-up approach with nationally determined contributions (NDCs) aimed at limiting global warming to well below 2 °C above pre-industrial levels, while pursuing efforts to limit the increase to 1.5 °C.

11 Susan Baker, 'The evolution of European Union environmental policy: from growth to sustainable development?' in Susan Baker and others (eds), *The Politics of sustainable development. Theory, policy and practice within the European Union* (Routledge 2012).

on environmental and social sustainability. Indeed, it necessitates a holistic perspective that evaluates the long-term availability of resources, the resilience of ecosystems, and the well-being of societies. The triple bottom line—a commonly-accepted modern framework for understanding sustainability—encompasses three fundamental, indispensable dimensions: environmental, economic, and social. The environmental dimension focuses on reducing ecological footprints, mitigating climate change, and preserving biodiversity. The economic aspect advocates for sustainable practices that promote resilient economies through green innovation, sustainable business models, and responsible consumption. The social dimension underscores the need for inclusivity, social justice, and equitable access to resources, emphasizing that sustainability must benefit all sectors of society, particularly marginalized communities disproportionately affected by environmental degradation.

As sustainability becomes a central pillar of global governance, an interdisciplinary approach bridging legal frameworks and scientific advancements becomes increasingly necessary. Legal scholars and policymakers must work collaboratively with scientists to develop adaptable regulatory structures that can accommodate our evolving understanding of environmental challenges. Climate science, for instance, plays a crucial role in shaping legal responses to environmental threats, informing policies on carbon emissions, land use, and energy consumption. Emerging fields such as environmental law and ecological economics contribute to the development of legal instruments that integrate scientific data into decision-making processes. The precautionary principle, a cornerstone of environmental law, exemplifies this intersection by advocating for pre-emptive action in cases of scientific uncertainty, thereby preventing irreversible environmental harm.[12]

Moreover, the integration of scientific and sustainability considerations into the legal domain has necessitated the development of compliance mechanisms, monitoring systems, and enforcement strategies to ensure accountability at both the national and international levels. Institutions such as the Intergovernmental Panel on Climate Change (IPCC), the United Nations Environment Programme (UNEP), and the European Environment Agency (EEA) play pivotal roles in conducting scientific assessments, setting regulatory benchmarks, and guiding policy implementation. The emergence of sustainability reporting standards, such as the Global Reporting Initiative (GRI) and the Task Force on Climate-related Financial Disclosures (TCFD), further

12 Nicolas de Sadeleer, 'The precautionary principle in EC health and environmental law' (2006) 12 European Law Journal 139.

underscores the importance of transparency and corporate responsibility in advancing sustainability goals.[13]

The evolving relationship between law, science, and sustainability underscores the need for dynamic, evidence-based regulatory systems capable of responding to complex global challenges. As environmental risks intensify and sustainability becomes a normative imperative, the integration of scientific insights into legal and policy frameworks will be essential for achieving long-term ecological resilience, social equity, and economic stability. Ultimately, a forward-looking, interdisciplinary approach offers the most effective path toward a sustainable future governed by both scientific rigor and legal accountability.

3.1 *Challenges and Potential Solutions to the Future of Sustainability*

Despite significant progress, challenges to fully integrating sustainability into global governance structures remain. One of the primary obstacles is the tension between economic interests and environmental imperatives, particularly in industries reliant on fossil fuels and resource extraction. The transition to a sustainable economy requires comprehensive policy frameworks that incentivize green investments while mitigating socio-economic impacts on labour markets and communities dependent on extractive industries. Carbon pricing mechanisms, green taxation, and subsidy reforms represent potential policy tools to drive the shift toward sustainable economic models while ensuring a just transition for affected populations.

Another key challenge lies in bridging the disparity between developed and developing nations in terms of sustainability capacity and financial resources. Though industrialized nations have historically contributed the most to environmental degradation, developing countries often bear the brunt of climate change consequences while having fewer resources to implement mitigation and adaptation strategies. International agreements, such as the Paris Agreement, emphasize the principle of 'common but differentiated responsibilities', recognizing that sustainability efforts must be tailored to the specific capacities and developmental needs of different nations. Financial instruments like the Green Climate Fund (GCF) have been established to provide financial assistance to developing countries, enabling them to pursue sustainable development pathways while addressing climate vulnerabilities.[14]

---

13 Philippe J Sands, 'The Environment, Community and International Law' (1989) 30 Harvard International Law Journal 393.

14 Christopher D Stone, 'Common but Differentiated Responsibilities in International Law' (2004) 98 American Journal of International Law 276.

Looking ahead, the future of sustainability hinges on the ability of global institutions, national governments, and local communities to collaborate in crafting and implementing inclusive, science-based policies that balance economic, environmental, and social objectives. The role of technological innovation cannot be overstated: advancements in renewable energy, circular economy models, and sustainable urban planning hold the potential to accelerate the transition toward a more resilient and equitable world. Furthermore, public awareness and civic engagement remain crucial in holding governments and corporations accountable, fostering a culture of sustainability that extends beyond policy frameworks to everyday decision-making.

4 The Role of European Law and Policy

Europe has often been a forerunner in not only integrating sustainability into its legal frameworks but also defining tangible metrics to measure success and ensure accountability. From the Maastricht Treaty in 1992, which enshrined the concept of sustainability into European Union (EU) charters, to the Treaty of Amsterdam in 1997, and 1996's 'Blue Book',[15] European policymaking has demonstrated a sustained effort to translate the abstract concept of sustainability into concrete, measurable goals. These initiatives represent a broad commitment to embedding sustainability into the fabric of European governance, ensuring that environmental, economic, and social considerations are not treated in isolation but as interconnected dimensions of sustainable development.[16]

4.1 *The Latest Developments and the European Green Deal*

In the European context, sustainability is no longer viewed solely as a regulatory obligation but as a strategic driver of competitiveness, innovation, and societal well-being. For example, the Europe 2020 initiative and European

15 The 1996 European Blue Book, formally known as 'European Sustainable Cities & Towns Campaign—The Lisbon Action Plan', is a policy document developed under the auspices of the European Commission. It outlines practical strategies and commitments for implementing sustainable development at the local level across Europe, following the principles set out in the 1994 Aalborg Charter. The Blue Book provides a framework for integrating environmental, social, and economic sustainability into urban governance and planning.

16 Nicolas de Sadeleer, 'Sustainable development in EU law: still a long way to go' (2015) 6 Jindal Global Law Review 39.

Green Deal are not limited to environmental sustainability but encompass economic and social dimensions as well. Europe 2020, launched in 2010, set ambitious targets for smart, sustainable, and inclusive growth, emphasizing the role of green innovation, digital transformation, and climate action in fostering long-term economic resilience. The 2019 European Green Deal lays out a comprehensive roadmap to achieve climate neutrality by 2050, promoting sustainable industries, biodiversity conservation, and cleaner energy sources while integrating stringent regulatory mechanisms to monitor progress.

The European Investment Bank (EIB) has played a crucial role in financing sustainable projects to enact this agenda, channelling resources toward renewable energy, circular economy initiatives, and green infrastructure development. Such financial instruments reinforce the EU's commitment to a green transition, demonstrating that sustainability can be both an ethical imperative and an economic opportunity.[17]

This paradigm shift reflects growing recognition that sustainability must be a cornerstone of any new development model, influencing not only environmental policy but also economic and social agendas. By aligning economic incentives with sustainability objectives, the EU is acknowledging that long-term prosperity cannot be achieved without maintaining ecological integrity

4.2 *National Implementations*

This shift extends beyond the supranational level. National governments, regional authorities, and even local municipalities have increasingly aligned their policies with the broader sustainability goals set forth by the EU. Many Member States have integrated sustainability targets into their national legislation, reinforcing the EU's overarching objectives through legally-binding commitments. For instance, Germany's Climate Action Plan 2050[18] offers a roadmap for achieving climate neutrality that aligns with EU targets while addressing country-specific challenges. Similarly, France's Energy Transition Law mandates a reduction in fossil fuel dependence and promotes renewable energy sources.

---

17 Sarah Wolf and others, 'The European Green Deal—more than climate neutrality' (2021) 56 Intereconomics 99 <https://www.intereconomics.eu/contents/year/2021/number/2/article/the-european-green-deal-more-than-climate-neutrality.html> accessed 23 June 2025.

18 Franziska Tanneberger and others, 'Towards net zero CO2 in 2050: An emission reduction pathway for organic soils in Germany' (2021) 27 Mires and Peat article 5 <http://mires-and-peat.net/pages/volumes/map27/map2705.php> accessed 23 June 2025.

Regional and local governments have also taken proactive measures to incorporate sustainability into urban planning, transportation, and waste management strategies. Cities such as Copenhagen, Amsterdam, and Vienna have emerged as global leaders in sustainable urban development, implementing innovative policies to reduce carbon emissions, promote green mobility, and enhance energy efficiency. Smart city initiatives leverage digital technologies to optimize resource use and minimize environmental impact. And the Covenant of Mayors—Europe brings together a network of local governments to achieve climate and energy targets at the grassroots level.

The integration of sustainability into policymaking at all levels underscores its transformative power and central role in shaping the future of law. The legal dimension of sustainability continues to evolve, with the European Court of Justice (ECJ) increasingly adjudicating cases that balance economic freedoms with environmental protections. Landmark rulings have reinforced the principle of sustainability as a fundamental legal consideration, driving new interpretations of existing EU treaties and directives. The precautionary principle, enshrined in EU Environmental Law, exemplifies this legal evolution by prioritizing preventive action in the face of scientific uncertainty.

Scientific advancements have played an equally crucial role in shaping sustainability policies and efforts across Europe by providing an empirical basis for regulatory decisions and policy frameworks. Research in climate science, ecological economics, and sustainable engineering has informed EU legislation, ensuring that policies are grounded in robust evidence. For example, the Horizon Europe program, the EU's largest funding initiative for science and innovation, has allocated substantial resources to sustainability-related research, which has resulted in renewable energy breakthroughs, advancements in carbon capture and storage technologies, and more. The program has also fostered interdisciplinary collaboration in its efforts to address pressing environmental challenges.

As Europe continues to refine its sustainability agenda, new challenges and opportunities will emerge. The transition to a green economy requires the careful balancing of economic, social, and environmental priorities, ensuring that vulnerable populations are not disproportionately affected by sustainability policies. The concept of a 'just transition', which aims to mitigate the socio-economic impacts of climate policies on workers and industries, has gained traction within EU discourse, emphasizing the need for inclusive and equitable sustainability strategies.

A good example of rollback in environmental regulations and of non-balanced policies on the other hand can be found in California where lawmakers enacted, in June 2025, a historic overhaul of the California Environmental Quality Act

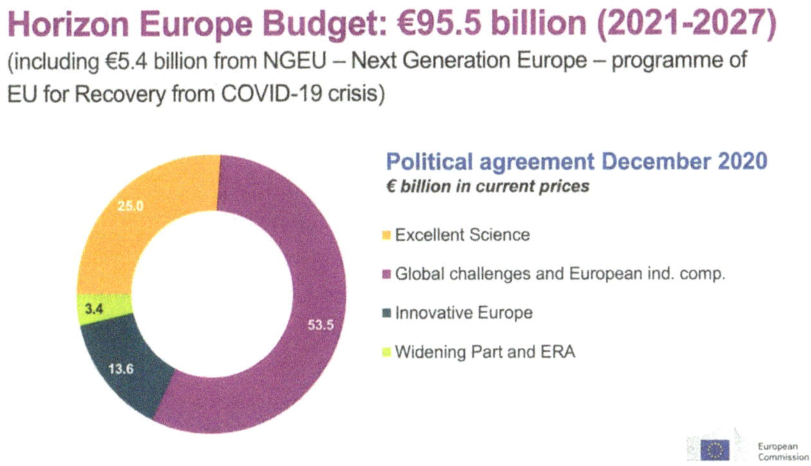

FIGURE 1.1 Horizon's programme funding for the period 2021–2027
SOURCE: EUROPEAN COMMISSION

(CEQA),[19] integrating two budget-trailer bills—AB 130 and SB 131—championed by assemblymember Buffy Wicks and Senator Scott Wiener and signed by Governor Gavin Newsom. The reforms exempt a broad range of infill housing and other public-interest projects (including childcare centres, health clinics, food banks, wildfire mitigation, broadband, water infrastructure, and advanced manufacturing in industrial zones) from environmental review and litigation under CEQA. Advocates argue that the streamlined process is necessary to alleviate California's acute housing crisis and accelerate construction, while critics warn that reducing CEQA's scope undermines environmental safeguards, public participation, and protections for vulnerable communities. The legislation represents the most significant rollback of CEQA in decades and signals a shift toward prioritizing development and affordability amid pressing fiscal and demographic pressures.

This policy represents a peculiar case of those policies that are not done adequately balancing the different interests at stake.

19 The California Environmental Quality Act (CEQA), enacted in 1970, is a state law that requires public agencies to identify, evaluate, and mitigate the environmental impacts of proposed projects before approval. It mandates environmental impact reports (EIRS) for projects with significant effects and provides mechanisms for public participation and judicial review. CEQA serves as California's principal legal framework for environmental protection in land use and infrastructure planning.

Moreover, geopolitical considerations and global supply chain dependencies add complexity to Europe's sustainability ambitions. The EU's push for sustainable trade agreements and carbon border adjustment mechanisms reflects an awareness that sustainability must be embedded into international economic relations due to the borderless nature of climate change. An example of this recognition by the European Union of the complexity of the international global supply chain but also of the necessity to regulate it is the Corporate Sustainability Due Diligence Directive.[20] By leveraging its regulatory influence, Europe seeks to set global standards for sustainability, encouraging trade partners to adopt environmentally responsible practices.[21]

Ultimately, science and sustainability's integration into European legal frameworks represents a fundamental shift in governance paradigms and recognition of the interconnectedness of environmental, economic, and social systems. As climate change and resource depletion pose unprecedented challenges, the EU's proactive and committed stance on sustainability not only sets a precedent but also serves as a blueprint and call to action for other regions, highlighting the imperative of coordinated, science-based policymaking to secure a resilient and prosperous future for all.

5 Sustainability and the Food Sector

One of the most critical areas where sustainability intersects with law and science is in the agrifood sector.[22] This issue is especially relevant in countries where food production is a key economic driver and deeply ingrained in the national identity. Ensuring sustainability within the food sector raises numerous regulatory and legal challenges, from promoting environmentally responsible agricultural practices to addressing social issues like food security and equitable access.

---

20 Directive (EU) 2024/1760 of the European Parliament and of the Council of 13 June 2024 on corporate sustainability due diligence, amending Directive (EU) 2019/1937 and Regulation (EU) 2023/2859, OJ L 123, 12.5.2016, p. 1.

21 Khalid Nadvi, 'Global standards, global governance and the organization of global value chains' (2008) 8 Journal of Economic Geography 323.

22 Davide Lanzoni and others, 'Cultured meat in the European Union: Legislative context and food safety issues' (2024) 8 Current Research in Food Science 100722 <https://www.sciencedirect.com/science/article/pii/S2665927124000480?via%3Dihub> accessed 23 June 2025.

The need for sustainability in agriculture has become more urgent as global challenges such as climate change, soil degradation, and resource depletion threaten food systems worldwide. As such, food sustainability is no longer viewed as a niche concern but as a guiding principle that informs broader economic policies and social welfare programs. This has significant implications for how industries like agriculture, where profit margins are slim, are regulated.

Creating a regulatory framework that addresses sustainability in the agrifood sector is challenging due to the inherent uncertainties in both agricultural and sustainability science. The effects of climate change, for example, introduce unpredictability in agricultural output and practices. How can laws that adapt to new scientific findings while providing clear and enforceable guidance to industry stakeholders be created? The answer requires a dynamic relationship between law and science that enables adaptable regulation that is grounded in current research yet responsive to future discoveries.

One way to approach this is by designing laws that encourage sustainable practices and incentivize innovation in the sector. For instance, regulations could provide farmers with financial support to adopt regenerative farming techniques which emphasize soil health and biodiversity as critical components of sustainable food production. By integrating science-backed methods, policies can promote practices that are both environmentally friendly and economically feasible for farmers, reducing the need for reactive regulatory changes down the line. This proactive approach not only benefits farmers but also helps ensure long-term food security and resilience against environmental shocks.

Furthermore, sustainability in the food sector requires adopting a comprehensive approach that addresses social and economic considerations such as food access and affordability. Regulatory frameworks must balance supporting sustainable farming practices with the need to keep food accessible and affordable for consumers. For example, subsidy programs that support sustainable practices among small-scale farmers can help make sustainable food options more widely available while contributing to rural economic stability.

In many cases, achieving sustainability in the agrifood sector also calls for international collaboration. Globalized food supply chains mean that sustainability issues often extend beyond national borders, necessitating harmonized standards and shared commitments to sustainable practices across regions. The interconnected nature of food production, distribution, and consumption highlights the need for coordinated efforts at the global level to ensure sustainable food systems. Initiatives such as the United Nations' Sustainable Development Goals (SDGs)—particularly Goal 2 (Zero Hunger) and Goal 12

(Responsible Consumption and Production)—serve as a foundation for policy development, encouraging nations to adopt practices that promote sustainability while addressing pressing challenges such as climate change, biodiversity loss, and food security.

Sustainability within the food sector demands a balanced regulatory framework that integrates evolving scientific knowledge with economic and social priorities. This integration requires policymakers to consider a range of factors, including environmental conservation, technological advancements in agriculture, and equitable access to food resources. Effective sustainability policies must support sustainable agricultural practices, ensuring that farming methods minimize environmental degradation while maintaining high productivity. This includes the promotion of regenerative agriculture, precision farming, and organic cultivation techniques that enhance soil health, reduce chemical inputs, and improve biodiversity. Moreover, sustainable food production must account for water conservation, responsible land use, and the reduction of greenhouse gas emissions associated with agriculture and food transport.

Ensuring food security is another crucial aspect of sustainability in the agrifood sector. A resilient food system must provide stable access to nutritious food for all populations, particularly vulnerable communities affected by economic disparities, political instability, or environmental disruptions. Legal frameworks must facilitate fair trade practices, support smallholder farmers, and encourage investment in local food systems to enhance food sovereignty. Additionally, regulations should promote responsible consumption patterns, reducing food waste and encouraging consumers to make environmentally conscious choices.

Adapting to new environmental challenges is essential for long-term sustainability in the food sector. Climate change presents significant risks, including shifting weather patterns, increased frequency of extreme weather events, and threats to crop yields. Legal and policy frameworks must anticipate these challenges, incorporating adaptive measures such as climate-resilient crops, improved irrigation techniques, and enhanced disaster preparedness in agricultural planning.

By fostering a collaborative relationship between law, science, and industry, we can build a more resilient and sustainable food system capable of meeting the needs of current and future generations. Strengthening international partnerships, investing in innovative solutions, and ensuring inclusive policy-making will be key to achieving sustainability in the agrifood sector. With concerted global efforts, the transition to a more sustainable food system is not only possible but imperative for the well-being of both people and the planet.

6 From Planning to Strategic Regulation

One of the critical insights emerging from recent research is the need to transition from a traditional, planning-based regulatory model to a more strategic, adaptable approach that accounts for the inherent uncertainty and evolving nature of scientific knowledge.[23] The conventional planning-based model assumes a relatively static set of facts and conditions, which served well during the welfare state era and the industrial development phase after World War II. However, in today's world—characterized by rapid advancements in science, technological innovation, and environmental shifts—this model is increasingly insufficient. Regulation today requires a fundamental rethinking of how we govern industries and social issues alike.

The traditional regulatory model focuses on pre-established rules and rigid structures that are often slow to change, prioritizing stability and predictability. Yet, this approach has limitations in a world where industries, scientific discoveries, and environmental conditions are constantly shifting. A more strategic approach to regulation—one that is designed to accommodate uncertainty—can better adapt to emerging knowledge and changing realities. This shift is not merely a technical adjustment but a change in mindset that extends to lawmakers, regulators, scientists, and industry stakeholders alike. Together, they must rethink how regulatory frameworks can be both stable enough to support long-term economic and social development and flexible enough to respond to new challenges and discoveries.

Strategic regulation requires developing adaptable regulatory instruments that can evolve alongside advancements in scientific understanding. For instance, the development of environmental regulations must consider that new findings in climate science may demand changes in policy or enforcement measures. This adaptive model does not mean discarding stability but rather achieving it through mechanisms that are responsive and flexible. Regulatory approaches must be designed to accommodate potential revisions, allowing regulators to respond effectively to shifting circumstances. Such frameworks ensure that regulation does not become outdated as new scientific knowledge emerges, promoting a proactive stance on challenges related to climate change and sustainability.

---

23 Michelle D Lazarus and Silvio Funtowicz, 'Learning together: facing the challenges of sustainability transitions by engaging uncertainty tolerance and post-normal science' (2023) 6 Sustainable Earth Reviews article 18 <https://sustainableearthreviews.biomedcentral.com/articles/10.1186/s42055-023-00066-3> accessed 23 June 2025.

In many ways, this transition is already underway across different sectors. One example is in the realm of social rights. Previously, regulations in areas like healthcare, education, and welfare were based on fixed standards designed to meet essential levels of service. However, these static models struggle to meet the complex, changing needs of contemporary society, where resource availability and population demographics can shift rapidly. Adaptive regulations allow for service levels to be re-evaluated based on real-time data and emerging social needs, ultimately providing a more tailored approach that can adjust to new realities while safeguarding social rights.

A good example of this kind of policy is represented by Spain's *Bono Social*; a government-subsidized electricity discount program designed to protect vulnerable consumers. Originally established by Royal Decree 897/2017 and updated through subsequent legislation, most notably in response to the COVID-19 crisis and the energy price surge of 2021–2022. The scheme adapts eligibility criteria and support levels based on real-time economic indicators and social data. During energy crises, the Spanish government has temporarily expanded the scope of beneficiaries, increased the discount rates, and introduced additional protections. This responsiveness demonstrates how adaptive regulation can ensure minimum essential service levels while adjusting to shifting social needs, such as inflation, unemployment, or extreme weather events.

The field of sustainability provides another example of this shift toward strategic regulation. For instance, regulatory frameworks in agriculture must be prepared to address sudden changes due to climate impacts, resource scarcity, or shifting ecological conditions. Strategic regulation in sustainability emphasizes adaptability, ensuring that regulations can evolve to reflect scientific advancements and changing environmental conditions without undermining the stability and predictability industries need for planning.

Moving toward strategic regulation also necessitates collaboration among scientists, policymakers, and industry leaders. Rather than operating in silos, these stakeholders can work together to develop flexible frameworks informed by the latest research. In fields such as public health, environmental protection, and technology, this collaborative approach ensures that regulations remain relevant, evidence-based, and responsive to current needs. By aligning regulatory strategies with scientific and technological progress, strategic regulation creates a foundation for sustainable development that is resilient in the face of change.

The shift from a planning-based regulatory model to one of strategic regulation represents a fundamental and necessary evolution in governance. This approach recognizes the dynamism of scientific knowledge and the need for adaptable, responsive frameworks in our increasingly complex world. Strategic regulation offers a way to address today's uncertainties while still providing the stability required for long-term economic and social development, paving the way for a regulatory landscape that can support innovation, protect social rights, and respond effectively to the environmental and technological challenges of our time.

7 Conclusion

The intersection of science, law, and sustainability presents both profound challenges and exciting opportunities. As we continue to explore this dynamic relationship, it is clear that we are only at the beginning of what promises to be a long and fruitful research pathway. The evolution of sustainability as a legal principle has already demonstrated its capacity to reshape regulatory frameworks, influencing policies at both the national and international levels. However, the road ahead remains complex, requiring continued collaboration between legal scholars, policymakers, and scientific communities to craft regulations that are not only coherent and evidence-based but also responsive to the ever-evolving realities of science and sustainability.

One of the key challenges lies in balancing economic development with environmental and social imperatives. Legal frameworks must evolve to accommodate new scientific findings while ensuring that sustainability initiatives do not disproportionately burden vulnerable populations. The principle of a 'just transition', which seeks to mitigate the socio-economic impacts of sustainability policies, will play a crucial role in determining the success of future regulations. Additionally, the precautionary principle, deeply embedded in environmental law, underscores the necessity of proactive policymaking in the face of scientific uncertainty, emphasizing the importance of preventive measures to avoid irreversible harm.

Moreover, as sustainability becomes an increasingly global concern, the harmonization of legal standards across jurisdictions will be essential. International treaties, trade agreements, and cross-border collaborations must reflect a shared commitment to sustainability, ensuring that regulatory disparities do not hinder collective progress. The role of supranational organizations, such as the European Union and the United Nations, in establishing common sustainability goals and enforcement mechanisms cannot be overstated. Through binding commitments and coordinated efforts, legal instruments can facilitate a more uniform approach to sustainability governance on a global scale.

Science, as a driving force behind sustainability regulations, will continue to play a crucial role in informing legal discourse. Advances in climate modelling, environmental monitoring, and green technologies will provide the empirical basis for policy decisions, making interdisciplinary collaboration indispensable. Legal frameworks must therefore remain adaptable, integrating the latest scientific developments while maintaining legal certainty for stakeholders. The intersection of science and law is not static but rather a dynamic process that demands continuous refinement and innovation.

Ultimately, the success of sustainability law depends on its ability to address the complexities of modern governance while fostering a long-term vision for environmental stewardship, economic resilience, and social equity. By embracing a strategic approach to regulation—one that recognizes the inherent uncertainty of scientific knowledge and the multifaceted nature of sustainability—lawmakers and legal scholars can contribute to shaping a future that is both sustainable and just. While the challenges ahead are significant, the potential rewards are even greater. Through continued research, dialogue, and cooperation, the legal community can play a transformative role in advancing sustainability as a guiding principle of governance. As this discourse evolves, it remains imperative to prioritize policies that safeguard both present and future generations, ensuring a legal framework that upholds sustainability as a cornerstone of modern law and society.

Bibliography

Baker S, 'The evolution of European Union environmental policy: from growth to sustainable development?' in Susan Baker and others (eds), *The Politics of sustainable development. Theory, policy and practice within the European Union* (Routledge 2012).

De Sadeleer N, 'The precautionary principle in EC health and environmental law' (2006) 12 European Law Journal 139.

De Sadeleer N, 'Sustainable development in EU law: still a long way to go' (2015) 6 Jindal Global Law Review 39.

Irti N, Severino E, *Dialogo su diritto e tecnica* (Editori Laterza 2001).

Jasanoff S (ed), *Reframing Rights: Bioconstitutionalism in the Genetic Age* (MIT Press 2011).

Lanzoni D and others, 'Cultured meat in the European Union: Legislative context and food safety issues' (2024) 8 Current Research in Food Science 100722.

Lazarus MD and Funtowicz S, 'Learning together: facing the challenges of sustainability transitions by engaging uncertainty tolerance and post-normal science' (2023) 6 Sustainable Earth Reviews article 18.

Martini D, Ragone G, and others, 'The Need for A Multidisciplinary Approach to Face Challenges Related to Food, Health, and Sustainability: The Contribution of CRC I-WE' (2021) 13 Sustainability 13720.

Mesias ER and Cateli Rosa AL, 'Sustainable Economic Development: The Necessary Dialogue between Environmental Law and Economics' (2022) 4 (1) Macro Management & Public Policies 21.

Nadvi K, 'Global standards, global governance and the organization of global value chains' (2008) 8 Journal of Economic Geography 323.

Ranchordás S, 'Innovation-Friendly Regulation: The Sunset of Regulation, the Sunrise of Innovation' (2015) 55 Jurimetrics 201.

Sands PJ, 'The Environment, Community and International Law' (1989) 30 Harvard International Law Journal 393.

Schrijver NJ, *The evolution of sustainable development in international law: inception, meaning and status* (Martinus Nijhoff Publishers 2008).

Stone CD, 'Common but Differentiated Responsibilities in International Law' (2004) 98 American Journal of International Law 276.

Tanneberger F and others, 'Towards net zero CO2 in 2050: An emission reduction pathway for organic soils in Germany' (2021) 27 Mires and Peat article 5.

Violini L (ed), *One Health. Dal paradigma alle implicazioni giuridiche* (Giappichelli 2023).

Wolf S and others, 'The European Green Deal—more than climate neutrality' (2021) 56 Intereconomics 99.

Burmeister, Fabian, et al. 'Toward Architecture-Driven Interdisciplinary Research: Learnings from a Case Study of COVID-19 Contact Tracing Apps'. *Proceedings of the 2022 Symposium on Computer Science and Law*. 2022.

Ioanna Pervou, Mpogiatzidis Panagiotis, 'Restrictive human rights measures against the spread of COVID-19: an interdisciplinary approach between law and health-care management'. *International Journal of Human Rights in Healthcare* 17.4, 2024, 475–486.

CHAPTER 2

Food Security and Scientific Innovation in International Law

Striking a Balance between Patent Rights on Plant Resources and Human Rights Protection

Ludovica Di Lullo

Summary

1 Introduction: Food Security and Innovation

Food security is defined as a state in which all people, at all times, have physical and economic access to sufficient, safe, and nutritious food that meets their dietary needs and food preferences for an active and healthy life.[1]

According to the annual report titled 'The State of Food Security and Nutrition in the World' (SOFI Report):

> [T]he reverse in progress and the persistently high levels of hunger, food insecurity, and malnutrition in recent years have put the world off track to meet Sustainable Development Goal (SDG) Targets 2.1 and 2.2—to end hunger, food insecurity and all forms of malnutrition by 2030.[2]

In terms of numbers, between 713 and 757 million people (8.9 and 9.4% of the global population, respectively) were estimated to have been undernourished

1 FAO World Food Summit, *Rome Declaration on World Food Security*, Rome 13 November 1996.
2 FAO, IFAD, UNICEF, WFP, and WHO, *The State of Food Security and Nutrition in the World 2024. Financing to end hunger, food insecurity and malnutrition in all its forms* (Rome 2024), 1.

in 2023 and about 152 million more people faced hunger in 2023 compared to 2019.[3]

Scientific and biotechnological innovation in this domain have the potential to enhance crop management and productivity, increase yields, adapt food production to the effects of climate change, and develop early warning systems to safeguard land, crops, and food production.[4]

The overarching objectives of this transformation are twofold: to enhance food accessibility and to improve nutritional outcomes. The aim is to contribute to the effective implementation of the 2030 Agenda for Sustainable Development,[5] which emphasises the role of technology as a fundamental enabler to achieve the Sustainable Development Goals (SDGs).[6]

From an international law perspective, innovation can present numerous legal challenges. Indeed, normative conflicts may emerge among different legal regimes. For example, the Intellectual Property Rights (IPR) regime imposes financial fees for the utilisation of inventions based on plant genetic resources, which can result in a detrimental impact on the ability of the most vulnerable populations to access food, particularly in developing and least developed countries (LDCs).[7]

Conversely, the international protection of human rights promotes economic and technological collaboration among States in part to safeguard and ensure the right to access to adequate and available food.

The main challenge regards the protection of traditional knowledge (TK) of indigenous peoples and local communities (IPLCs)—the cultivation, conservation, use, and application of natural resources—from commercialisation by the biotechnology industry of genetic resources from plants, animals, and micro-organisms. If a private actor, such as a multinational company, can appropriate TK through patents, this could lead to an increase in the cost of seeds, and thus a reduction in their availability to farmers and those peoples

3 ibid 8,14.

4 See for instance UNCTAD, *The role of science, technology and innovation in ensuring food security by 2030* (New York and Geneva 2017), 11–20; Rui Benfica and others, 'Food System Innovations and Digital Technologies to Foster Productivity Growth and Rural Transformation' in Joachim von Braun and others (eds), *Science and Innovations for Food Systems Transformation* (Springer 2023).

5 FAO, *Introducing the Agrifood Systems Technologies and Innovations Outlook* (Rome 2022), 1.

6 UN Interagency Task Team on Science, Technology and Innovation for the SDGs (IATT), *Science, Technology and Innovation for the SDGs Roadmaps—Framework and Working Method* (2018) <https://sdgs.un.org/documents/policy-brief-1-science-technology-and-innovation-sdgs-roadmaps-framework-and-working> accessed 24 June 2025.

7 Philippe Cullet, 'Intellectual Property Rights and Food Security in the South' (2004) 7 Journal of World Intellectual Property 261.

whose economies and livelihoods are largely based on agriculture. This can drive the erosion of biological diversity at all levels—genetic, species, and ecosystem. Several studies dealing with IPLCs highlight not only a decline in the transmission of ancestral knowledge,[8] but also a shift in dietary habits towards cheap and low-nutrient alternatives that has led to a rise in malnutrition and food insecurity.[9]

Against this backdrop, the present chapter provides an overview of the international norms governing both IPR and the protection of human rights—and the normative tensions between them. Methodologically, this paper does not address international jurisprudence on this issue, due to limitations in available length. The paper concludes with possible legal developments, emphasising potential synergies and the complementarity between the two regimes.

2 International Intellectual Property Law and Food Innovation

The legal instrument providing for international binding rules with respect to IPR is the Agreement on Trade Related Aspects of Intellectual Property Rights (TRIPS Agreement). Adopted in 1994 under the umbrella of the Marrakesh Agreement Establishing the World Trade Organisation (WTO), today TRIPS counts 166 States parties.[10]

The rationale of the TRIPS Agreement is to regulate exclusive IP rights, pertaining to inventors of patentable goods. These rights are typically considered by States to be an incentive to facilitate innovation and technology transfer, which ultimately benefits producers and users alike.

As will be illustrated below, additional international instruments are involved when laying down a specific legal framework protecting intellectual property rights over resources essential for innovation in the food sector.

8 International Development Research Centre, 'Valuing Indigenous knowledge for climate-resilient food systems' (IDRC·CRDI, 2 June 2023) <https://idrc-crdi.ca/en/research-in-action/valuing-indigenous-knowledge-climate-resilient-food-systems> accessed 23 June 2025.

9 For instance, the Ecuador National Institute of Statistic in 2018 found that 39% of Indigenous children were chronically malnourished, compared with a national average of 27%. See Instituto Nacional de Estadísticas y Censos—Encuesta Nacional de Salud, Salud Reproductiva y Nutrición (ENSANUT) (2018).

10 WTO, *Agreement on Trade-Related Aspects of Intellectual Property Rights*, Marrakesh 15 April 1994.

2.1 *The TRIPS Agreement*

The international protection of IPR is primarily achieved through the granting of patents to an invention in any field of technology, whether a product or a process. For a patent to be granted in accordance with TRIPS, the invention must be novel, involve an inventive step and be capable of industrial application. Patent holders are entitled to the right to grant licenses for the utilisation of their invention to third parties[11] in order to prevent third parties not having the owner's consent from making, using, offering for sale, selling, or importing for these purposes that product.[12]

As set forth in Articles 7 and 8 of the TRIPS Agreement, which inform the interpretation of the treaty, such guarantee is afforded with a view to promoting social and economic welfare, protecting public health, and advancing the public interest in vital areas, such as nutrition.[13]

To achieve these objectives, under certain circumstances, exclusive rights may be limited or suspended on the grounds of the legitimate interests of third parties. States parties to TRIPS may suspend patents and grant compulsory licenses for the use of the patent without the authorisation of the patent holder. These limitations should not unduly impede the normal exploitation of the patent and must not prejudice the legitimate interests of the patent owner. According to Article 31, a waiver may be granted in the event of a national emergency or extreme urgency, for non-commercial public use or the supply of the domestic market, provided that specific procedural and substantive conditions are met.[14] In any case, the patent holder is entitled to receive an economic fee ('royalty').

---

11 ibid art 27, para 1.

12 ibid art 28.

13 ibid arts 7–8, para 1.

14 ibid art 31, letters from (a) to (k). Article 31 provides for a non-exhaustive list of grounds for excluding patentability, since the Doha Declaration on TRIPS and Public Health explicitly mentions public health crises and epidemics as falling within the situations of 'national emergency or extreme urgency', these exceptions have been increasingly discussed in relation to health and, in particular, to the production and distribution of medicines, diagnostics, and vaccinations. See Justin Malbon, Charles Lawson and Mark Davison, *The WTO Agreement on Trade-Related Aspects of Intellectual Property Rights. A Commentary* (Elgar 2014), 499; Carlos M Correa, *Trade Related Aspects of Intellectual Property Rights: A Commentary on the TRIPS Agreement* (2nd edn, OUP 2020), 306. With regard to health see, among others, Frederick M Abbott, 'The Trips-Legality of Measures Taken to Address Public Health Crises: A Synopsis' (2001) 7 Widener Law Symposium Journal 71; id, 'The Doha Declaration on the TRIPS Agreement and Public Health: Lighting a Dark Corner at the WTO' (2002) 5 Journal of International Economic Law 469; Haochen Sun, 'The Road to Doha and Beyond: Some Reflections on the TRIPS Agreement and Public Health' (2004) 15 European Journal of International Law 123; Wenwei Guan, 'IPRs, Public Health,

Specific attention has been paid to the circumstances of WTO Member States with inadequate or no manufacturing capabilities (Least Developed Countries, or LDCs). The TRIPS Agreement provides for a general waiver for LDCs (except for Articles 3, 4, and 5),[15] for a period of ten years, which may be extended by a special decision of the TRIPS Council. Moreover, according to Article 66, paragraph 2, industrialised States parties to the Agreement are required to provide incentives to their enterprises and institutions to facilitate technology transfer to LDC Members.[16] In the same vein, States parties are required to fulfil obligations pertaining to technical and financial cooperation in favor of LDC Members.

The specific legal framework governing innovations in the field of agrifood systems is a bit more complex. Article 27 of the TRIPS Agreement provides that States may exclude the patentability of inventions whose commercial exploitation is necessary to protect ordre public or morality,[17] including to protect human or animal life or environmental health. For this reason, 'plants and animals other than micro-organisms, and essentially biological processes for the production of plants or animals other than non-biological and microbiological processes' can be excluded from patentability.[18] However, States parties shall provide for 'plant genetic resources' protection 'either by patents or by an effective *sui generis* system or by any combination thereof'.[19]

These norms pose some challenges to the TK of IPLCs, ie the methods employed in the conservation, utilisation, and processing of natural resources to produce basic goods for the communities concerned, such as food, medicines, and cultural products.[20]

---

and International Trade: An International Law Perspective on the TRIPS Amendment' (2016) 29 Leiden Journal of International Law 411.

15 Articles 3, 4, and 5 of the TRIPS deal, respectively, with the principle of national treatment, the most-favoured-nation treatment principle, and a clause concerning the relation between multilateral agreements on acquisition or maintenance of protection.

16 TRIPS (n 10), art 66, paras 1–2.

17 On the definition of 'ordre public and morality' see Malbon, Lawson, and Davison (n 14), 430; Correa (n 14), 279.

18 TRIPS, art 27, para 3, letter. (b).

19 ibid.

20 A considerable number of cases involving a wide range of plant species have been documented over the years, such as those concerning, namely, neem trees, turmeric, ayahuasca, hoodia cactus, katempfe, serendipity berry, and basmati rice. See Naomi Roht-Arriaza, 'Of Seeds and Shamans: The Appropriation of the Scientific and Technical Knowledge of Indigenous and Local Communities' (1996) 17 Michigan Journal of International Law 919; Bernard O'Connor, 'Protecting Traditional Knowledge: An Overview of a Developing Area of Intellectual Property Law' (2003) 6 Journal of World Intellectual Property 677.

While intellectual property rights are individual and private, the concept of TK refers to collective ancestral know-how, orally transmitted through generations. This means that TK lacks the essential element of being novel. Nonetheless, TK should be protected due to the essential role it plays in the daily lives of IPLCs.

The challenges posed by traditional IP governance and the lack of appropriate legal protection for TK may indeed raise various concerns.[21] First, the commercialisation of natural resources has the potential to accelerate the loss of biodiversity by increasing monoculture crops that erode the diversity of landraces, or traditional crop varieties. Second, the commodification of food products can diminish accessibility to food, owing to the considerable costs associated with patent rights. Third, and consequently, the consumption of low-priced and unhealthy food results in an increase in malnutrition.[22]

A *sui generis* regime, thus, represents a practical legal solution for balancing competing interests and facilitating the harmonisation of various elements, including IPR, TK, biodiversity, and food security.

2.2 *Applicable Norms to* Sui Generis *Regimes*

The implementation of a *sui generis* regime for patents or 'any other combination'[23] means the establishment of a system based on other international instruments which provide for the protection of plant varieties and their genetic resources, the essential material for both farmers and plant breeders, namely those who professionally breed, discover, or develop plant varieties.[24]

A specific regime for the protection of plant breeders is set out in the International Union for the Protection of New Varieties of Plants (UPOV).[25] Since its adoption in 1978, UPOV has sought to achieve a balance between the rights of plant breeders to produce and sell plant varieties and the rights of farmers and researchers to utilise them. The act's efficacy, which did not

21 Francis Kariuki, 'Traditional Governance Institutions and the Holistic Protection of Traditional Knowledge' in Laura Pineschi (ed), *Cultural Heritage, Sustainable Development and Human Rights. Towards an Integrated Approach* (Routledge 2024).

22 UN General Assembly, *The right to food, Seed policies and the right to food: enhancing agrobiodiversity and encouraging innovation, Report of the Special Rapporteur on the right to food*, UN Doc. A/64/170, 23 July 2009.

23 TRIPS (n 18).

24 For an overview see Laurence R Helfer, *Intellectual Property Rights in Plant Varieties. International Legal Regimes and Policy Options for National Governments* (FAO 2004).

25 The Acts are set down in the International Convention for the Protection of New Varieties of Plants, 2 December 1961, as revised at Geneva on 10 November 1972, on 23 October 1978, and on 19 March 1991 (hereinafter, in note, UPOV Act 1991).

address any concern related to food (in)security,[26] was downgraded due to the lack of a broad membership.[27] For this reason, the UPOV Act was revised in 1991.[28]

In accordance with the actual provisions, a plant's eligibility for protection is contingent on the fulfilment of specific criteria. Primarily, the plant variety must demonstrate novelty, distinctness, uniformity, and stability.[29] This protection requires those seeking to utilise reproductive or vegetative propagating material of the plant variety for the purpose of production or reproduction; conditioning for the purpose of propagation; offering for sale; selling or marketing; exporting; importing; and stocking for any of these purposes to obtain prior authorisation from the designated breeder.[30] However, this protection risks facilitating the role of the breeder, but limiting the rights of farmers.

There are a limited number of exceptions to the general rule, pertaining to the private, non-commercial activities of individuals; acts performed for research and experimental purposes within the appropriate scientific context; and so-called 'farmers' privilege'[31]—the permission granted to farmers to utilise the product of their harvest for propagating purposes on the condition that the protected variety in question has been obtained through planting on their own holdings.[32]

Some authors criticise the approach of the UPOV Acts, since they encourage crop monocultures without safeguarding agricultural biodiversity.[33] Furthermore, the privilege does not provide farmers with the authorisation needed to engage in the sale or exchange of seeds with other farmers for the purpose of propagating new varieties.[34] Such provisions, again, risk hav-

---

26 Shelley Edwardson, 'Reconciling TRIPS and the Right to Food', in Thomas Cottier, Joost Pauwelyn and Elisabeth Bürgi (eds), Human Rights and International Trade (OUP 2005).

27 Only 17 of 79 Member States to the UPOV are bound by the 1978 Act. See Laurent Manderieux, 'Right to Food versus Food Quality and Safety in Plant Variety Protection Regimes', in Angela Lupone, Carola Ricci, and Andrea Santini (eds), *The Right to Safe Food Towards a Global Governance* (Giappichelli 2013).

28 As per January 2025, only 60 states and 2 international organisations (the African Intellectual Property Organisation and the European Union) are bound by the 1991 Act.

29 UPOV Act 1991, arts 7–9.

30 ibid art 14.

31 ibid art 15.

32 ibid art 15, para 2.

33 United Nations Development Programme (UNDP), *Towards a Balanced 'Sui Generis' Plant Variety Regime: Guidelines to Establish a National PVP Law and an Understanding of TRIPS-plus Aspects of Plant Rights* (New York 2008).

34 Dan Leskien, Michael Flitner, *Intellectual Property Rights and Plant Genetic Resources: Options for a* Sui Generis *System* (IPGRI 1997).

ing a detrimental impact on developing countries, where a large proportion of the population depends on agriculture for employment and income, thus multiplying inequalities.[35]

Alternatively, States may decide to base their systems on the 2001 FAO International Treaty on Plant Genetic Resources for Food and Agriculture (ITPGRFA), which today counts 152 Contracting Parties.[36] The ITPGRFA imposes obligations on States concerning the conservation and sustainable use of plant genetic resources, with a view to ensuring sustainable agriculture and food security.[37]

The negotiation process for ITPGRFA took place after the Conference for the Adoption of the Convention on Biological Diversity (CBD).[38] In this context, States parties agreed to undertake a comprehensive review of the existing non-binding FAO International Undertaking on Plant Genetic Resources (IU)[39] to explore means to develop complementarity and cooperation between these legal instruments.[40]

The harmonisation between the CBD and the ITPGRFA ensures—or at least should ensure—the protection of agricultural biodiversity, TK, and farmers' rights. With regard to conservation of natural resources, the CBD provides that each States party shall:

> [R]espect, preserve, and maintain knowledge, innovations, and practices of indigenous and local communities embodying traditional lifestyles relevant for the conservation and sustainable use of biological diversity

35 Graham Dutfield, *Intellectual Property, Biogenetic Resources and Traditional Knowledge* (Routledge 2004).

36 FAO, *International Treaty on Plant Genetic Resources for Food and Agriculture*, Rome 3 November 2001.

37 ibid, art 1, para 1 states that 'The objectives of this Treaty are the conservation and sustainable use of plant genetic resources for food and agriculture and the fair and equitable sharing of the benefits arising out of their use, in harmony with the Convention on Biological Diversity, for sustainable agriculture and food security'. See Gerald Moore and Witold Tymowsky, *Explanatory Guide to the International Treaty on Plant Genetic Resources for Food and Agriculture* (IUCN 2005).

38 UN, *Convention on Biological Diversity*, Rio de Janeiro 5 June 1992.

39 FAO, *International Undertaking on Plant Genetic Resources: Resolution 8/83 of the Twenty-second Session of the FAO Conference*, Rome 5–23 November1983. The International Undertaking was based on the principle that plant genetic resources are a heritage of mankind and consequently should be available without restriction.

40 FAO, Nairobi Final Act of the Conference for the Adoption of the Agreed Text of the Convention on Biological Diversity, Resolution 3, *The Interrelationship Between the Convention on Biological Diversity and the Promotion of Sustainable Agriculture*, Nairobi 22 May 1992, para 2.

> and promote their wider application with the approval and involvement of the holders of such knowledge, innovations, and practices and encourage the equitable sharing of the benefits arising from the utilisation of such knowledge, innovations, and practices.[41]

The ITPGRFA does not provide an exhaustive list of the relevant rights of farmers. Article 9 refers to three objectives that governments should achieve: (a) the protection of traditional knowledge relevant to plant genetic resources for food and agriculture; (b) the right to equitably participate in sharing benefits arising from the utilisation of plant genetic resources for food and agriculture; and (c) the right to participate in making decisions, at the national level, on matters related to the conservation and sustainable use of plant genetic resources for food and agriculture.[42] Moreover, the last paragraph of Article 9 provides that '[n]othing in this Article shall be interpreted to limit any rights that farmers have to save, use, exchange, and sell farm-saved seed/propagating material, subject to national law and as appropriate'.[43]

The ITPGRFA imposes obligations on States to balance the right to access and control genetic resources with their sovereign rights over natural resources.[44] At the same time, a reading consistent with the CBD entails the implementation of the international tools provided thereby for the fair and equitable sharing of benefits arising out of the utilisation of genetic resources.[45] To this end, the ITPGRFA aims to establish a Multilateral System (MS) which lists crops and forages to be made available to all countries for the purpose of utilisation and conservation for research, breeding, and training for food and agriculture,

41 CBD, art 8, letter (j).

42 ITPGRFA, art 9, paras 1–2.

43 ibid para 3.

44 Mary Elisabeth Footer, 'Agricultural Biotechnology, Food Security and Human Rights' in Francesco Francioni, Tullio Scovazzi, *Biotechnology and International Law* (Bloomsbury 2006).

45 This represents one of the main objectives of the CBD, as set out in art 1 and further developed through the Bonn Guidelines and the Nagoya Protocol to the CBD. See Secretariat of the Convention on Biological Diversity, *Bonn Guidelines on Access to Genetic Resources and Fair and Equitable Sharing of the Benefits Arising out of their Utilization* (Montreal 2002); UN, *Nagoya Protocol on Access to Genetic Resources and the Fair and Equitable Sharing of Benefits Arising from their Utilization to the Convention on Biological Diversity* (Nagoya 2010). Among scholars see Elisa Morgera, Elsa Tsioumani, and Matthias Buck, *Unraveling the Nagoya Protocol: A Commentary of the Protocol on Access and Benefit-Sharing to the Convention on Biological Diversity* (Brill 2015).

and/or other non-food/feed industrial uses, free of charge.[46] Moreover, according to Article 13:

> [B]enefits arising from the use, including commercial, of plant genetic resources for food and agriculture under the Multilateral System shall be shared fairly and equitably through the following mechanisms: the exchange of information, access to and transfer of technology, capacity-building, and the sharing of the benefits arising from commercialisation.[47]

Article 12 also provides that '[r]ecipients shall not claim any intellectual property or other rights that limit the facilitated access to the plant genetic resources for food and agriculture, or their genetic parts or components, in the form received from the Multilateral System'.[48] Additionally, the ITPGRFA requires that:

> [A] recipient who commercialises a product that is a plant genetic resource for food and agriculture and that incorporates material accessed from the Multilateral System, shall pay to [an appropriate mechanism, such as a Trust Account] an equitable share of the benefits arising from the commercialisation of that product, except whenever such a product is available without restriction to others for further research and breeding, in which case the recipient who commercialises shall be encouraged to make such payment.[49]

Consequently, the provisions of the ITPGRFA may be considered incompatible or conflicting with TRIPS, which require Members to ensure that patents are available, and patent rights are enjoyed without discrimination in all fields of technology.[50]

To effectively balance all the variables associated with food innovation, alternative solutions have been proposed at both the national and international level.

---

46 ITPGRFA, art 12, para 3, letters (a) and (b). See Elsa Tsioumani, *Fair and Equitable Benefit-Sharing in Agriculture. Reinventing Agrarian Justice* (Routledge 2021), 16.

47 ibid art 13, para 2.

48 ibid art 12, para 3, letter (d).

49 ibid art 13, para 2, letter (d).

50 TRIPS, art 27, para 1. See Helfer (23), 91.

On the one hand, domestic legislation has combined rights and duties deriving from the international instruments illustrated above by establishing different flexibilities and incentives for technological innovation.[51] For instance, the Organisation of African Unity (OAU) has drafted model legislation entitled 'African Model Legislation for the Protection of the Rights of Local Communities, Farmers and Breeders, and for the Regulation of Access to Biological Resources'.[52] This model legislation encourages the full participation and approval of the IPLCs concerned in the development of contracts regulating the collection of biological resources.[53]

The need to balance intellectual property rights and access to genetic resources has been discussed internationally, even by the WTO. In this sense, in the Ministerial Declaration adopted at the end of the 2001 'Doha Round', Member States instructed the Council for TRIPS to include in its agenda:

> [T]he review of Article 27, para 3, letter (b), the review of the implementation of the TRIPS Agreement under Article 71, para 1, and the work foreseen pursuant to paragraph 12 of this declaration, to examine, *inter alia*, the relationship between the TRIPS Agreement and the CBD, the protection of TK, folklore, and other relevant new developments.[54]

Notwithstanding this request, the review of Article 27 has not yet been undertaken by the TRIPS Parties. However, an innovative proposal has been developed under the auspices of the World Intellectual Property Organisation (WIPO).

2.3 *The WIPO Treaty on Intellectual Property, Genetic Resources, and Associated Traditional Knowledge*

In May 2024—after more than twenty years of negotiations—WIPO Member States adopted the Treaty on Intellectual Property, Genetic Resources, and

---

51 Hans Morten Haugen, Manuel Ruiz Muller, and Savita Mullapudi Narasimhan, 'Food security and intellectual property rights: Finding linkages' in Tzen Wong and Graham Dutfield (eds), *Intellectual Property and Human Development. Current Trends and Future Scenarios* (CUP 2010). For an overview, see UNCTAD, *Systems and National Experiences for Protecting Traditional Knowledge, Innovations and Practices, Background Note by the UNCTAD Secretariat*, 22 August 2000.

52 Organisation of African Unity (OAU), *African Model Legislation for the Protection of the Rights of Local Communities, Farmers and Breeders, and for the Regulation of Access to Biological Resources*, (Algeria 2000), art 22.

53 ibid.

54 WTO, *Ministerial Declaration*, WT/MIN(01)/DEC/1, 14 November 2001, para 19.

Associated Traditional Knowledge (WIPO Treaty), a unique treaty dedicated to IP, TK, and folklore.[55] The WIPO Treaty, which entered into force after fifteen ratifications, regulates a new international disclosure requirement for patent applicants whose inventions are based on genetic resources and/or associated TK.

According to the new treaty, States parties have a duty to disclose pertinent information in instances where a patent application pertains to an invention that is derived from genetic resources or traditional knowledge associated with genetic resources. This disclosure requirement encompasses the following elements: the country of origin of the genetic resources in question; the specific source of these resources; the indigenous peoples or local community associated with these resources; and the origin of the traditional knowledge associated with the genetic resources.[56]

In the event of the requisite information not being disclosed, appropriate, effective, and proportionate, sanctioning measures will be implemented. Patent applicants will be afforded the opportunity to rectify a failure to disclose the required information, unless fraudulent conduct or intent can be demonstrated.[57]

The introduction of these preconditions represents a significant international achievement in IP law, given the pivotal role that natural resources and traditional knowledge play in food production within indigenous communities. While the introduction of a specific protection regime related to the intangible heritage of indigenous people is a laudable result, the threshold of disclosure required is considered relatively low.[58] For instance, if the applicant is unaware of the IPLC or the TK's source, the applicant can 'make a declaration to that effect, affirming that the content of the declaration is true and correct to the best knowledge of the applicant'.[59] In conclusion, it remains unclear whether the actual system, which is complex and not harmonised, is

55 WIPO, *Treaty on Intellectual Property, Genetic Resources and Associated Traditional Knowledge*, 13–24 May 2024. On this topic see Daniel F Robinson, Ahmed Abdel-Latif, and Pedro Roffe (eds), *Protecting Traditional Knowledge. The WIPO Intergovernmental Committee on Intellectual Property and Genetic Resources, Traditional Knowledge and Folklore* (Routledge 2019).

56 ibid art 3, paras 1 and 2.

57 ibid art 5.

58 Ayla do Vale Alves, 'WIPO's New Treaty on Intellectual Property, Genetic Resources, and Traditional Knowledge—A Turning Point for Indigenous Heritage?' (2024) 13 (11) ESIL Reflections <https://esil-sedi.eu/esil-reflection-wipos-new-treaty-on-intellectual-property-genetic-resources-and-traditional-knowledge-a-turning-point-for-indigenous-heritage/> accessed 23 June 2025.

59 WIPO, *Treaty on Intellectual Property* (n 55), Art. 3.3.

adequate to ensure respect for the right to food access and other fundamental human rights.

3 Human Rights Protection and Food Innovation

International legal instruments governing IP rights have been criticised for establishing norms that are often perceived to conflict with the protection of human rights.[60] The economic burden on developing countries deriving from IP regimes on genetic resources and plant varieties have the potential to hinder the realisation of the right to adequate food. Furthermore, restrictions on access to and transfer of technology can impact the ability of the most vulnerable people and farmers to improve their livelihoods.[61]

The norms provided for by the two distinct regimes, if read as working towards the shared objective of establishing food security, can lead to an alternative international solution to the challenges posed by intellectual property protection.

For this purpose, it is crucial to grasp the essence of some fundamental rights, namely the right to access to food and right to science.

3.1 *The Right to Food*

Since the adoption of the International Covenant on Economic, Social, and Cultural Rights (the Covenant or ICESCR),[62] the right to food, provided for in Article 11, represents a cornerstone of the international human rights system, and nowadays its content is consolidated in international customary law.[63] According to this provision, the right to food has two dimensions: the right to an adequate, available, and accessible level of food, and the 'fundamental' right to be free from hunger.[64]

As interpretated by the Committee on Economic, Social, and Cultural Rights (ESCR Committee or CESCR) in its 1999 General Comment No. 12 on the right to food, this right is primarily concerned with two central aspects. On the one hand, the availability of food in sufficient quantity and quality to meet

60 Laurence R Helfer, 'Human Rights and Intellectual Property: Conflict or Co-Existence?' (2004) 22 Netherlands Quarterly of Human Rights 167.

61 UN, *Report of the Special Rapporteur on the right to food* (n 22).

62 UN, *International Covenant on Economic, Social and Cultural Rights*, New York 16 December 1966, art 11.

63 William A Schabas, *The Customary International Law of Human Rights* (OUP 2021), 303.

64 Philip Alston, 'International Law and the Human Rights to Food' in Philip Alston, Katarina Tomaševski (eds), *The Right to Food* (Netherlands Institute of Human Rights 1984).

the nutritional needs of individuals, and on the other, accessibility, in the physical and economic sense, such that it does not interfere with the enjoyment of other rights.[65] The ESCR Committee also affirms that the right to food must be guaranteed in accordance with the requirements of adequacy and sustainability, which apply to both the characteristics of food and the obligations of States parties in realising this right.[66]

The notion of adequacy depends on a number of factors, such as prevailing social, economic, cultural, climatic, and environmental conditions.[67] The requirement of sustainability, as interpreted by the CESCR, concerns the long-term availability of food, ie its accessibility for present and future generations.[68] In line with the concept of sustainability developed in international law since the 1992 Rio Declaration on Environment and Development, this characteristic implies that States parties to the Covenant shall implement food policies that ensure the most sustainable management and use of natural and other resources for food, at the national, regional, local, and household levels.

The norms set forth by the ICESCR are programmatic.[69] This signifies that States parties are obliged to guarantee at least the 'minimum core obligation'—namely freedom from hunger—and to adopt all appropriate measures to guarantee its progressive realisation and non-regression. This may be achieved through the adoption of appropriate domestic measures at the legislative, administrative, and judicial levels, as well as through the development of targeted strategies. States parties to the ICESCR, thus, bear the duty to create the conditions that facilitate the implementation of the obligations deriving from the right to food. This includes regulating the conduct of private actors, adopting national measures and strategies that ensure the food and nutritional security of every individual, and establishing monitoring mechanisms and judicial or other remedies to seek redress in case of a human rights violation.

---

65 CESCR, *General Comment n°12: The Right to Adequate Food (Art. 11)*, UN Doc. E/C.12/1999/5, 12 May 1999. See also Sven Söllner, 'The "Breakthrough" of the Right to Food: The Meaning of General Comment No.12 and the Voluntary Guidelines for the Interpretation of the Human Right to Food' (2007) 11 Max Planck Yearbook of United Nations Law 391.

66 CESCR, *General Comment n°12* (n 63), para 8.

67 Ben Saul, David Kinley and Jacqueline Mowbray, *The International Covenant on Economic, Social and Cultural Rights. Commentary, Cases and Materials* (OUP 2014), 870.

68 ibid.

69 UN, *International Covenant on Economic, Social and Cultural Rights* (n 60) art 2; Maria M Sepúlveda Carmona, *The Nature of the Obligations under the International Covenant on Economic, Social and Cultural Rights* (Intersentia 2003), 157.

It is worth noting that Article 11 also explicitly defines the duties of States in relation to the fundamental right to be 'free from hunger'. This provision specifies that these duties consist of improving methods of food production, preservation, and distribution, making full use of technical and scientific knowledge, disseminating information on nutritional principles, and developing or reforming agrarian systems to ensure the most efficient use of natural resources. States parties to the ICESCR, thus, should adopt measures aimed at the production, conservation, and distribution of food, taking into consideration 'the problems of both food-importing and food-exporting countries, to ensure an equitable distribution of world food supplies in relation to need'.[70]

Against this background, the ESCR Committee argued that the Parties shall recognise the essential role of international cooperation and that in order to achieve the full realisation of the right to adequate food, it is incumbent on them to take measures to ensure the enjoyment of this right in other countries as well.[71] States parties, thus, shall refrain from restricting food products in a manner that endangers food production and access to food in other countries, and to provide food aid in a manner that does not adversely affect local producers and markets and facilitates the food self-sufficiency of beneficiaries.

This wording reiterates what was foreseen in the 1990 General Comment No.3 on the obligations of States parties to the Covenant. More precisely, the Committee argued that in accordance with established principles of international law, international cooperation on the realisation of economic, social, and cultural rights is an obligation of all Parties, particularly of those States in a position to assist others to that end.[72]

Against this background, it proves challenging to reconcile the prerogatives of the right to food with the elevated costs associated with patented food technologies which should serve as instruments for international technical and economic cooperation to facilitate the realisation of the right, especially in developing countries.

3.2 *The Right to Science*

Within the context of the rights enshrined in the Covenant, the right to benefit from scientific progress and its applications is particularly salient to this research.[73] When read in conjunction with Article 27 of the 1948 Universal

70 ICESCR, (n 60), art 11, para 2.

71 CESCR, 1999 (n 63) para 36.

72 CESCR, *General Comment No.3: The Nature of States Parties' Obligations (Art. 2, Para. 1, of the Covenant)*, UN Doc. E/1991/23, 14 December 1990.

73 ICESCR, (n 60), art 15.

Declaration of Human Rights (UDHR or the Universal Declaration), the 'right to science' also includes the right to enjoy and share scientific advancement and its benefits.[74]

In addition, as confirmed within the *travaux preparatoires* of the Universal Declaration, the term 'share' here is understood to signify 'participate'.[75] Consequently, the right to science is also considered to encompass a participatory dimension.[76]

The right to science is understood to cover both natural and social sciences, the processes and methodologies employed, and the outcomes of these processes and their tangible results, or 'benefits'.[77]

The Committee has further elucidated the normative content of the right, stressing the following elements:

> (a) access to the benefits of science by everyone, without discrimination; (b) opportunities for all to contribute to the scientific enterprise and freedom indispensable for scientific research; (c) participation of individuals and communities in decision-making; and (d) an enabling environment fostering the conservation, development, and diffusion of science and technology.[78]

According to the ICESCR, States parties have a duty to undertake measures to the maximum extent of their available resources to ensure the full realisation of the right to science. This right is to be achieved in a progressive manner, without the adoption of regressive or discriminatory measures.[79]

---

74 UN General Assembly, Resolution 217A (III), *Universal Declaration of Human Rights*, UN Doc. A/RES/217(III), 10 December 1948, art 27.

75 Johannes Morsink, *The Universal Declaration of Human Rights: Origins, Drafting and Intent* (University of Pennsylvania Press 1999). For an overview, see William A Schabas, 'Looking Back: How the Founders Considered Science and Progress in Their Relation to Human Rights' [2015] European Journal of Human Rights 504.

76 Samantha Besson, 'The "Human Right to Science" *qua* right to participate in science. The participatory good of science and its human rights dimensions' (2024) 28 The International Journal of Human Rights 497, 510.

77 CESCR, *General Comment No.25 (2020) on science and economic, social and cultural rights (article 15(1)(b), (2), (3) and (4) of the International Covenant on Economic, Social and Cultural Rights)*, UN Doc. E/C.12/GC/25, 30 April 2020, paras 4–8.

78 UN Human Rights Council, *The right to enjoy the benefits of scientific progress and its applications, Report of the Special Rapporteur in the field of cultural rights, Farida Shaheed*, UN Doc. A/HRC/20/26, 14 May 2012, para 25.

79 UN Committee on Economic, Social and Cultural Rights, *General Comment No. 25* (n 75), 23–27. See also General Comment no 3.

This right to science is inextricably linked to other economic, social, and cultural rights, the realisation and enjoyment of which are significantly reliant on scientific progress[80]—the right to food in particular.[81] As emphasised in the Venice Statement on the Right to Enjoy the Benefits of Scientific Progress and its Applications, adopted in 2009 by a group of experts convened by UNESCO:

> [I]n the area of food production, although scientific advances have significantly increased crop yields, they may also reduce crop genetic diversity, widen the gap between poor farmers and large-scale producers, and thus affect the right to food.[82]

For this reason, IP rights have been recognised as a distinct challenge to the right to science. CESCR has addressed this topic in General Comment No. 25 on science and economic, social, and cultural rights,[83] where it stressed that the interaction between private scientific research and IP has substantial influence on the right to science. While IP norms offer incentives for innovation through mechanisms such as patents, they can also impede scientific advancement and equitable access. This is achieved, for instance, by distorting research funding towards profitable projects, restricting information sharing through IP regulations, and creating barriers to accessing essential products due to high costs set by patent holders.[84] Furthermore, States should strive to find a balance between the protection of intellectual property rights and the promotion of open access and the sharing of scientific knowledge, in accordance with

---

80 UNESCO, *Venice Statement on the Right to Enjoy the Benefits of Scientific Progress and its Applications*, (Venice, 2009), para 12, letter d. For an overview see Amrei Müller, 'Remarks on the Venice Statement on the Right to Enjoy the Benefits of Scientific Progress and its Applications (Article15(1)(b) ICESCR)' (2010) 10 Human Rights Law Review 765.

81 For instance ICESCR, art 11(2)(a); Convention on the Rights of the Child, UN Doc. A/44/49, 20 November 1989, Art.24(2)(c); Additional Protocol to the American Convention on Human Rights in the Area of Economic, Social and Cultural Rights (Protocol of San Salvador), 1988, art 12(2). See also Kerstin Mechlem, Terri Raney, 'Agricultural Biotechnology and the Right to Food' in Francesco Francioni (ed), *Biotechnologies and International Human Rights* (Hart 2007); Olivier De Schutter, 'The Right of Everyone to Enjoy the Benefits of Scientific Progress and the Right to Food: From Conflict to Complementarity' (2011) 33 Human Rights Quarterly 304.

82 UNESCO, *Venice Statement on the Right to Enjoy the Benefits of Scientific Progress and its Applications*, (n 78) para 1(i).

83 UN, *General Comment No. 25* (n 77), paras 58–62.

84 ibid para 61.

international human rights obligations.[85] Finally, the Committee emphasised that:

> [I]ntellectual property is a social product and has a social function and consequently, States parties have a duty to prevent unreasonably high costs for access to essential medicines, plant seeds, or other means of food production, or for schoolbooks and learning materials, from undermining the rights of large segments of the population to health, food, and education.[86]

In a similar vein, the Special Rapporteur in the field of cultural rights, following an earlier examination of the connection between the right to science and IP rights,[87] dedicated a report to the implications of patent policy on the human right to science and culture.[88] From the human rights perspective, it is vital to consider the social function and human dimension of intellectual property, as well as the public interests involved, when discussing patents. In her opinion, these themes are often overlooked when patents are discussed in terms of trade, as in the TRIPS Agreement.

The obligations of States under IP treaties must not jeopardise the implementation of their obligations under human rights treaties.[89] Patent laws should impose no limitations on the rights to health, food, science, and culture, unless the State can demonstrate that the limitation pursues a legitimate aim, is compatible with the nature of these rights, and is strictly necessary for the promotion of general welfare.[90] Furthermore, the Special Rapporteur emphasised that international norms governing plant variety should not impede the right of farmers to utilise, conserve, exchange, and commercialise farm-saved seeds, and that engaging in experimentation, notably within local contexts, should continue.[91]

---

85 ibid.

86 ibid. The Committee previously furnished analogous indications in CESCR, *General Comment No. 17 (2005), The right of everyone to benefit from the protection of the moral and material interests resulting from any scientific, literary or artistic production of which he or she is the author (article 15, paragraph 1 (c), of the Covenant)*, UN Doc. E/C.12/GC/17.

87 *Report of the Special Rapporteur in the field of cultural rights*, 14 May 2012, paras 56–65.

88 UN General Assembly, *Cultural rights, Report of the Special Rapporteur in the field of cultural rights*, UN Doc. A/70/279, New York 4 August 2015.

89 ibid para 89.

90 ibid para 100.

91 ibid para 110.

4 Conclusion: (the Need for) Innovating the Law-Making Agenda

A thorough analysis of the present state of the agrifood sector and its impact on human life reveals certain inadequacies in the existing legal context which necessitate further international efforts to address them.[92]

International law provides for legal instruments that protect the individual right to food through international States' obligations to ensure effective access to food to their populations and, in particular, for the most vulnerable. Nevertheless, international IP norms may impede the advancement of such protections for two different consequential reasons.

Technology can play a key role as a driver of international norm change[93] with the aim of achieving a better balance between the protection of the IP of food innovations and the protection of human rights. To this end, some hypotheses could be further explored both in research activities and in the promotion of future international law-making activities.

On the one hand, the time may be ripe to undertake a revision of the requirements provided for by Article 27(3)(b) for excluding certain innovations from patentability. Indeed, rather than proposing the termination of the TRIPS Agreement, as some prominent scholars have suggested,[94] and which is typically considered 'necessary and impossible',[95] an amending procedure could prove more fruitful.

According to the requirement provided for by Article 71, '[t]he [TRIPS] Council may also undertake reviews in the light of any relevant new developments which might warrant modification or amendment of this Agreement'. The current challenges threatening food security, sustainable development, biodiversity conservation, climate change, and the protection of human rights could be considered a 'relevant new development' that may warrant a

92 UN General Assembly, *Seeds, right to life and farmers' rights, Report of the Special Rapporteur on the right to food, Michael Fakhri,* UN Doc. A/HRC/49/43, New York 30 December 2021.

93 Sandra Schwindenhammer, 'The Future We Want? Interlinking Global Sustainability Norm Change, Technology Innovation, and Regime Complexity' in Heike Krieger and Andrea Liese, *Tracing Value Change in the International Legal Order. Perspectives from Legal and Political Science* (OUP 2023).

94 Anne Orford, 'The 2022 Annual Kirby Lecture in International Law: Why It's Time to Terminate the TRIPS Agreement' (2024) 41 The Australian Yearbook of International Law Online 3 <https://brill.com/view/journals/auso/41/1/article-p3_1.xml?srsltid=AfmBOor8MarULuPmoyflouAdAMK91xiIgllFat8eP6FOwNH9fzlG7XNE> accessed 24 June 2025.

95 Siva Thambisetty, 'Termination of the TRIPS Agreement: Necessary And Impossible' (2023) Opinio Juris <https://opiniojuris.org/2023/01/11/termination-of-the-trips-agreement-necessary-and-impossible/>, accessed 30 May 2025.

modification to Article 27. As other authors have observed, the preservation and exploitation of TRIPS flexibilities should be recommended when the intellectual property system presents impediments for the eradication of hunger.[96]

In 1998, States parties to TRIPS commenced discussions regarding the potential for a review of the exclusion from patentability of plants and animal inventions. This need has been reflected in different proposals, particularly by developing countries, in different fora within the WTO.[97]

Nevertheless, as the debate surrounding IP of technology and food is inextricably linked to that of effective human rights protection, a multilateral discourse between the relevant international organisations may prove more appropriate.

On the other hand, *sui generis* regimes allow for the incorporation of any measures deemed essential for the advancement of specific objectives, including those regarding food security.[98] Therefore, relevant amendments to domestic legislation should be considered, with a view to integrating concerns around food security into the existing domestic legislation. A comprehensive approach should also be adopted to achieve an up-to-date integration of specific norms that balance IP rights and human rights obligations. This implies that further development should not be restricted to considering only the right to adequate food; rather, it should be expanded to encompass the protection of other rights concerned, such as the right to access scientific innovation, and even the emerging right to seeds.[99] The strengthening of protection of the rights of farmers has proved to balance the incentives for innovation for professional plant breeders and the reward to farmers for their role in the preservation of plant resources.[100] In other worlds, human rights can offer a fertile ground for restoring a balance in IP law,[101] and for this reason distinguished scholars consider the development of norms within non-traditional fora as a

96 Claudio Chiarolla, 'Commodifying Agricultural Biodiversity and Development-Related Issues' (2006) 9 The Journal of World Intellectual Property 41.

97 Edward Kwakwa, 'International Legal Argumentation Outside the Courtroom: A Focus on Intellectual Property' in Ian Johnstone, Steven Ratner (eds), *Talking International Law. Legal Argumentation Outside the Courtroom* (OUP 2021).

98 Matthew T Stilwell, *Review of Article 27.3(b)*, (CIEL 2001).

99 Francesco Seatzu, 'The day after no tomorrow?: the right to seeds as a new and distinct human right?' (2024) 4 Federalismi.it 215.

100 De Schutter, 'The Right of Everyone to Enjoy the Benefits of Scientific Progress' (n 79). See for instance at the domestic level, n° DL-33004/2001, The Protection of Plan Varieties and Farmers Rights Act 2001, Gazette of India, 30 October 2001.

101 Lea Shaver, 'The Right to Science and Culture' [2010] Wisconsin Law Review 121, 127.

possible, effective long-term strategy to contribute to making the IP regime more equitable.[102]

In conclusion, with respect to the discretionary authority granted by Article 27 for the *sui generis* option, the harmonisation of national legislation, rather than the establishment of competing systems for the protection of heterogeneous and non-global objectives is a desirable option.

More generally, it is crucial to reiterate that '[a]chieving food security and nutrition goals is not only good for those suffering from food insecurity and malnutrition, it is good for everyone. A healthier, more just and equal world is better for all'.[103]

Bibliography

Abbott FM, 'The Trips-Legality of Measures Taken to Address Public Health Crises: A Synopsis' (2001) 7 Widener Law Symposium Journal.

Abbott FM, 'The Doha Declaration on the TRIPS Agreement and Public Health: Lighting a Dark Corner at the WTO' (2002) 5 Journal of International Economic Law 469.

Alston P, 'International Law and the Human Rights to Food' in Alston P, Tomaševski K (eds), *The Right to Food* (Netherlands Institute of Human Rights 1984).

Benfica R and others, 'Food System Innovations and Digital Technologies to Foster Productivity Growth and Rural Transformation' in von Braun J and others (eds), *Science and Innovations for Food Systems Transformation* (Springer 2023).

Besson S, 'The "Human Right to Science" *qua* right to participate in science. The participatory good of science and its human rights dimensions' (2024) 28 The International Journal of Human Rights 497.

Chiarolla C, 'Commodifying Agricultural Biodiversity and Development-Related Issues' (2006) 9 The Journal of World Intellectual Property 41.

Correa CM, *Trade Related Aspects of Intellectual Property Rights: A Commentary on the TRIPS Agreement* (2nd edn, OUP 2020).

Cottier T, Pauwelyn J and Bürgi E (eds), *Human Rights and International Trade* (OUP 2005).

102 ibid 183; Laurence R Helfer, 'Regime Shifting: The TRIPs Agreement and New Dynamics of International Intellectual Property Lawmaking' (2004) 29 Yale Journal of International Law 1.

103 FAO, IFAD, UNICEF, WFP, and WHO, The State of Food Security and Nutrition in the World 2023. Urbanization, Agrifood systems transformation and healthy diets across the rural-urban continuum (Rome 2023).

Cullet P, 'Intellectual Property Rights and Food Security in the South' (2004) 7 Journal of World Intellectual Property 261.

De Schutter O, 'The Right of Everyone to Enjoy the Benefits of Scientific Progress and the Right to Food: From Conflict to Complementarity' (2011) 33 Human Rights Quarterly 304.

do Vale Alves A, 'WIPO's New Treaty on Intellectual Property, Genetic Resources and Traditional Knowledge—A Turning Point for Indigenous Heritage?' (2024) 13 (11) ESIL Reflections.

Dutfield G, *Intellectual Property, Biogenetic Resources and Traditional Knowledge* (Routledge 2004).

Edwardson S, 'Reconciling TRIPS and the Right to Food' in Cottier T, Pauwelyn J and Bürgi E (eds), *Human Rights and International Trade* (OUP 2005).

Footer ME, 'Agricultural Biotechnology, Food Security and Human Rights' in Francioni F and Scovazzi T, *Biotechnology and International Law* (Bloomsbury 2006).

Francioni F and Scovazzi T (eds), *Biotechnology and International Law* (Bloomsbury 2006).

Guan W, 'IPRs, Public Health, and International Trade: An International Law Perspective on the TRIPS Amendment' (2016) 29 Leiden Journal of International Law 411.

Helfer LR, 'Human Rights and Intellectual Property: Conflict or Co-Existence?' (2004) 22 Netherlands Quarterly of Human Rights 167.

Helfer LR, *Intellectual Property Rights in Plant Varieties. International Legal Regimes and Policy Options for National Governments* (FAO 2004).

Kariuki F, 'Traditional Governance Institutions and the Holistic Protection of Traditional Knowledge' in Laura Pineschi (ed), *Cultural Heritage, Sustainable Development and Human Rights. Towards an Integrated Approach* (Routledge 2024).

Kwakwa E, 'International Legal Argumentation Outside the Courtroom: A Focus on Intellectual Property' in Johnstone I, Ratner S (eds), *Talking International Law. Legal Argumentation Outside the Courtroom* (OUP 2021).

Leskien D, Flitner M, *Intellectual Property Rights and Plant Genetic Resources: Options for a sui generis system* (IPGRI 1997).

Lupone A, Ricci C and Santini A (eds), *The Right to Safe Food Towards a Global Governance* (Giappichelli 2013).

Malbon J, Lawson C and Davison M, *The WTO Agreement on Trade-Related Aspects of Intellectual Property Rights. A Commentary* (Elgar 2014).

Moore G, Tymowsky W, *Explanatory Guide to the International Treaty on Plant Genetic Resources for Food and Agriculture* (IUCN 2005).

Morgera E, Tsioumani E and Buck M, *Unraveling the Nagoya Protocol: A Commentary of the Protocol on Access and Benefit-Sharing to the Convention on Biological Diversity* (Brill 2015).

Morsink J, *The Universal Declaration of Human Rights: Origins, Drafting and Intent* (Pennsylvania University Press 1999).

Morten Haugen H, Ruiz Muller M and Mullapudi Narasimhan S, 'Food security and intellectual property rights: Finding linkages' in Tzen Wong and Graham Dutfield (eds), *Intellectual Property and Human Development. Current Trends and Future Scenarios* (CUP 2010).

Müller A, 'Remarks on the Venice Statement on the Right to Enjoy the Benefits of Scientific Progress and its Applications (Article15(1)(b) ICESCR)' (2010) 10 Human Rights Law Review 765.

O'Connor B, 'Protecting traditional knowledge: an overview of developing area of intellectual property law' (2003) 6 Journal of World Intellectual Property 677.

Orford A, 'The 2022 Annual Kirby Lecture in International Law: Why It's Time to Terminate the TRIPS Agreement' (2024) 41 The Australian Yearbook of International Law Online 3.

Pineschi L (ed), *Cultural Heritage, Sustainable Development and Human Rights. Towards an Integrated Approach* (Routledge 2024).

Roht-Arriaza N, 'Of seeds and shamans: the appropriation of the scientific and technical knowledge of indigenous and local communities' (1996) 17 Michigan Journal of International Law, 919.

Saul B, Kinley D and Mowbray J, *The International Covenant on Economic, Social and Cultural Rights. Commentary, Cases and Materials* (OUP 2014).

Seatzu F, 'The day after no tomorrow?: the right to seeds as a new and distinct human right?' (2024) 4 *Federalismi.it* 215.

Sepúlveda Carmona MM, *The Nature of the Obligations under the International Covenant on Economic, Social and Cultural Rights* (Intersentia 2003).

Schabas WA, 'Looking Back: How the Founders Considered Science and Progress in Their Relation to Human Rights' [2015] European Journal of Human Rights 504.

Schabas WA, *The Customary International Law of Human Rights* (OUP 2021).

Schwindenhammer S, 'The Future We Want? Interlinking Global Sustainability Norm Change, Technology Innovation, and Regime Complexity' in Krieger H and Liese A, *Tracing Value Change in the International Legal Order. Perspectives from Legal and Political Science* (OUP 2023).

Shaver L, 'The Right to Science and Culture' [2010] Wisconsin Law Review 121.

Söllner S, 'The "Breakthrough" of the Right to Food: The Meaning of General Comment No.12 and the Voluntary Guidelines for the Interpretation of the Human Right to Food' (2007) 11 Max Planck Yearbook of United Nations Law 391.

Stilwell MT, '*Review of Article 27.3(b)*' (CIEL 2021).

Sun H, 'The Road to Doha and Beyond: Some Reflections on the TRIPS Agreement and Public Health' (2004) 15 European Journal of International Law 123.

Thambisetty S, 'Termination of the TRIPS Agreement: Necessary and Impossible' (2023) Opinio Juris, <https://opiniojuris.org/2023/01/11/termination-of-the-trips-agreement-necessary-and-impossible/>, accessed 30 May 2025.

Tsioumani E, *Fair and Equitable Benefit-Sharing in Agriculture. Reinventing Agrarian Justice* (Routledge 2021).

Wong T and Dutfield G (eds), *Intellectual Property and Human Development. Current Trends and Future Scenarios* (CUP 2010).

CHAPTER 3

The European Union's Action in Promoting Agrifood Innovation: Fostering through Funding

Nicola Bergamaschi

Summary

1. Introduction. 2. EU Funds as a Policy Instrument in the Context of Agrifood Innovation. 3. The Focus of EU Funds on Agrifood Innovation. 3.1 Horizon Europe. 3.2 CAP funds. 4. Sustainable Development as a Guiding Star: Purpose and Limits of Funding Agrifood Innovation. 5. Conclusions.

1 Introduction

'Agrifood innovation' is not a predefined domain of legal intervention of the European Union (EU). It is neither mentioned by the EU's founding Treaties—the Treaty on the European Union (TEU) and the Treaty on the Functioning of the European Union (TFEU)—nor is there a specifically dedicated legal basis or, even, an ad hoc normative regime regulating it. Nonetheless, if intended as 'innovation' within 'the agrifood system' of the Union, the topic assumes relevance for the EU action. This emerges clearly in the Commission's Communication, 'A Vision for Agriculture and Food', where innovation is considered fundamental for the future of the EU's farming and food sectors.[1]

In EU law, a variety of legal acts provide definitions of innovation. Although they may present slight differences depending on the specific purposes of each act's normative regime, they do not significantly diverge. A good example, useful for this work, is the one presented in Regulation 2021/819:

> Innovation means the process, including its outcome, by which new ideas respond to societal, economic or environmental needs and demand and generate new products, processes, services, or business, organisational and social models that are successfully introduced into an existing

1 Commission, *A Vision for Agriculture and Food. Shaping Together an Attractive Farming and Agri-food Sector for Future Generations* COM(2025) 75 final.

> market or that are able to create new markets and that provide value to society.[2]

Interestingly, the term 'innovation' here refers to both the activity of innovating and the outcome of such an activity, which respectively represent two distinct moments in the innovation process.[3] Also, it must be noted that the definition includes a policy orientation of innovation towards certain societal interests and objectives.[4]

As for the notion of an 'agrifood system', the Commission refers to it as one of the 14 industrial ecosystems identified in the updated New Industrial Strategy. It is described as covering:

> [A]ll operators in the food supply chain (farmers, food industry, food retail and wholesale, and food service) and their suppliers of inputs and services (seeds, pesticides, fertiliser, machinery, packaging, repair, transport, finance, advice, and logistics).[5]

---

2 Regulation (EU) 2021/819 of the European Parliament and of the Council of 20 May 2021 on the European Institute of Innovation and Technology [2021] OJ L189/61, art 2, para 1. This definition has not been subject to interpretation by the European Court of Justice. A similar definition is in art 2, para 22, of Directive 2014/24/EU of the European Parliament and of the Council of 26 February 2014 on public procurement [2014] OJ L94/65. At the international level, see OECD and Eurostat, *Oslo Manual 2018. Guidelines for Collecting, Reporting and Using Data on Innovation* (4nd edn, OECD Publishing 2018), 20. Even if not explicitly mentioned or defined, the concept of innovation may find relevance in various areas of the EU legal framework, such as biotechnological inventions' patentability (Directive 98/44/EC of the European Parliament and of the Council of 6 July 1998 on the legal protection of biotechnological inventions [1998] OJ L213/13). However, this does not imply that rules or legal categories elaborated in a specific context can be automatically transposed to others; cf Case T-561/14 *One of Us and Others v Commission* [2018] EU:T:2018:210, paras 173–174.

3 As confirmed in Commission, *Guidance on Innovation Procurement* [2021] OJ C267/01, 6. The same approach is adopted in OECD and Eurostat (n 2), 20.

4 This seems consistent with TEU art 3 which refers to the promotion of research and technological advances and the EU's sustainable development as being based on 'a highly competitive social market economy, aiming at ... social progress', as EU objectives related to the establishment of the internal market.

5 Commission, *Annual Single Market Report 2021* SWD(2021) 351 final, 82. The EU notion does not diverge from that shared at the international level; see High-Level Panel of Experts (HLPE) on Food Security and Nutrition of the Committee on World Food Security, *Food losses and waste in the context of sustainable food systems* (Roma 2014), 12. Cf Commission, *Co-creation of a transition pathway for a more resilient, sustainable and digital agrifood ecosystem* SWD(2023) 263 final, 2.

The scope of the 'agrifood innovation' concept in the EU legal order is, thus, remarkably broad, touching upon several domains of the Union's action. In fact, within the EU legal framework, 'food' is classically seen as a multifaceted issue, falling within the scope of multiple EU policies and normative fields.[6] The Common Agricultural Policy (CAP), the Common Fisheries Policy (CFP), and the internal market regime play important roles, but also policies covering health, trade, environment, competition, consumer protection, intellectual property, cohesion, research, and industry may address food or food-related issues.[7] This explains why the agrifood sector is one of the 'most heavily regulated economic sectors' in the EU,[8] making it difficult to draw a comprehensive picture of the EU food legal discipline. Among the mentioned EU policies, one is specifically dedicated to innovation: the EU Research and Technological Development policy (referred to hereafter as the 'research policy').[9] However, most of the policies mentioned above may entail issues concerning innovation. Consequently, it is reasonable to claim that, within the EU's legal order, agrifood innovation represents a topic composed of many components, linked to different areas of EU law.

Moreover, since innovation refers to the innovating activity and its outcome, it is subject to various lines of normative intervention, each dealing with one of these two moments. On the one hand, EU law steps in downstream of the innovation process to regulate many issues concerning the marketability of the products that are the fruit of innovation.[10] This is visible, for example, in

6 For a thorough analysis, see Hanna Schebesta and Kai Purnhagen, *EU Food Law* (OUP 2024), 34–35. A definition of 'food' is provided in art 2 of Regulation (EC) 178/2002 of the European Parliament and of the Council of 28 January 2002 (General Food Law Regulation) laying down the general principles and requirements of food law, establishing the European Food Safety Authority, and laying down procedures in matters of food safety [2002] OJ L31/1.

7 Eg the General Food Law Regulation is grounded in four legal bases, concerning four different policies.

8 See Bernd Van der Meulen and Bart Wernaart (eds), *EU Food Law Handbook* (BRILL | Wageningen Academic Publishers 2020), 161.

9 TFEU, arts 179–190.

10 For an overview of the EU law's role in this domain see Laura Salvi, 'Agri-Food Law and Innovation through the Lenses of Better Regulation' and Irene Canfora, '"Products of Innovation" in Agri-Food Markets. Legal Rules for the Access of Innovating Products and Paradigms in the Agri-Food Market' in AIDA-IFLA (ed), *Innovation in Agri-Food Law between Technology and Comparison* (Wolters Kluwer 2019). For an example of innovative production methods, see the case of vertical farming in the chapter by Simone Pitto in this volume.

the case of so-called 'Novel Foods',[11] or in that of food produced through innovative biotechnology techniques.[12]

On the other hand, EU law also plays an upstream role in the innovation process, addressing the innovation activity itself. As the present study will demonstrate, the key instrument at the EU's disposal to promote innovation in the agrifood system is its budgetary funds. Moving on from the above, the chapter focuses on the role and the use of EU funds in this field, exploring the legal framework of the EU's action in fostering agrifood innovation through its spending power, instead of its regulatory one. To this end, Section 2 will examine the main features of the EU funds as a policy instrument in this context, with special reference to the cases of Horizon Europe and the Common Agricultural Policy (CAP) funds, representing the two main EU funding programmes addressing innovation.

Subsequently, Section 3 will bring the analysis to a more substantial level, illustrating in detail the space that Horizon Europe and CAP funds devote to agrifood innovation. Section 4 then moves to the purpose of innovation, focusing on the orientation towards sustainability which characterises agrifood innovation funding instruments and its main implications, especially regarding the interplay between innovation and precaution, and the limits to innovation. Finally, the main findings are summarised in Section 5.

2 EU Funds as a Policy Instrument in the Context of Agrifood Innovation

A variety of means are available for the EU to carry out its policies. In the legal sphere, this includes normative and non-normative (ie soft law) measures. It can also rely on tools with both a legal and financial nature, such as EU funds. By using these funds, the EU channels financial resources, gathered mainly from Member States' contributions,[13] towards EU objectives according to criteria set at the supranational level.

Currently, more than 40 EU funding programmes—the so-called 'budgetary galaxy' of the EU[14]—exist covering a wide range of sectors and policies. These

11 See the chapters by Maria Laura Grilli and Giacomo Degli Antoni, Marco Faillo and Giulia Formici in this volume.

12 See the chapter by Maria Chiara Errigo in this volume.

13 Cf Council Decision (EU, Euratom) 2020/2053 of 14 December 2020 on the system of own resources of the European Union [2020] OJ L424/1.

14 Richard Crowe, 'The European Budgetary Galaxy' (2017) 13 European Constitutional Law Review 428.

programmes are funded through the Multiannual Financial Framework (MFF), the long-term budget of the EU (which typically spans a seven-year period).[15] The creation of each funding programme requires a dedicated, legally-binding act that establishes the fund, outlines its specific functioning rules, and sets its objectives.[16] Like all legal acts adopted by the EU institutions, these acts require appropriate legal bases in the Treaties, depending on the Union policies under which the funds are established.[17]

Agrifood innovation is among the objectives that various EU funds serve. As shown in the previous section, such a topic can be addressed (more or less intensively) by several EU policies and, consequently, by an array of funding programmes.[18] The two main programmes among these are Horizon Europe and the CAP's funds,[19] which illustrate well the role that EU funds play as a policy instrument in the context of agrifood innovation.

Horizon Europe was established for the financial period of 2021–2027,[20] with a double-policy legal basis, under the EU research policy and the EU industrial policy.[21] Its general objective is to 'deliver scientific, technological, economic, and societal impact from the EU's investments in Research and Innovation (R&I)'.[22] In broad terms, it can be described as providing financial support to R&I projects in different areas, including the agrifood system, as discussed below in Section 3. With a budget of nearly 95.5 billion EUR, Horizon Europe represents the main funding tool of EU research policy. Indeed, as anticipated, allocating funding could be a helpful measure the EU

15 For the period 2021–2026, the budget's resources are accompanied by the extra-MMF resources of the Recovery and Resilience Facility. See Regulation (EU) 2021/241 of the European Parliament and of the Council of 12 February 2021 establishing the Recovery and Resilience Facility [2021] OJ L57/17.

16 TFEU, art 310, para 3.

17 Cf Bruno de Witte, 'Integration Through Funding. The Union's Finances as Policy Instrument' in Ruth Weber (ed), *The Financial Constitution of European Integration. Follow the Money?* (Hart Publishing 2023), 222–224.

18 For an infographic overview see OECD, 'Policies for the Future of Farming and Food in the European Union' (OECD Publishing 2023), 229.

19 Other funds may have a role in fostering innovation in sectors related to the agrifood system. See, for instance, Regulation (EU) 2021/1139 of the European Parliament and of the Council of 7 July 2021 establishing the European Maritime, Fisheries and Aquaculture Fund [2021] OJ L247/1.

20 Regulation (EU) 2021/695 of the European Parliament and of the Council of 28 April 2021 establishing Horizon Europe—the Framework Programme for Research and Innovation, laying down its rules for participation and dissemination [2021] OJ L170/1.

21 Respectively, under the TFEU, arts 182, para 1, art 183 and art 188 and under the TFEU, art 173, para 3.

22 Regulation (EU) 2021/695 (n 20), art 3, para 1.

can employ to reach its policy goals, of which the promotion of scientific and technological advances is one.[23] In accordance with this goal, Article 179 TFEU provides for the creation of a European Research Area (ERA) as the main aim of the EU research policy and, in pursuing it, the EU should carry out a set of activities 'complementing' the action of Member States in this field.[24] In fact, given that the EU's role is supportive in nature, it has the power to act on research and technological development, without preventing the Member States from doing the same.[25] The EU should thus cooperate and coordinate Member State action, with the EU's role being to ensure that its policy and national ones are consistent.[26] In a similar vein, EU industrial policy consists of supporting and coordinating the action of Member States through 'specific measures' aimed at pursuing the objective of the policy—to ensure the conditions for industry competitiveness[27]—without harmonising the laws and regulations of the Member States.[28] Horizon Europe corresponds to one of these specific measures. It is therefore no accident that a funding programme such as Horizon Europe is a central instrument in the context of both research and industrial policy. This is due to the nature of the competences the EU has in this domain,[29] where the EU shall refrain from setting strict and uniform mandatory standards. Indeed, instead of more top-down rule-making, the research and industrial policies are conducted through other instruments, including the use of budgetary resources of the EU, which, while 'softer', remain effective.[30]

In short, Horizon Europe enacts the EU's mandate to promote and support research and innovation by financing relevant projects. This activity takes place via direct contact between the EU and funding recipients; in fact, Horizon Europe is mostly implemented under the 'direct management regime'.[31] Accordingly, the Commission is responsible for all the implementation steps, including the evaluation and selection of the funded activities, the disbursement of the fund, and the control over it. These duties are carried

23 See n 4.
24 TFEU, art 180.
25 TEU, art 4, para 3.
26 TFEU, art 181.
27 TFEU, art 173, para 1.
28 TFEU, art 173, para 4.
29 Cf TFEU, art 3, para 6.
30 Cf de Witte (n 17), 227. What is said does not imply that the adoption of legislative or other binding acts is prevented. As mentioned, their use is required by the Treaties to establish the funding programmes.
31 Regulation (EU, Euratom) 2024/2509 of the European Parliament and of the Council of 23 September 2024 on the financial rules applicable to the general budget of the Union (recast) [2024] OJ L239/1, art 62, para 1, lett a).

out directly by the Commission or through the executive agencies it has created, which are considered extensions of the Commission itself. Thus, the EU (through the Commission) is directly in charge of Horizon Europe's political or administrative discretionary choices at all stages, from the establishment of the programme to its implementation.

As for CAP funds, they represent the most important instrument of EU agricultural policy and one of the longest-standing EU funding instruments. And at over 386 billion EUR (in the current MFF), it accounts for roughly one-quarter of the EU budget. CAP funds consist of two funding programmes, the European Agricultural Guarantee Fund (EAGF) and the European Agricultural Fund for Rural Development (EAFRD).[32] The first is mainly dedicated to direct payments for Member State farmers, while the second finances national-level interventions for rural development. So, unlike Horizon Europe, these funds are not prima facie intended to support R&I activities. Indeed, CAP funds primarily aim to pursue the CAP's general objectives,[33] for which research and innovation can be instrumental. Innovation is thus addressed by the CAP not as an end per se, but as a way to reach its more general goals. Interestingly, the CAP was the first policy for which the Treaty of Rome mentioned scientific research as a means to pursue its objectives,[34] whereas Article 41 TFEU now explicitly envisages the possibility of the EU adopting measures under the CAP framework to pursue effective coordination of research efforts.

The use of financial investment as a policy instrument in the CAP domain is not due to the EU's lack of other possible instruments. Indeed, the agricultural policy falls under the shared competence of the EU,[35] meaning that in the context of the CAP, the EU is endowed with powers that are more cogent than those within the research and industrial fields. Accordingly, EU intervention within the framework of the CAP is not limited to a supportive or coordinating role and, once it takes place, supersedes any autonomous initiatives of Member States. The fact that funding programmes represent the main means of EU action—even in this context where the EU is also endowed with fully-fledged

32 Regulation (EU) 2021/2115 of the European Parliament and of the Council of 2 December 2021 establishing rules on support for strategic plans to be drawn up by Member States under the common agricultural policy (CAP Strategic Plans) and financed by the European Agricultural Guarantee Fund (EAGF) and by the European Agricultural Fund for Rural Development (EAFRD) [2021] OJ L435/1.

33 TFEU, art 39, para 1, combined with TFEU, art 11. See Commission, *Impact Assessment Accompanying the Documents COM(2018) 392 final, COM(2018) 393 final, COM(2018) 394 final, SEC(2018) 305 final* SWD/2018/301 final, 19; cf de Witte (n 17), 226.

34 Treaty establishing the European Economic Community (TCEE), art 41.

35 TFEU, art 4, para 2, lett d).

regulatory powers—underscores the potentialities the EU perceives this tool as possessing. As noted by de Witte:

> The current EU funding landscape is marked by the increased eagerness of European institutions to use EU funding in a strategic way so as to advance Europe-wide policy objectives rather than (or in addition to) redistribution among the Member States.[36]

In fact, the EAGF and the EAFRD are not only about handing out money to farmers or rural communities. Rather, their general objective is to improve 'sustainable development of farming, food, and rural areas' in the 'economic, environmental, and social spheres',[37] with research and innovation being instrumental in this sense.[38] It is on these premises that, as will be illustrated in Section 3, CAP funds address innovation issues, namely through EAFRD resources.

Against this background, CAP funds' approach of introducing innovation into the agricultural sector can be reconsidered under what de Witte describes as the 'policy steering role of EU funding' which characterises CAP funds too.[39] In this sense, funds are utilised by the EU to guide policy choices made at the national level by Member States and other stakeholders. It must be noted that the EU does not manage CAP funds directly, as is the case with Horizon Europe. EAGF and EAFRD are implemented according to the 'shared management regime'[40] under which the programmes' implementation jointly falls on the Commission and Member States. More precisely, according to the current CAP funds' new performance delivery model, each Member State shall adopt a National Strategic Plan (NSP) explaining and justifying how the finances will be used nationally.[41] The NSPs should adhere to the objectives and basic rules of EAGF and EAFRD and must be approved by the Commission.[42] The funds are then managed by the Member States' national authorities, which select the beneficiaries and disburse the resources, while the Commission supervises

36 De Witte (n 17) 235.

37 Regulation 2021/2115, art 5.

38 Regulation 2021/2115, art 6, para 2.

39 De Witte (n 17) 226.

40 Regulation (EU, Euratom) 2024/2509, (n 31) art 63.

41 Regulation 2021/2115, art 1, para 1, lett c. This practice substantively corresponds to the partnership principle operating in the field of the EU cohesion policy funds. See Katerina Pantazatou, 'European Union Funds' in Herwig CH Hofmann, Gerard C Rowe, and Alexander H Türk, *Specialized Administrative Law of the European Union* (OUP 2018) 537.

42 Regulation 2021/2115, art 118.

all operations. The results are then subject to regular monitoring and evaluation of performance and results by the Member States and, in a second stage, by the EU. Consistent with the subsidiarity and proportionality principles, under the described performance delivery mechanism the Member States are thus endowed with a certain flexibility in deciding the interventions to be funded, with an emphasis shift 'from compliance with detailed EU-level rules towards … achieving results against the policy's common objectives, defined and agreed at EU level'.[43]

3 The Focus of EU Funds on Agrifood Innovation

3.1 *Horizon Europe*

Horizon Europe corresponds to what Article 182 TFEU calls a 'multiannual framework programme' of the research policy,[44] which is to be established by a legislative act (Regulation 2021/695, HE Regulation)[45] with the following goals: to determine the scientific and technological objectives and relevant priorities for EU action in the research field; to define the broad categories of activities to be carried out; and to set the overall funds to finance selected R&I projects.[46] The detailed rules for the framework programme's implementation (concerning operational objectives, project duration, and budgets) are provided in the 'specific programme', contained in a decision adopted by the Council.[47] Under the framework of Horizon Europe, the EU finances R&I projects of selected beneficiaries through grants and other funding forms (eg, procurement). Eligible activities are those that intend to pursue the research objectives listed in Article 3. Any legal entity may apply for funding. As discussed previously,[48] the Commission is the main institutional actor managing the entire funding process, supported by the European Research Council (ERC), the European Innovation Council (EIC), and the European Institute of Innovation & Technology (EIT). The EIT is assigned operational tasks covering

43 See SWD/2018/301 final, 21. The described delivery model can be—at least partially—seen through the lens of the new planning method described in Paul Dermine, 'The Planning Method: An Inquiry into the Constitutional Ramifications of a New EU Governance Technique' (2024) 61 Common Market Law Review 959.

44 TFEU, art 182, para 1.

45 See (n 20).

46 TFEU, art 182, para 1.

47 TFEU, art 182, para 3. Council Decision (EU) 2021/764 of 10 May 2021 establishing the Specific Programme implementing Horizon Europe [2021] OJ L167/1.

48 See Section 2.

education, business creation and acceleration services, and innovation-driven research projects, mainly working through Knowledge and Innovation Communities (KICs).[49]

The agrifood system occupies an important place among Horizon Europe's thematic areas. Indeed, it is one of the sectors that receives the most funding (around 10 billion EUR), permeating the entire programme's articulations. Horizon Europe is structured in three pillars: 1) Excellent science; 2) Global challenges and European industrial competitiveness, and 3) Innovative Europe.

'Excellent science' consists of funding researchers' work and formation experiences, to, for instance, support early-stage researchers and sustain the creation and diffusion of scientific excellence. The ECR is the main arm of the pillar and, with a budget of 16 billion EUR under the current programme, funds thousands of R&I projects in several fields, including the agrifood system.[50] Pillar two, 'Global Challenges and European Industrial Competitiveness', aims to stimulate and support R&I solutions to sensitive issues affecting seven selected areas, or 'clusters'. Cluster 6 among these is dedicated to 'Food, Bioeconomy, Natural Resources, Agriculture, and Environment'. Financed with nearly 9 billion EUR, Cluster 6 covers seven fields of intervention, all of which are bound to the agrifood system.[51] One of these seven fields, 'food systems', deals with safety, security, and sustainability issues concerning food production and consumption.[52] Finally, the third pillar, 'Innovative Europe', is not thematically organised, rather it aims to foster all forms of innovation with a special focus on Small and Medium Enterprises (SMEs). It includes the funding activities of EIC and EIT, some of which are expressly focused on agrifood innovation. For instance, among the funding calls launched by EIC, one targets projects on nature-inspired alternatives for food packaging and films, while another concerns projects aimed at obtaining food from precision

49 KICs are large-scale, institutionalised, European partnerships (as referred to in the HE Regulation; see below in this section) of higher education institutions, research organisations, companies, and other stakeholders in the innovation process in the form of a strategic network, based on joint mid- to long-term innovation planning to meet EIT challenges and contribute to attaining the objectives established under Horizon Europe; Regulation (EU) 2021/819 (n 2) art 2, para 2.

50 Cf European Research Council Executive Agency, 'Mapping ERC frontier research sustainable food production and consumption' (Publications Office 2023) <https://op.europa.eu/en/publication-detail/-/publication/59edf0fa-0e5c-11ee-b12e-01aa75ed71a1> accessed 27 June 2025.

51 HE Regulation, Annex I.

52 ibid.

fermentation and algae. As for EIT, in 2016 it started a KIC specifically focused on food, called 'EIT Food'.

Furthermore, 'missions' and 'European Partnerships' can be established to implement the programme, in particular its second pillar.[53] The missions focus on five predetermined thematic areas, one of which relates to 'Soil Health and Food'. The European Partnerships can be co-programmed, co-funded, or institutionalised. They are grouped because of their thematic link to the seven clusters' fields. Of 49 European Partnerships, eight pertain to food-related matters under Cluster 6 (EIT Food should be added to this group since it is formally qualified as an 'institutionalised partnership').

Interestingly, Article 180 TFEU requires EU actions in the research policy context to ensure the involvement of all actors taking part in the innovation process, including the private sector, encouraging the work of undertakings, research centres, universities, and researchers. Horizon Europe embraces this attitude, which is reflected in the multi-actor approach that is expected to be followed by activities funded under Cluster 6,[54] including involving those who are:

> [E]ssentially the (end-) users of the project results who are backed up by any other useful intermediaries and actors who can contribute with further expertise and innovative ideas relevant to the topic's objectives, and support communication and dissemination.[55]

Finally, it is worth noting that Horizon Europe should be implemented in synergy with other EU funding programmes relating to different EU policies, including the CAP.[56]

3.2 *CAP Funds*

Although the two CAP funds, ie the EAGF and the EAFRD, support diverse kinds of interventions with different functions, they have common objectives and follow the same set of rules, which regulate their functioning and their performance delivery mechanism.[57] As anticipated, the programmes' implementation centres around the adoption of NSPs by Member States, which

53 HE Regulation, arts 8 and 10 and Annex IV.
54 Council Decision 2021/764 (n 47), Annex I.
55 Commission Implementing Decision 2024/2371, Annex IX, 22.
56 HE Regulation, rec. 7 and Annex I.
57 The basic act is Regulation (EU) 2021/2115.

contain the interventions to be funded under both of the funds and are subject to the same performance monitoring and assessment framework.

It has been mentioned that, under the CAP, innovation is considered a functional part of the more general objectives of the policy. This is reflected within CAP fund rules, in particular in Article 6 of Regulation 2021/2115. The norm lists the specific objectives of the EAGF and the EAFRD through which the general objectives of the funds (enshrined in Article 5 of the regulation) shall be pursued. Among those specific objectives, the second paragraph of Article 6 includes:

> [T]he cross-cutting objective of modernising agriculture and rural areas by fostering and sharing of knowledge, innovation, and digitalisation in agriculture and rural areas and by encouraging their uptake by farmers, through improved access to research, innovation, knowledge exchange, and training.[58]

Hence, in light of the quoted provision, innovation, at large, is instrumental to agricultural modernisation, which in turn is a cross-cutting, specific objective that contributes to the reach of the EAGF and EAFRD's general objective.

More specifically, agricultural innovation is addressed by CAP fund rules by two main, interconnected sides. One side relates to the infrastructural and networking dimension. It revolves around the European Innovation Partnership for agricultural productivity and sustainability (EIP),[59] which is a 'policy and networking initiative designed to speed up innovation on the ground through the interactive innovation model'.[60] This model corresponds to the same multi-actor approach found in Horizon Europe. The EIP is integrated into the structure of CAP networks, which are established at the European and national levels, respectively by the Commission and each Member State.[61] In the background of EIP, there are the Agricultural Knowledge and Innovation Systems (AKISs) of the EU and the Member States, which are 'the combined organisation and knowledge flows between persons, organisations, and institutions

58 Regulation 2021/2115, art 6, para 2.

59 Regulation 2021/2115, art 127. See Communication from the Commission to the European Parliament and the Council on the European Innovation Partnership 'Agricultural Productivity and Sustainability' COM(2012) 079 final.

60 EU SCAR AKIS, *Preparing for Future AKIS in Europe* (European Commission 2nd edn, 2019) 17. See Reg 2021/2115, art 127, para 2, letts a) and d).

61 Regulation 2021/2115, art 126.

who use and produce knowledge for agriculture and interrelated fields'.[62] The EU and Member States' AKISs thus represent an environment and driver for agricultural innovation to grow and take root.[63]

The second side concerns the financial dimension. In particular, EAFRD resources may be used by Member States to fund different types of interventions aimed at pursuing the cross-cutting objective of agricultural modernisation,[64] including on agri-environment-climate commitments.[65] In addition, Member States may grant support for cooperation in preparing and implementing projects of EIP operational groups.[66] These groups can include different actors carrying out a plan to develop or implement an innovative project.[67]

Remarkably, Member States' efforts towards agricultural modernisation are embedded in the performance delivery mechanism of the funding programmes for both the planning and monitoring and evaluation phases. Indeed, each NSP should contain a section describing 'the elements that ensure modernisation of the CAP',[68] including an illustration of how the AKIS is organised at the national level and the Member State's strategy for the development of digital technologies in agriculture and rural areas.[69] Furthermore, achievements resulting from the cross-cutting objective of modernisation are assessed by the common indicators that form the basis of the performance framework of the NSPs objective.[70]

Specularly to the HE Regulation, Regulation 2021/2115 affirms the need for synergies between the use of EAFRD funds and Horizon Europe, to 'make the best use of research and innovation results, in particular those stemming from projects funded by Horizon Europe and the [EIP], leading to innovations in the farming sector and rural areas'.[71] The EIP is placed at the centre of the funding programmes interaction,[72] together with the Standing Committee on Agricultural Research (SCAR), which was established by the Council in 1974 in

---

62 Regulation 2021/2115, art 3, para 9. See Commission, *Agricultural knowledge and innovation systems in transition—A reflection paper* (Publications Office of the European Union 2012) <https://scar-europe.org/images/AKIS/Documents/AKIS_reflection_paper.pdf> 8 accessed 26 June 2025.

63 Further on the topic, see OECD (n 18) 218–223.

64 See Reg 2021/2115, arts 71–73, 75, 76, and 78.

65 ibid, art 70.

66 ibid, art 77, para 1 and 2.

67 ibid, art 127, para 3.

68 ibid, art 107, para 1, lett g).

69 ibid, art 114.

70 ibid, art 7, para 1 and Annex I.

71 ibid, rec 6. Cf Reg 2021/2115, art 79, para 4.

72 See OECD (n 18) 255.

order to strengthen the coordination of agricultural research in Europe (candidate and associated Countries may be observers),[73] also referring to the lines of action funded under the research policy.

4 Sustainable Development as a Guiding Star: Purpose and Limits of Funding Agrifood Innovation

From the above, one may conclude that the EU legislator has taken agrifood innovation seriously in drafting the design of Horizon Europe and CAP funds. This does not come as a surprise, as it is fully in line with the EU agenda on agrifood matters within the wider context of the EU's sustainability transition, as emerges from the relevant EU policy papers in this field.

R&I and other innovation aspects are defined as 'critical to achieve the objectives of the European Green Deal'.[74] Accordingly, the Farm to Fork Strategy stresses the importance of research, innovation, and technology as key drivers to encourage the transition towards sustainability in the agrifood system.[75] In both cases, EU funding is referred to as an important instrument of this transition. The point is further explored in Food 2030,[76] which provides a 'vision and a policy narrative' for the role of R&I in reaching sustainable, healthy, and inclusive food systems. The report outlines ten pathways to guide EU action following the EU Green Deal and the UN's Sustainable Development Goals (SDGs), as defined in the 2030 Agenda.[77] Food 2030 thus represents the strategy that frames food-related initiatives under Horizon Europe, and which is also recognised by the HE Regulation. In fact, according to it, the general objective of the programme on scientific and technological development and industrial competitiveness is meant to contribute to 'the realisation of Union objectives and policies, to tackle global challenges, including the SDGs by

73 Council Regulation (EEC) 1728/74 of 27 June 1974 on the coordination of agricultural research [1974] OJ L182/1.

74 Commission, *The European Green Deal* COM(2019) 640 final, 18.

75 Commission, *A Farm to Fork Strategy for a fair, healthy and environmentally-friendly food system* COM(2020) 381 final, 15–16. See also Commission, *The Energy Transition of the EU Fisheries and Aquaculture Sector* COM(2023) 100 final, 14–17.

76 Karen Fabbri and Irene Ndongosi (eds), *Food 2030 Pathways for Action Research and Innovation Policy as a Driver for Sustainable, Healthy and Inclusive Food Systems* (Publications Office of the European Union 2020) Giulia Bizzo and others, *Food 2030—Pathways for Action 2.0* (Publications Office of the European Union 2023); SWD(2023) 263 final (n 5).

77 UN General Assembly, *Resolution adopted by the General Assembly on 25 September 2015. Transforming our world: the 2030 Agenda for Sustainable Development* [2015] A/RES/70/1.

following the principles of the 2030 Agenda and the Paris Agreement'.[78] This is made tangible in all the programme's components relating to the agrifood system, which present multiple references to sustainability as a priority towards which efforts should be directed. The strategy echoes CAP fund goals, which view innovation as a driver of agricultural modernisation which, in turn, supports the general objectives of the funds—the development of an agricultural model that is sustainable economically, socially, and environmentally and thus contributes to the 2030 Agenda.[79] All in all, it has been observed in this paper's introduction that innovation is not a neutral notion in the EU's conception: it is oriented towards social good by its very definition. The pursuit of sustainability of the agrifood system thus answers the question about what kind of innovation is fostered through the EU funds and to what end. In short, it gives substance to the idea of innovation and prevents it from being an otherwise empty or ambiguous flag.

The consequences of innovation being an empty objective can be visualised if innovation is viewed as a force that potentially contrasts with another one: precaution.[80] Precaution finds legal acknowledgement in EU law through the precautionary principle.[81] This is intended to guide the action of authorities to prevent serious adverse effects on the environment and human and animal health that may arise from circumstances of scientific uncertainty. More specifically, it applies when 'there are reasonable grounds for concern that potential hazards may affect the environment or human, animal or plant health, and when at the same time the available data preclude a detailed risk evaluation',[82] And it could require abstention from action if necessary. Although provided in the context of EU environmental policy,[83] the principle informs the entire

78 HE Regulation, art 3, para 1.

79 See Alexandra Langlais, 'The New Common Agricultural Policy: Reflecting an Agroecological Transition. The Legal Perspective' (2023) 104 Review of Agricultural, Food and Environmental Studies 51.

80 Among others, Paolo Borghi, 'The "Myth" of Precaution in EU Law', in AIDA-IFLA (ed), *Innovation in Agri-Food Law between Technology and Comparison* (Wolters Kluwer 2019); Peter-Tobias Stoll, 'Of Fear and Prudence: Precaution Through Better Regulation and Innovation' in Lorenzo Squintani and others (eds), *Managing Facts and Feelings in Environmental Governance* (Edward Elgar 2019).

81 Among others, Kristel de Smedt and Ellen Vos, 'The Application of the Precautionary Principle in the EU' in Harald A Mieg (ed), *The Responsibility of Science* (Springer 2022).

82 Commission, *Communication from the Commission on the precautionary principle* COM(2000) 1 final, 8.

83 TFEU, art 191, para 2.

EU legal framework,[84] including the EU research policy. Indeed, the specific programme implementing Horizon Europe expressly mentions it by listing, among the operative objectives, the promotion of 'responsible R&I, taking into account the precautionary principle' as one.[85] The precautionary principle may thus pose bounds to R&I activities supported by the programme, and, in this sense, it could constrain the pursuit of innovation in the agrifood system.[86] The possible tensions between the precautionary principle and innovation have been highlighted with the introduction of the so-called 'innovation principle' by the Commission.[87] Contrary to the precautionary principle, the latter is not endowed with normative force.[88] Rather, it is a policy approach,[89] ensuring that 'the innovation dimension is considered when preparing and implementing EU legislation'.[90] This reflects the high importance paid to innovation, especially within EU regulatory activity,[91] which might otherwise be at odds with an overly cautious attitude caused by strict application of the precautionary principle. To conclude, if agrifood innovation were to

84 TFEU, arts 7, 9, and 11 and Charter of Fundamental Rights, art 37. Cf Case T-74/00 *Artegodan and Others v Commission* (2002) ECR II-04945 para 184. See Anna Szajkowska, 'The Impact of the Definition of the Precautionary Principle in EU Food Law' (2010) 47 Common Market Law Review 173.

85 Council Decision 2021/764 (n 47), art 2, para 2, lett d).

86 Contrasts between the promotion of innovation through the funds and the other principles envisaged by TFEU, art 191, para 2, ie prevention, rectifying pollution at source, and 'polluters pay' are less likely to arise. On the contrary, funded projects may provide innovative solutions to facilitate compliance with those principles (especially prevention and rectifying pollution at source) in the context of the activities in the agrifood sector.

87 Commission, *A renewed European Agenda for Research and Innovation* COM(2018) 306 final, 10. On the topic, Kathleen Garnett, Geert Van Calster and Leonie Reins, 'Towards an Innovation Principle: An Industry Trump or Shortening the Odds on Environmental Protection' (2018) 10 Law Innovation and Technology 1; Ellen Vos and Kristel de Smedt, 'WP1 Report: Taking stock as a basis for the effect of the precautionary principle since 2000' <https://recipes-project.eu/sites/default/files/2021-01/Report_Taking%20stock%20as%20a%20basis%20for%20the%20effect%20of%20the%20precautionary%20principle%20since%202000_Final.pdf>, 25–39 accessed 26 June 2025.

88 Garnett, Van Calster and Reins (n 87) 11. For a different view, European Political Strategy Centre, 'Towards an innovation principle endorsed by better regulation' <https://op.europa.eu/en/publication-detail/-/publication/53b6d635-ac93-11e6-aab7-01aa75ed71a1/language-en#>, 2–3 accessed 26 June 2025.

89 Andrea Renda and Felice Simonelli, 'Study supporting the interim evaluation of the innovation principle. Final report' (Publications Office of the European Union 2019) <https://op.europa.eu/en/publication-detail>.

90 Commission, *'Better regulation' toolbox* (July 2023 edition) <https://commission.europa.eu>, 172.

91 Reference to the innovation principle can also be found in HE Regulation, rec 6.

be pursued as an end in itself, it could clash with the precautionary principle and the societal interests the latter protects. On the contrary, considering the above, it is possible to claim that the orientation of R&I in the field of agrifood innovation towards sustainable development, in principle, obviates the potential contradictions between innovation and precaution, the first being aligned with the aims of the second.

However, the sustainability orientation of agrifood innovation does not mean the absence of limits or conditions to its support through funding. On the contrary, it underscores their presence. Accordingly, agrifood innovation should be aligned with the different components of sustainable development in accordance with an integrated approach.[92] Indeed, as the Commission stressed, innovations to be introduced in the agrifood sector should be assessed 'in an inclusive way that also considers social, ethical, economic, environmental, and cultural aspects of food innovation'.[93]

In particular, two forms of constraints to agrifood innovation funding, relevant to this discussion, can be found in the EU regime. The first relates to the context in which financed activities take place. It is linked to sustainability as a general objective of CAP funds. More specifically, the delivery of EAFRD resources destined for (inter alia) innovation purposes requires recipients to respect preexisting requirements concerning agricultural sustainability. Indeed, some types of interventions under the EAFRD are subject to the beneficiary's compliance with a set of requirements, standards, and rules about the fight against climate change, the protection of the environment, human and plant health, animal welfare, and social and labour conditions of agricultural workers.[94] In other words, the EAFRD can be used to support certain interventions concerning innovation on the condition that the beneficiaries do not otherwise undermine the sustainability of their agricultural activity.

The second form of constraint regards the boundaries within which innovation can be pushed. This limitation concerns other important interests whose protection may justify a restriction on innovation, and which contribute to

92 See the International Law Association New Delhi Declaration, ILA Resolution 3/2002, annexed to UN Doc. A/57/329, para 7. Cf Christina Voigt, *Sustainable Development as a Principle of International Law* (Martinus Nijhoff 2009), 35–55; Dominic McGoldrick, 'Sustainable Development and Human Rights: An Integrated Conception' (1996) 45 The International and Comparative Law Quarterly 796.

93 COM(2025) 75 final (n 1), 24.

94 See Reg 2021/2115, arts 12–14 and Annexes III and IV. Cf Daniel Bianchi, 'Cross Compliance: The New Frontier in Granting Subsidies to the Agricultural Sector in the European Union' (2007) 19 Georgetown Environmental Law Review 817; Irene Canfora and Vito S Leccese, 'Social Sustainability as the Milestone for a Sustainable Food System: The Essential Role of People Working in Agriculture' (2024) 15 European Journal of Risk Regulation 253.

defining the sustainability of the financed activities. The HE Regulation contains specific provisions in this sense. Namely, it excludes funding for research in certain fields where human life's dignity is at stake.[95] Moreover, it provides for the respect of ethical principles and relevant EU, national, and international laws,[96] including the Charter of Fundamental Rights (Charter) and the European Convention for the Protection of Human Rights and Fundamental Freedoms,[97] so as not to endanger human rights and other priorities such as 'the need to ensure protection of the environment and high levels of human health protection'.[98] Similarly, CAP fund rules require Member States to ensure the design of the interventions in their NSPs complies with the Charter.[99] Accordingly, the Commission shall assess the conformity of project proposals under Horizon Europe,[100] and that of the Member States' NSPs,[101] using the listed criteria.

At least in part, this reflects the need to follow the above-mentioned integrated approach in the pursuit of the SDGs.[102] Nonetheless, the challenge of ensuring the sustainability of agrifood innovation lies in the evaluation and balancing of the various aspects of sustainability on a case-by-case basis. As explained by Voigt, 'integration is eventually about making compromises. But these compromises have to be sustainable and—even more crucially—the *sum* of all compromises has to be sustainable'.[103]

5 Conclusions

Agrifood innovation, although not a predetermined subject of EU law, finds wide coverage in the EU's legal framework. Indeed, it may be potentially targeted by several EU policies that could address innovation in the agrifood

---

95 HE Regulation, art 18. Cf Case T-561/14 (n 2). Such a restraint is consistent with the fundamental rights of science freedom under art 13 of the Charter of Fundamental Rights, which can be legitimately restricted in order to protect human dignity under art 1 of the same instrument.

96 Article 19 para 1, first alinea, of the HE Regulation.

97 Convention for the Protection of Human Rights and Fundamental Freedoms, 1950, ETS No. 005.

98 HE Regulation, art 19, para 1, second alinea.

99 Regulation 2021/20115, art 9.

100 HE Regulation, art 19, para 3. Cf Case T-158/19 *Breyer v REA* [2021] EU:T:2021:902, para 198.

101 Regulation 2021/2011, art 118, para 2. Cf Case T-39/23 *Acqua & Sole v Commission* [2024] EU:T:2024:710 para 56.

102 For a critical view, see Alexandra Langlais, 'Le Droit de l'Environnement, Caution de la Dimension Agroécologique de la PAC 2023 ?' [2022] Revue de l'Union Européenne 631.

103 Voigt (n 92), 54.

system in terms of both the activity of innovation and its outcome. This chapter focused on innovation in the first sense, exploring the legal framework of the EU's action in fostering innovation through its budgetary funds. The funding programmes analysed are Horizon Europe and CAP funds, whose contribution to agrifood innovation follows different and inverse dynamics. The first is intended to be a stimulus for innovation in various selected areas, among which the agrifood system is included. The second considers innovation as a factor in pursuing EU policy goals in a principal sector, namely the agrifood system. Still, both represent useful instruments for the EU to support and promote agrifood innovation in the context of its research and common agricultural policies. Within their contents, the two programmes dedicate wide coverage to agrifood innovation issues, financing different kinds of projects and interventions at the European, national, and local levels involving all the relevant stakeholders, and operating in synergy. In doing so, the funding programmes aim to contribute to the wider EU strategy on the sustainability of the agrifood system by directing innovation towards such a goal. This gives shape to agrifood innovation, as fostered through funding, determining its purpose and limits too.

Bibliography

Bianchi D, 'Cross Compliance: The New Frontier in Granting Subsidies to the Agricultural Sector in the European Union' (2007) 19 Georgetown Environmental Law Review 817.

Bizzo G, Fabbri K, Gajdzinska M, Haentjens W, Lueth D, Lutzeyer HJ, Luvarà G, Meloni G, Molina Villanueva J, Sain Lopez N, Schoumacher C, Zampoukas N, 'Food 2030—Pathways for action 2.0' (Publications Office of the European Union 2023).

Borghi P, 'The "Myth" of Precaution in EU Law', in AIDA-IFLA (eds), *Innovation in Agri-Food Law between Technology and Comparison* (Wolters Kluwer 2019).

Canfora I, '"Products of Innovation" in Agri-Food Markets. Legal Rules for the Access of Innovating Products and Paradigms in the Agri-Food Market' in AIDA-IFLA (eds), *Innovation in Agri-Food Law between Technology and Comparison* (Wolter Kluwer 2019).

Canfora I, Leccese VS, 'Social Sustainability as the Milestone for a Sustainable Food System: The Essential Role of People Working in Agriculture' (2024) 15 European Journal of Risk Regulation 253.

Crowe R, 'The European Budgetary Galaxy' (2017) 13 European Constitutional Law Review 428.

Dermine P, 'The Planning Method: An Inquiry into the Constitutional Ramifications of a New EU Governance Technique' (2024) 61 Common Market Law Review 959.

De Smedt K, Vos E, 'The Application of the Precautionary Principle in the EU' in Mieg HA (ed), *The Responsibility of Science* (Springer 2022).

de Witte B, 'Integration Through Funding. The Union's Finances as Policy Instrument' in Weber R (ed), *The Financial Constitution of European Integration: Follow the Money?* (Hart Publishing 2023).

Fabbri K and Ndongosi I (eds), 'Food 2030 Pathways for Action Research and Innovation Policy as a Driver for Sustainable, Healthy and Inclusive Food Systems' (Publications Office of the European Union 2020).

Garnett K, Van Calster G and Reins L, 'Towards an Innovation Principle: An Industry Trump or Shortening the Odds-on Environmental Protection' (2018) 10 Law Innovation and Technology 1.

Langlais A, 'Le Droit de l'Environnement, Caution de la Dimension Agroécologique de la PAC 2023?' (2022) Review of Agricultural, Food and Environmental Studies 631.

Langlais A, 'The New Common Agricultural Policy: Reflecting an Agro-ecological Transition. The Legal Perspective' (2023) 104 Review of Agricultural, Food and Environmental Studies 51.

McGoldrick D, 'Sustainable Development and Human Rights: An Integrated Conception' (1996) 45 The International and Comparative Law Quarterly 796.

Pantazatou K, 'European Union Funds' in Hofmann HCH, Rowe GC and Türk AH, (eds), *Specialized Administrative Law of the European Union* (OUP 2018).

Renda A, Simonelli F, 'Study supporting the interim evaluation of the innovation principle. Final report' (Publications Office of the European Union 2019).

Salvi L, 'Agri-Food Law and Innovation through the Lenses of Better Regulation' in AIDA-IFLA (ed), *Innovation in Agri-Food Law between Technology and Comparison* (Wolter Kluwer 2019).

Schebesta H, Purnhagen K, *EU Food Law* (OUP 2024).

Stoll PT, 'Of Fear and Prudence: Precaution Through Better Regulation and Innovation' in Squintani L, Lavrysen L, Darpö J, Stoll PT (eds), *Managing Facts and Feelings in Environmental Governance* (Edward Elgar 2019).

Szajkowska A, 'Impact of the Definition of the Precautionary Principle in EU Food Law' (2010) 47 CMLR 173.

Van der Meulen B, Bart Wernaart B, *EU Food Law Handbook* (Brill | Wageningen Academic 2020).

Voigt C, *Sustainable Development as a Principle of International Law* (Martinus Nijhoff 2009).

CHAPTER 4

Edible Insects on the EU Plate: Navigating Regulatory Challenges and Future Prospects

Maria Laura Grilli

Summary

1 Introduction

The[1] rapid growth of the global population and escalating environmental pressures call for a profound reconsideration of the global food system. The urgent need to identify alternative protein sources that can address growing demand for food while mitigating environmental impact has driven the development of innovative options, such as edible insects, as a viable solution for future dietary strategies.

Traditionally consumed in many parts of the world, insects represent a promising protein alternative for the European market due to their production efficiency, low environmental footprint, and high nutritional value. Despite their potential, the integration of edible insects into European diets faces significant obstacles, including complex legal frameworks and cultural resistance. The European Union, through Regulation (EU) 2015/2283 on Novel Foods, has laid the groundwork for authorising and commercialising insects as food. Nevertheless, the approval procedures remain intricate and multifaceted.

1 Research activity funded under the National Recovery and Resilience Plan (NRRP), Mission 4 Component 1 Investment 3.4 and 4.1. Call for tender No. 351 of 09/04/2022 of Italian Ministry of University and Research funded by the European Union – NextGenerationEU CUP D92B22000500005.

Further challenges to widespread adoption include food safety concerns, the absence of harmonised guidelines, and consumer perception issues.

This chapter examines the current European framework governing the use of edible insects as food, highlighting key procedural hurdles and the opportunities presented by this emerging sector. Finally, it explores future developments, assessing potential policy advancements and market trends, with particular emphasis on the contribution edible insects could make to global food security and sustainability goals.

2 Defining Food Sustainability and Sustainable Food Systems

Before delving deeper, it is essential to explore the connection between food and sustainability, clarifying key definitions that can inform food policy discussions. This is particularly important in light of the absence of a universally accepted and legally defined framework for food sustainability and sustainable food systems.[2]

The Food and Agriculture Organisation (FAO) provides a valuable reference, as it extensively discusses the concepts of sustainable food systems and sustainable diets, both of which enjoy international recognition and are supported by broad academic consensus.[3] The same approach is reflected in various European documents, especially in the recent reform of the Common Agricultural Policy (CAP 2023–2027), which integrates sustainability goals in line with the European Green Deal and the Farm to Fork Strategy.[4]

Various sources agree that food sustainability is closely linked to the adequacy and accessibility of food. According to FAO,[5] a sustainable food system ensures food security and proper nutrition for all while safeguarding the economic, social, and environmental foundations necessary for future generations. Sustainable diets are characterised by their capacity to minimise environmental impact while promoting food security, good nutrition, and overall

2 Simone Pitto, 'Tutela ambientale e sostenibilità dei sistemi alimentari. Una comparazione tra possibili soluzioni normative: environmental protection and sustainability of food systems. A comparison of possible regulatory solutions' (2023) DPCE Online 58 723 <https://www.dpceonline.it/index.php/dpceonline/article/view/1915/1922> accessed 20 June 2025.

3 FAO and WHO, *Sustainable healthy diets. Guiding principles*, (Rome 2019).

4 Commission, 'A Farm to Fork Strategy for a fair, healthy and environmentally-friendly food system', COM(2020) 381 final.

5 High Level Panel of Experts on Food Security and Nutrition (HLPE), *Food Losses and Waste in the Context of Sustainable Food Systems: A Report by the High Level Panel of Experts on Food Security and Nutrition of the Committee on World Food Security* (Rome, 2014).

well-being. Such diets support biodiversity and ecosystem health, respect cultural traditions, ensure economic fairness and accessibility, meet nutritional needs, and make efficient use of both natural and human resources.

The principal dimensions of food sustainability include:

- environmental sustainability: focusing on development that is compatible with the balance and conservation of natural resources, the protection of biodiversity, and the preservation of climatic equilibrium; and
- social sustainability: building societies that promote individual well-being through the protection of rights, the improvement of communities, and the valuing of communal cooperation.

It includes food security, which covers:

- food safety—the healthiness of food;
- food security—the guarantee of an existence free from hunger and access to adequate food;[6] and
- economic sustainability, which is dependent on resilient food systems that are capable of responding to imbalances and crises without compromising food self-sufficiency and the right to adequate food. An efficient system reduces waste, optimises production processes, and promotes innovation.[7]

2.1 *The Role of Innovation in Food Sustainability*

The relationship between scientific and legal innovation can be further understood through the lens of reactive and proactive legal innovation—where the law either follows technological change to mitigate risks or actively shapes future developments through anticipatory regulation.[8]

Legal innovation plays a crucial role in food sustainability by addressing the need for funding solutions that support healthy and environmentally-sustainable

---

6 Luigi Costato, 'Dalla Food Security alla Food Insecurity' [2011] Rivista di Diritto Agrario 3; Emily Webster and Peer Zumbansen, 'Introduction: transnational food (in)security' in Emily Webster, Ankita Gupta and Ruth Ambros (eds), *Transnational Food Security* (Routledge 2020). FAO, *An introduction to the basic concept of food security* (Rome 2008). To better understand the denomination of food safety, see Ferdinando Albisinni, *Strumentario di diritto alimentare europeo* (4th edn, Wolters Kluwer 2020) 5–6, in which the author argues that '*In accordance with internationally recognized definitions as formalized by European Union law, food safety denotes the hygienic and sanitary safety of food products in relation to the protection of human health, understood in its broadest sense as encompassing the entire food chain and including consumer communication measures. Food security, by contrast, refers to the economic and physical availability of sufficient food to meet normal nutritional requirements*'.

7 World Commission on Environment and Development (WCED), *Our Common Future* (OUP 1987).

8 Ferdinando Albisinni, 'Reactive and proactive innovation in European Food Law', in Fernando Leonini, Mariachiara Tallacchini and Matteo Ferrari, *Innovating Food, Innovating the Law. An interdisciplinary approach to the challenges in the agro-food sector* (Libellula edizioni 2014).

discoveries. For that reason, investing in new protein sources is fundamental to responding to the urgent challenges faced by the current food system.[9] Innovation should not be limited to products derived from new technologies but should also encompass foods that are newly integrated into common dietary practices in Europe. For instance, while insects are a traditional food source in many regions worldwide, they are classified as a 'novel food' in Europe and, in accordance with Regulation (EU) 2015/2283 could, consequently, be introduced as an alternative protein source in European diets.

As previously mentioned, however, the introduction of edible insects into the European food market extends beyond regulatory challenges; it necessitates deeper consideration of their intrinsic value as a sustainable food resource. Before delving into the complex regulatory dynamics and cultural barriers to this, it is crucial to understand the environmental and nutritional benefits that insects can offer in order to fully assess their potential impact on the global food system and European consumption patterns.

The first aspect to examine is environmental sustainability. Insect farming is known for its low consumption of water, land, and energy.[10] Being cold-blooded, insects do not require energy-intensive temperature control, which significantly reduces the energy needed to raise them. Moreover, their water consumption and land use are extremely low, particularly when compared to intensive livestock farming.[11] Among agricultural activities, livestock farming is one of the most environmentally impactful sectors. It occupies approximately 70% of global agricultural land and is responsible for a substantial portion—between 72% and 78%—of greenhouse gas emissions produced by agriculture. Key contributors to the high environmental impact of livestock farming include enteric fermentation in ruminants, manure management emissions, and the inefficiency of feed conversion typical of conventional farming practices, in addition to intensive water and land use.[12]

9 Ferdinando Albisinni, 'Diritto agroalimentare innanzi alle sfide dell'innovazione' [2020] (2) BioLaw Journal 25 <https://teseo.unitn.it/biolaw/article/view/1583/1587> accessed 20 June 2025.

10 Arnold van Huis and others (eds), *Edible insects: Future prospects for food and feed security* (FAO 2013) 171.

11 Francesco Montanari, Ana Pinto de Moura and Luís M Cunha, *Production and Commercialization of Insects as Food and Feed. Identification of the Main Constraints in the European Union* (Springer 2021) 9–14.

12 Dennis GAB Oonincx and Imke JM de Boer, 'Environmental impact of the production of mealworms as a protein source for humans—a life cycle assessment' (2012) 7 (12) PLoS ONE 1 <https://journals.plos.org/plosone/article?id=10.1371/journal.pone.0051145> accessed 20 June 2025. See also Arnold van Huis, 'Insects as food and feed, a new emerging agricultural sector: a review' (2020) 6 Journal of Insects as Food and Feed 27.

In contrast, insects require significantly less feed than traditional livestock to produce an equivalent amount of protein. In fact, producing 1 kg of beef requires 25 kg of feed, while pork requires 9.1 kg and poultry 4.5 kg. In comparison, crickets require only 2.1 kg of feed.[13] The superior feed conversion efficiency of insects is due to their ectothermic nature, which allows them to rely on external environmental factors to regulate their metabolic processes.[14] Additionally, insect farming, also known as mini-livestock, typically requires less land and water for large-scale production. Certain species, such as mealworms and crickets, require five times less land and three times less water than livestock.

Preliminary studies indicate that the overall carbon footprint of certain edible insects (eg *T. molitor*, *A. domesticus*, and *L. migratoria*) is lower than that of large ruminants and comparable to that of poultry. However, it should be noted that a large portion of the carbon footprint of insect farming depends on the type of feed used. From a circular economy perspective, feeding insects with unused organic waste could offer a more sustainable solution than using traditional feed.[15]

It is crucial to emphasise that for the production of insects to be regarded as a genuinely beneficial contribution to sustainability within the food system, several critical criteria must be satisfied. First, the use of renewable throughout the insect farming process is essential. This practice not only mitigates the carbon footprint associated with insect production but also aligns with global initiatives aimed at fostering sustainable energy solutions.

Moreover, the utilisation of organic waste as insect feed significantly enhances the sustainability profile of this practice. By repurposing food waste and agricultural by-products into high-quality protein sources, insect farming can contribute to waste reduction and promote a circular economy. This strategy not only diminishes the environmental impact of food waste but also addresses pressing food security challenges by providing an alternative nutrient-dense protein source.

Furthermore, a comprehensive focus on sustainable practices throughout the entire supply chain is necessary to optimise the benefits of insect production. This encompasses the responsible sourcing of raw materials, efficient water management, and the minimisation of the ecological footprint associated with insect farming operations. Implementing best practices in these

13 Montanari, Pinto de Moura and Cunha (n 11).

14 Arnold van Huis, 'Potential of insects as food and feed in assuring food security' (2013) 58 Annual Review of Entomology 563.

15 ibid, 295. Darja Dobermann, Judy A Swift and Linda M Field 'Opportunities and hurdles of edible insects for food and feed' (2017) 42 Nutrition Bulletin 293.

areas can enhance the resilience and sustainability of the food system as a whole.

3 Edible Insects as a Protein and Healthy Food Source

In addition to the high degree of environmental sustainability associated with the production of edible insects, another remarkable factor that positions them as a promising and innovative food resource is their exceptional nutritional profile. Certain types of insects, which have already been approved for consumption in Europe, are notable for their high content of protein, essential minerals, and other nutrients.

Many edible insects contain substantial levels of high-quality protein, often comparable to or exceeding that of traditional animal sources. Additionally, they provide a wide array of micronutrients such as iron, zinc, and magnesium, which are vital for human health. Some species of insects are also rich in beneficial fats, such as omega-3 and omega-6 fatty acids, which are essential for cardiovascular and brain health. These nutritional attributes highlight the potential of edible insects not only as a sustainable food source but also as a contributor to improved human health and nutrition.[16] By contrast, conventional animal proteins—particularly red and processed meats—have been increasingly scrutinised by public health authorities due to their nutritional composition, especially their saturated fat content, which has been associated with an increased risk of non-communicable diseases, including cardiovascular and metabolic disorders. Institutions such as the World Health Organisation have recommended limiting the intake of foods high in saturated fatty acids, particularly those of animal origin, in order to reduce diet-related health risks.[17]

Interestingly, the 2015 EU Regulation on Novel Foods does not require that a novel food possess specific nutritional or health-enhancing properties to be authorised for the market. Yet many Novel Foods, including edible insects, do demonstrate significant nutritional benefits that can positively impact human health.[18]

---

16 International Platform of Insects for Food and Feed (IPIFF), *Edible insects on the European market* (June 2020).

17 World Health Organisation (WHO), *Saturated fatty acid and trans-fatty acid intake for adults and children: WHO guideline* (WHO 2023), <https://www.who.int/publications/i/item/9789240073630> accessed 14 July 2025.

18 Stefano Sforza, 'Food (In)Security: The Role of Novel Foods on Sustainability', in Lucia Scaffardi and Giulia Formici (eds), *Novel Food and Edible Insect in the European Union* (Springer 2022).

In fact, studies show that edible insects like ants, beetle larvae, and caterpillars already serve as nutrient-rich sources of essential proteins, fats, and micronutrients in traditional and indigenous diets.[19] For example, in the Ingano community in Colombia, ants and beetle larvae are consumed for their high protein and fat content, crucial for energy and growth. In regions such as the Amazon Basin and the Democratic Republic of the Congo, insects contribute significantly to daily protein intake, especially during times when other animal protein sources, like fish or game, are scarce. Insects, therefore, offer a sustainable alternative to conventional livestock, additionally positioning them as a valuable resource for global food security.

Edible insects pose not only an environmentally sustainable option but also a nutritionally advantageous alternative within the evolving food market. Expanding research on the nutritional composition of various insect species will be essential to fully understand and leverage their benefits at scale, further strengthening their role as a novel food resource with significant potential for human diets.[20] Edible insects, therefore, present a compelling case for inclusion in the global food system with their potential to address key challenges related to food security and human health making them a valuable addition to the European food market and beyond.[21]

4 The Current Regulation on Novel Foods: Edible Insects

The concept of Novel Foods was first introduced into the European regulatory framework with the adoption of Regulation (EC) No. 258/1997. This regulation established the initial legal basis for assessing and authorising food products that had not been widely consumed within the European Union prior to May 15, 1997. However, with rapid advancements in technology and the continuous development of innovative production techniques in the agrifood sector, the limitations of the original regulation became increasingly evident. This technological evolution highlights the interconnected dynamic between scientific and disciplinary innovation within the agrifood sector.[22] Legal frameworks are increasingly required to evolve in tandem with technological progress—either through reactive innovation, adapting to changes

19 Birgit A Rumpold and Oliver K Schlüter, 'Nutritional composition and safety aspects of edible insects', in (2013) 57 Molecular Nutrition & Food Research 802.

20 Arnold van Huis and others (n 13) 568.

21 ibid, 569.

22 For a discussion of this topic, see Chapter 1 of this volume.

after they emerge, or through proactive innovation, anticipating and shaping future developments in the field.[23]

In response to these challenges, the European Union introduced Regulation (EU) No. 2015/2283, which was adopted on November 25, 2015, and came into effect on January 1, 2018. This regulation replaced its predecessor while retaining key foundational elements, such as the definition of Novel Foods. However, it also introduced significant procedural and structural modifications aimed at streamlining the approval process, enhancing transparency, and ensuring a science-based evaluation of food safety. One of the most notable changes—that occurred even before the new Regulation come into force with a modification of the first Regulation 258/97 in 2003—was the shift from a Member State-based authorisation system to a centralised approval process managed at the EU level, with the European Food Safety Authority (EFSA) playing a pivotal role in conducting scientific risk assessments.[24]

Over the years, the regulatory framework governing Novel Foods in the European Union has undergone significant transformation, particularly due to the initial absence of an independent public authority responsible for food safety assessments. Prior to the establishment of EFSA, the authorisation process for Novel Foods was decentralised, with each Member State designating its own national authority to conduct safety evaluations and grant market approval. This fragmented system resulted in regulatory discrepancies across the EU, as individual countries adopted divergent approaches with some implementing stricter standards, thereby restricting the commercialisation of Novel Foods, and others pursuing more permissive policies, facilitating their market introduction.[25]

---

23 See Giulia Formici, 'L'evoluzione della disciplina normativa in materia di Novel Food: una sfida sul tavolo del Legislatore europeo' (2018) 1 Diritto Pubblico Europeo Rassegna Online <https://doi.org/10.6093/2421-0528/9408> accessed 20 June 2025; Annalisa Volpato, 'La riforma del regolamento sui Novel Food: alla ricerca di un impossibile equilibrio?' (2015) 4 Rivista di Diritto Alimentare 26; Sebastiano Rizzioli, 'Novel Foods' in Luigi Costato and Ferdinando Albisinni, *European and Global Food Law* (2nd edn, Wolters Kluwer 2016); Albisinni (n 8), 403; Valeria Paganizza, 'I nuovi alimenti ("Novel Foods")' in Paolo Borghi and others (eds), *Trattato di diritto alimentare italiano e dell'Unione europea* (Lefebvre Giuffrè 2021); Valeria Paganizza, 'I nuovi alimenti (*Novel Foods*)' in Luigi Costato and others, *Compendio di diritto alimentare* (9th edn, Wolters Kluwer 2019).

24 Giulia Formici, 'Novel Food e insetti per il consumo umano tra interventi legislativi e Corte di giustizia: alla ricerca di un difficile equilibrio' (2020) 14 (4) Rivista di Diritto Alimentare.

25 Michael Hermann, 'The impact of the European Novel Food Regulation on trade and food innovation based on traditional plant foods from developing countries' (2009) 34 Food Policy 499.

The establishment of EFSA represented a crucial step towards regulatory harmonisation and scientific consistency in food safety assessments. As an independent authority, EFSA plays a central role in evaluating the safety of Novel Foods, including edible insects, through rigorous scientific methodologies and risk assessment procedures. Its expertise ensures that food products entering the EU market meet uniform safety standards, thereby eliminating disparities that previously existed among Member States. The centralisation of risk assessment within EFSA has also enhanced consumer confidence by ensuring that all approved Novel Foods undergo an objective, evidence-based evaluation process, free from national biases or political influence.[26]

Furthermore, EFSA's role extends beyond mere risk assessment. By providing scientific opinions that inform policy decisions at the EU level, EFSA contributes to a more predictable and transparent regulatory environment. This has been particularly relevant in the case of edible insects, an emerging category within the novel food sector. EFSA's independent assessments have facilitated the structured and science-driven integration of insects into the European diet, ensuring that their nutritional benefits and safety profiles are thoroughly examined before market approval.[27]

Regarding its definition, Article 3 para 2 lett a) of Regulation (EU) No. 2283/2015 defines a novel food as 'any food that was not used for human consumption to a significant degree within the Union before May 15, 1997, irrespective of the date of accession of the Member State'. This temporal criterion, already established in the 1997 regulation, remains a key element in determining whether a food falls into the Novel Foods category.[28]

One of the most notable innovations of the 2015 regulation is the introduction of a detailed list aimed at identifying different types of food that qualify as Novel Foods. These categories include foods with modified molecular structures, foods derived from microorganisms, fungi, or algae, as well as products of animal or plant origin, mineral-based foods, foods obtained from cell cultures, and those containing engineered nanomaterials.[29] The regulation's scope extends beyond foods produced using new technologies or innovative

26 Daniela Martini, Cristian Del Bo' and Patrizia Riso, 'Legislazione europea e ruolo di EFSA nella valutazione della sicurezza d'uso dei Novel Foods: Principi e prospettive' (2020) 2 BioLaw Journal 9 <https://teseo.unitn.it/biolaw/article/view/1584> accessed 27 June 2025.

27 Annalisa Volpato, 'Novel Foods in the EU Integrated Administrative Space: An Institutional Perspective' in Scaffardi and Formici (n 16).

28 Formici (n 21).

29 Giulia Formici, 'Legislative and Judicial Challenges on Insects for Human Consumption: From Member States to the EU, Passing Through the Court of Justice of the EU' in Scaffardi and Formici (n 16).

processes. It also covers foods that, while being part of the traditional diet in non-EU countries, have not been widely consumed within the EU. From a regulatory perspective, these are considered novel despite their historical and cultural significance in other parts of the world.[30]

A crucial clarification brought about by the 2015 regulation concerns the status of edible insects. The 1997 regulation did not explicitly include whole insects in the category of Novel Foods, leading to varying interpretations among Member States. Some countries, such as the Netherlands, permitted the sale of insect-based products, while others prohibited their circulation unless they had been previously authorised through the Novel Foods procedure, discussed below.[31]

Although Regulation (EU) 2015/2283 does not explicitly mention insects in the main text, they are clearly encompassed within its scope. Article 3, para 2, lett a), point (v) includes within the definition of Novel Foods:

> [F]oods consisting of, isolated from, or produced from animals or their parts, except animals obtained through traditional breeding practices used for food production in the Union before May 15, 1997, provided those foods from such animals have a history of safe consumption in the Union.

This broad definition applies to insects and their parts, as confirmed in Recital 8 of the Regulation, which states that 'the categories of food which constitute Novel Foods should cover whole insects and their parts'. As a result, edible insects must undergo the pre-authorisation process established for Novel Foods before they can be legally placed on the EU market.

This pre-authorisation process involves a rigorous and detailed evaluation designed to ensure food safety for consumers. Any party interested in placing a novel food on the European market must submit an application to the European Commission. This application must contain several key components, such as identification of the novel food (the applicant must provide a detailed description of the food, including its name, origin, and production methods) and a scientific dossier (a comprehensive review demonstrating that the novel food is safe for human consumption). This dossier must include data on the food's composition, nutritional profile, and potential allergenic or toxicological effects, as well as any relevant historical consumption data. For products such as edible insects, it is essential to show that the insects are farmed,

---

30 Lucia Scaffardi, 'I novel food, un futuro ancora da definire' (2020) 2 Biolaw Journal 43 <https://teseo.unitn.it/biolaw/article/view/1582> accessed 27 June 2025.

31 Formici (n 29); Volpato (n 27), 20.

processed, and prepared in ways that eliminate any risks to human health, such as microbial contamination or allergenicity.[32]

Once submitted, the European Commission forwards the application to the European Food Safety Authority (EFSA) for a thorough scientific evaluation. EFSA's primary role is to assess the safety of the novel food by reviewing the data provided in the dossier. This review process includes a comprehensive risk assessment, where EFSA examines possible contaminants, allergens, or harmful compounds, as well as the nutritional benefits of the food.[33]

Although EFSA's scientific opinion is not legally binding, it plays a central role in the authorisation process. Based on EFSA's assessment, the European Commission prepares a draft implementing act to authorise the novel food. This draft must then be submitted to the Standing Committee on Plants, Animals, Food, and Feed (PAFF) within seven months of EFSA's opinion. The novel food cannot be authorised unless the PAFF Committee, composed of representatives from the Member States and chaired by a representative of the Commission, delivers a positive opinion through a qualified majority vote.

If the Commission reaches a favourable conclusion, the novel food is added to the EU list of authorised Novel Foods, which is regularly updated. However, if additional scientific data are required, the process may be extended beyond the standard, one-year time frame. In practice, completing the authorisation process typically takes at least two years, as further studies or clarifications are often needed.[34]

Since the adoption of Regulation (EU) No. 2283/2015, several insect species have successfully completed the pre-authorisation process. For instance, the European Commission Implementing Regulation (EU) 2021/882 adopted on June 1, 2021, authorised the marketing of dried *Tenebrio molitor* (yellow mealworm larvae). This was a significant milestone, as it marked the first authorisation of an insect species as a novel food within the EU.

Subsequent authorisations followed: Similarly, *Acheta domesticus* (house cricket) underwent a safety assessment by EFSA, leading to the authorisation for its marketing in frozen, dried, and powdered forms through Implementing Regulation (EU) 2022/188 of February 10, 2022. Following the same procedure, EFSA's safety assessment for *Locusta migratoria* (migratory locust) was published on May 25, 2021. Subsequently, the European Commission authorised the marketing of its frozen, dried, and powdered forms through Implementing

32 Valeria Paganizza, *Bugs in Law: Insetti e regole dai campi alla tavola* (Wolters Kluwer 2019).

33 Gabriela Precup and others, 'The Safety Assessment of Insects and Products Thereof As Novel Foods in the European Union' in Scaffardi and Formici (n 16), 128–129.

34 Volpato (n 27), 20.

Regulation (EU) 2021/1975 of November 12, 2021, which came into effect on December 5, 2021. *Alphitobius diaperinus* (lesser mealworm) received EFSA's safety assessment, leading to the approval of its frozen, paste, dried, and powdered forms under Implementing Regulation (EU) 2023/58 of January 5, 2023. Finally, in January 2025, a new form of production of the already approved *Tenebrio molitor* was authorised, specifically the UV-treated powder of whole larvae, under Implementing Regulation (EU) 2025/89 of January 20, 2025.[35]

5 Regulatory Challenges and Opportunities in the Market Introduction of Edible Insects

The increasing interest in edible insects as a sustainable protein source has placed considerable emphasis on their regulatory framework within the European Union. While Regulation (EU) No. 2015/2283 on Novel Foods provides the overarching procedure for market authorisation, several challenges remain, particularly concerning the specificities of insect-based food production. Unlike conventional food categories, edible insects have unique characteristics that require tailored regulatory provisions to ensure both consumer safety and market accessibility.[36]

Despite recent legislative advancements, the regulatory landscape governing edible insects remains complex and, in some respects, inadequate. Many of the current rules were originally designed for conventional agricultural and food systems, meaning they do not fully accommodate the distinctive aspects of insect farming and processing. Furthermore, bureaucratic hurdles, the duplication of scientific research for authorisation purposes, and gaps in labelling and allergen management contribute to delays in market entry and limit the growth potential of the sector. To facilitate the integration of insect-based foods into European diets, a more refined and adaptive regulatory framework is needed—one that balances food safety requirements with the promotion of innovation and sustainability.[37]

---

35 EFSA, *Scientific Panel on Nutrition, Novel Foods and Food Allergens, Minutes of the 53rd meeting of the working group on foods allergies* (Parma 12 December 2022); Dominique Turck and others, 'Guidance on the scientific requirements for an application for authorisation of a novel food in the context of Regulation (EU) 2015/228' (2024) 22 EFSA Journal.

36 Giovanni Sogari and others, 'The future is crawling: Evaluating the potential of insects for food and feed security' (2023) 6 Current research in Food Science 100504 <https://www.sciencedirect.com/science/article/pii/S2665927123000722> accessed 20 June 2025.

37 Gabriele Spatola and others, 'Assessment of the information to consumers on insects-based products (Novel Food) sold by e-commerce in the light of the EU legislation: when

A critical issue arises from Article 26 of Regulation (EU) No. 2015/2283, which establishes that scientific data submitted in support of a novel food application remain protected for at least five years. While this provision was introduced to safeguard intellectual property and incentivise investment into research and development, it also creates a significant barrier for new entrants in the edible insect sector. If another food business operator seeks to commercialise a similar insect-based product, they must conduct independent studies rather than rely on pre-existing data. This requirement leads to unnecessary duplication of scientific research, resulting in significant financial and time expenditures. The lack of data-sharing mechanisms prolongs approval processes and places an excessive burden on small and medium-sized enterprises, which often lack the resources to fund extensive toxicological and nutritional studies. A more flexible approach that allows for shared scientific data—while maintaining appropriate safeguards for proprietary research—could enhance regulatory efficiency and encourage market innovation.[38]

While Regulation (EU) No. 2015/2283 outlines the market approval process for edible insects, it does not provide specific provisions governing their production. As a result, insect farmers and processors must adhere to general food production laws, including the General Food Law (Regulation (EC) No. 178/2002), which establishes fundamental principles for food safety and risk management, and Regulation (EC) No. 852/2004, which sets out hygiene requirements for all food businesses. Additionally, they must comply with Regulation (EC) No. 183/2005 on feed hygiene standards.[39]

A notable regulatory gap is the absence of insect-specific welfare regulations. Directive 98/58/EC on the welfare of farmed animals applies exclusively to vertebrates and does not extend to insects, leaving uncertainty regarding the ethical treatment of insects in farming and processing. While insects are biologically distinct from traditional livestock, there is growing scientific and ethical discourse on the need to establish welfare standards that address issues such as appropriate rearing conditions, slaughter methods, and feeding practices.

The lack of dedicated legislation tailored to edible insect production creates multiple challenges. First, there is considerable ambiguity regarding the

labelling compliance becomes a matter of accuracy' (2024) 162 Food Control 110440 <https://www.sciencedirect.com/science/article/pii/S0956713524001579> accessed 20 June 2025.

38 Krystyna Żuk-Gołaszewska and others, 'Edible Insect Farming in the Context of the EU Regulations and Marketing—An Overview' (2022) 13 Insects 446 <https://www.mdpi.com/2075-4450/13/5/446> accessed 20 June 2025.

39 Spatola and others (n 37).

types of feed that can be legally used for insect rearing. Unlike traditional livestock, insects can be reared on organic by-products, which raises questions about the legal classification of feed sources. A more precise regulatory framework is needed to define permitted feed sources while ensuring food safety. Second, hygiene and processing standards for insect farming remain insufficiently detailed in current EU regulations. Insect farming and processing involve unique methodologies that differ from conventional meat production, necessitating regulatory clarity on processing techniques, storage conditions, and contamination risk management. Finally, the absence of standardised EU-wide regulations tailored to insect farming has led to fragmented national approaches. Some Member States have introduced stricter or more lenient rules, creating a lack of harmonisation that complicates market access and trade. Addressing these regulatory shortcomings requires targeted reforms that recognise the distinct nature of insect-based food production while maintaining rigorous safety standards.

Beyond production and authorisation challenges, the regulation of edible insects must also address consumer protection through effective labelling and allergen management. Labelling serves a dual function: it ensures compliance with legal requirements and fosters consumer trust in Novel Foods. Regulation (EU) No. 1169/2011 on food information to consumers applies to insect-based products, mandating transparent and accurate labelling. However, given the novelty of these foods, additional considerations arise.

One key issue is the choice between using scientific names or common names for insect species. While scientific names provide taxonomic precision, they may be unfamiliar to consumers, potentially leading to confusion. Conversely, common names may vary across languages and cultural contexts, affecting clarity and standardisation. A potential solution would be to require both designations on packaging to enhance consumer understanding.[40]

Another critical aspect is allergen disclosure. Some insect species contain proteins structurally similar to those found in crustaceans, molluscs, and dust mites, common allergens that could pose health risks to sensitive individuals. While Regulation (EU) No. 1169/2011 mandates allergen labelling, the introduction of edible insects necessitates more specific guidelines to ensure that labels clearly indicate cross-reactivity risks, warn of possible cross-contamination, and provide standardised allergen labelling practices across all EU Member States. As research on insect allergens remains ongoing, a prudent and risk-informed regulatory framework should be adopted. This includes not only mandatory

40 Precup and others (n 33). FAO, *Looking at edible insects from a food safety perspective. Challenges and opportunities for the sector* (Rome 2021).

labelling but also consumer education campaigns to inform the public about possible allergic reactions and the safe consumption of insect-based foods.

The regulation of edible insects in the European Union is at a pivotal juncture. While significant progress has been made in integrating insect-based products into the legal framework, the current regulations remain insufficiently tailored to the unique characteristics of insect production and consumption. The absence of dedicated legislative provisions creates uncertainty for producers and consumers alike, highlighting the urgent need for targeted reforms.

A more adaptive regulatory framework—one that facilitates market access while maintaining stringent safety standards—will be crucial for unlocking the full potential of edible insects. This includes refining data protection rules, clarifying production and hygiene standards, and implementing comprehensive labelling requirements. By fostering a well-regulated and consumer-friendly market, the EU can position itself as a global leader in sustainable food innovation, advancing edible insects from a niche curiosity to a mainstream dietary solution that addresses food security and environmental challenges.

6 Conclusion

Edible insects represent a promising alternative to conventional protein sources, offering substantial benefits in terms of environmental sustainability and nutritional value. Yet, their market presence in Europe remains marginal. To unlock their full potential, it is crucial to develop targeted legislative measures that establish clear rules for all production and marketing stages. These should include specific guidelines on feed use, farming conditions, hygiene standards, and safety assessments, thereby reducing legal ambiguities and facilitating compliance for industry stakeholders.

The current regulatory landscape reflects growing pressure on European legislators to adapt existing laws, which were not originally designed to govern insect-based food production. Unlike traditional livestock farming, insect farming presents unique challenges, such as the use of organic waste as feed, distinct hygiene requirements, and the need to define appropriate welfare standards for farmed insects. As a result, the existing frameworks may not always be adequate to regulate the sector effectively. Addressing these gaps requires a balanced approach that ensures food safety while fostering innovation and sustainability.

Beyond purely technical aspects, the regulatory challenges surrounding edible insects must be considered within a broader context of social acceptance and market integration. In recent years, significant progress has been made in positioning edible insects as a viable food source, largely due to the implementation of new regulations. However, the complex and costly pre-authorisation process, the absence of tailored legislation and the limited availability of long-term scientific data on the consumption of these Novel Foods continue to hinder their widespread adoption. Moreover, cultural resistance and consumer scepticism remain substantial barriers to market expansion.

Labelling, for instance, is not merely a legal or food safety requirement, it is also a fundamental tool for consumer education and awareness. Clear, transparent, and reliable information on the production processes of insect-based foods, their nutritional benefits, and potential allergenic risks is essential for fostering public trust. Clearly defined rules on labelling and allergen management will not only protect consumers but also facilitate the transition towards a more sustainable food system. A dedicated regulatory framework specifically designed for edible insects could play a crucial role in enhancing consumer acceptance by addressing these concerns in a systematic and science-driven manner.

Harmonised administrative procedures and a continuous dialogue between legislators, scientists, and industry representatives are essential to creating a regulatory framework that balances consumer protection with the promotion of novel food solutions. Both the European Union and national authorities play an essential role in shaping the future of edible insects as a sustainable food and feed source.

While a robust regulatory framework is indispensable to ensuring consumer safety, it must also be proportionate to the specific needs of the edible insect sector. In this context, edible insects should no longer be viewed as a mere gastronomic novelty but as a concrete and scientifically supported solution to the global challenges of food security and environmental sustainability. Through well-structured regulation and effective public communication, Europe can take significant steps towards a more resilient and resource-efficient food system, one that not only meets human nutritional needs but also addresses urgent ecological challenges.

Bibliography

Albisinni F, 'Reactive and proactive innovation in European Food Law', in Leonini F, Tallacchini M, and Ferrari M, *Innovating Food, Innovating the Law. An interdisciplinary approach to the challenges in the agro-food sector* (Libellula edizioni 2014).

Albisinni F, *Strumentario di diritto alimentare europeo* (4th edn, Wolters Kluwer 2020).

Albisinni F, 'Diritto agroalimentare innanzi alle sfide dell'innovazione' [2020] (2) BioLaw Journal 25 <https://teseo.unitn.it/biolaw/article/view/1583/1587> accessed 20 June 2025.

Costato L, 'Dalla Food Security alla Food Insecurity' [2011] Rivista di Diritto Agrario 3.

Costato L and Albisinni F, *European and Global Food Law* (2nd edn, Wolters Kluwer 2016).

Dobermann D, Swift JA, and Field LM, 'Opportunities and hurdles of edible insects for food and feed' (2017) 42 Nutrition Bulletin 293.

Formici G, 'L'evoluzione della disciplina normativa in materia di Novel Food: una sfida sul tavolo del Legislatore europeo' in (2018) 1 Diritto Pubblico Europeo Rassegna Online 1.

Formici G, 'Novel Food e insetti per il consumo umano tra interventi legislativi e Corte di giustizia: alla ricerca di un difficile equilibrio' (2020) 14 (4) Rivista di Diritto Alimentare 48.

Formici G, 'Legislative and Judicial Challenges on Insects for Human Consumption: From Member States to the EU, Passing Through the Court of Justice of the EU', in Scaffardi L and Formici G (eds.), *Novel Food and Edible Insect in the European Union* (Springer 2022).

Hermann M, 'The impact of the European Novel Food Regulation on trade and food innovation based on traditional plant foods from developing countries' (2009) 34 Food Policy 499.

Martini D, Del Bo' C, and Riso P, 'Legislazione europea e ruolo di EFSA nella valutazione della sicurezza d'uso dei Novel Foods: Principi e prospettive' (2020) 2 BioLaw Journal 9.

Montanari F, Pinto de Moura A, and Cunha LM, *Production and Commercialization of Insects as Food and Feed* (Springer 2021).

Oonincx DGAB, de Boer IJM. 'Environmental impact of the production of mealworms as a protein source for humans—a life cycle assessment', (2012) PLoS ONE 7 (12) 1.

Paganizza V, *Bugs in Law: Insetti e regole dai campi alla tavola* (Wolters Kluwer 2019).

Paganizza V, 'I nuovi alimenti (*Novel Foods*)' in Costato L and others, *Compendio di diritto alimentare* (Wolters Kluwer 2019).

Paganizza V, 'I nuovi alimenti ("Novel Foods")' in Borghi P and others (eds), *Trattato di diritto alimentare italiano e dell'Unione europea* (Lefebvre Giuffrè 2021).

Pitto S, 'Tutela ambientale e sostenibilità dei sistemi alimentari. Una comparazione tra possibili soluzioni normative: Environmental protection and sustainability of food systems. A comparison of possible regulatory solutions' (2023) DPCE Online 58 723.

Precup G, Ververis E, Azzollini D, Rivero-Pino F, Zakidou P, and Germini A, 'The Safety Assessment of Insects and Products Thereof As Novel Foods in the European Union', in Scaffardi L and Formici G (eds.), *Novel Food and Edible Insect in the European Union* (Springer 2022).

Rizzioli S, 'Novel Foods' in Luigi Costato and Ferdinando Albisinni, *European and Global Food Law* (2nd edn, Wolters Kluwer 2016).

Rumpold BA, Schlüter OK, 'Nutritional composition and safety aspects of edible insects' (2013) 57 Molecular Nutrition & Food Research 802.

Scaffardi L, 'I novel food, un futuro ancora da definire' (2020) 2 Biolaw Journal 43.

Sforza S, 'Food (In)Security: The Role of Novel Foods on Sustainability', in Scaffardi L and Formici G (eds), *Novel Food and Edible Insect in the European Union* (Springer 2022).

Sogari G and others, 'The future is crawling: Evaluating the potential of insects for food and feed security' (2023) 6 Current Research in Food Science 100504.

Spatola G and others, 'Assessment of the information to consumers on insects-based products (Novel Food) sold by e-commerce in the light of the EU legislation: when labelling compliance becomes a matter of accuracy' (2024) 162 Food Control 110440.

Turck D and others, 'Guidance on the scientific requirements for an application for authorisation of a novel food in the context of Regulation (EU) 2015/228' (2024) 22 EFSA Journal.

van Huis A, 'Potential of insects as food and feed in assuring food security' (2013) 58 Annual Review of Entomology 563.

van Huis A and others (eds), Edible insects: Future prospects for food and feed security (FAO 2013) 171.

van Huis A, 'Insects as food and feed, a new emerging agricultural sector: a review' (2020) 6 Journal of Insects as Food and Feed 27.

Volpato A, 'La riforma del regolamento sui Novel Food: alla ricerca di un impossibile equilibrio?' (2015) 4 Rivista di Diritto Alimentare 26.

Volpato A, 'Novel Foods in the EU Integrated Administrative Space: An Institutional Perspective', in Scaffardi L and Formici G (eds.), *Novel Food and Edible Insect in the European Union* (Springer 2022).

Webster E and Zumbansen P, 'Introduction: transnational food (in)security' in Emily Webster, Ankita Gupta and Ruth Ambros (eds), Transnational Food Security (Routledge 2020).

World Commission on Environment and Development (WCED), *Our Common Future* (OUP 1987).

Żuk-Gołaszewska K and others, 'Edible Insect Farming in the Context of the EU Regulations and Marketing—An Overview' (2022) 13 Insects 446.

CHAPTER 5

Innovating Food, Shaping Trust: Insights from a Consumer Survey on EU Novel Foods and Cell-Based Meat Regulation

Giacomo Degli Antoni, Marco Faillo and Giulia Formici

Summary

1 Innovation in the Agrifood Sector and the Linkages between the Market, Consumer Choice, and Regulatory Solutions: Novel Foods as a Case Study[1]

Against the backdrop of climate change, the depletion of natural resources, and a continuously growing global population,[2] building resilient and sustainable food systems has become critically important. Ensuring food security—defined as the guarantee of access to adequate, nutritious, and sufficient food for all, including future generations[3]—requires a profound paradigm shift. It is no longer sufficient to merely enhance the capacity of food

1 While this chapter has been jointly written by the coauthors, Sections 1, 2, and 5 were written by Giulia Formici, and Sections 3 and 4 by Giacomo Degli Antoni and Marco Faillo.

2 FAO, IFAD, UNICEF, WFP, and WHO, *The State of Food Security and Nutrition in the World 2024. Financing to end hunger, food insecurity and malnutrition in all its forms* (Rome 2024).

3 Emily Webster, Ankita Gupta and Ruth Ambros (eds), *Transnational Food Security* (Routledge 2020); Luigi Costato, Ferdinando Albisinni, and Theodore Georgopoulos (eds), *European and Global Food Law* (3rd edn, Wolters Kluwer 2025).

systems to meet evolving dietary needs, both in terms of quality and quantity. What is fundamentally demanded is the promotion of sustainable food production methods that minimise the environmental impact of the agrifood sector on biodiversity, natural resources such as air, soil, and water, while also addressing socioeconomic inequalities.[4]

In recent decades, significant technical and scientific advancements have been made to pave the way for the development of unprecedented food products and production methods. These improvements offer valuable tools to support the transition toward more sustainable food systems.[5] Innovations such as the 'Internet of farming' and Artificial Intelligence,[6] New Genomic Techniques,[7] and Novel Foods[8] are emerging as potential drivers of transformative solutions to challenges such as climate change, pollution, food waste,[9] environmental degradation, and resource scarcity.

However, innovation brings both potential and risk, raising new questions and concerns particularly around the need to foster scientific progress while safeguarding consumer health. In other words, it is crucial to guarantee that new foods or food production techniques entering the market do not pose risks to human health, the environment, and/or animal welfare.

Striking an appropriate balance between food safety, food security, food sustainability, and innovation necessitates thoughtful regulatory and policy interventions. Lawmakers and policymakers are increasingly called upon to craft comprehensive strategies as well as sophisticated normative frameworks to govern technological advancements in the agrifood sector. These legal mechanisms may significantly influence consumer acceptance and freedom of choice

---

4 Francesco Rossi Dal Pozzo and Vito Rubino (eds), *La sicurezza alimentare tra crisi internazionali e nuovi modelli economici* (Cacucci 2023); Simone Pitto, *La rilevanza costituzionale e globale della sicurezza alimentare. Una lettura olistica e comparata della food security* (Editoriale Scientifica 2024).

5 Stefano Sforza, 'Food (In)Security: The Role of Novel Foods on Sustainability' in Lucia Scaffardi and Giulia Formici (eds), *Novel Foods and Edible Insects in the European Union* (Springer 2022); AIDA-IFLA (ed), *Innovation in Agri-Food Law Between Technology and Comparison* (Wolters Kluwer 2019).

6 See Corazza in this Volume. Valeria Paganizza, 'Artificial Intelligence in the Food Sector' in Luigi Costato, Ferdinando Albisinni and Theodore Georgopoulos (eds), *European and Global Food Law* (3rd edn, Wolters Kluwer 2025).

7 See Errigo in this Volume.

8 See Grilli in this Volume; Daniele Pisanello and Giorgia Caruso, *Novel Foods in the European Union* (Springer 2018).

9 See Cerbone in this Volume.

while also affecting business investments—especially in terms of research and development—, ultimately shaping the entire food market.[10]

Within this broader scenario, Novel Foods constitute a particularly relevant and interesting case study. Focusing on the European Union (EU), the marketing of such foods is governed by Reg. (EU) 2015/2283,[11] which establishes a centralised pre-market authorisation procedure. This Regulation aims to ensure a high level of consumer protection, while simultaneously promoting innovation that contributes to food security and sustainability.[12]

Despite these legislative efforts, current regulation of Novel Foods remains under scrutiny and, in some cases, has faced criticism, prompting growing calls for reform.[13] This ongoing legislative and political debate has also been fuelled by certain specific categories of new foods—most notably insects-based products and cell-based meat[14]—which are at the centre of a lively discourse involving civil society, stakeholder organisations, media, politicians, and the academic community. Therefore, the future of Novel Foods appears to be clearly intertwined with legislative decisions and regulatory approaches, both at the national and supranational levels, that have the power to influence the internal market and the strategic choices of key players in the sector. At the same time, public knowledge and trust in the regulatory system may serve as essential factors for lawmakers, helping to assess the need for reform and guiding efforts to better inform and educate citizen-consumers, thereby fostering more conscious consumer choices.

As part of the On Foods Project,[15] a survey was conducted in Italy involving a representative sample of adults, in terms of age, gender, and

10 Bernd Van Der Meulen, *Reconciling Food Law to Competitiveness. Report on the regulatory environment of the European Food and dairy sector* (Wageningen Academic Publisher 2009).

11 Regulation (EU) 2015/2283 of the European Parliament and of the Council of 25 November 2015 on Novel Foods, amending Regulation (EU) 1169/2011 of the European Parliament and of the Council and repealing Regulation (EC) 258/97 of the European Parliament and of the Council and Commission Regulation (EC) 1852/2001 [2015] OJ L327/1.

12 ibid Recital 29.

13 Valeria Paganizza, 'I nuovi alimenti ("Novel Foods")' in Paolo Borghi and others (eds), *Trattato di diritto alimentare italiano e dell'Unione europea* (2nd edn, Giuffrè 2024); Alessandro Monaco, 'Data Protection under the Novel Food Regulation: Valuable Instrument or Barrier to Innovation? Insights from the Insect Sector' (2023) 18 European Food and Feed Law Review 172.

14 Giulia Formici, Maria Cecilia Mancini and Lucia Scaffardi (eds), *Cell-Based Meat in the European Union and Beyond. An Interdisciplinary Study* (Springer 2025).

15 Project funded by the European Union under the Next Generation EU initiative, National Recovery and Resilience Plan (NRRP)—Mission 4, Component 2, Investment 1.3—Ministerial Call No. 341 of 15 March 2022 issued by the Ministry of University and

macro-geographical area of residence.[16] Among its objectives, the survey also aimed to explore: a) consumer awareness and understanding of the existing Novel Foods discipline in the EU and b) citizen-consumer preferences regarding how such rules should ideally be shaped. The study paid particular attention to the roles and responsibilities of different institutional actors, including national and supranational authorities as well as independent agencies. It also investigated the relevance of scientific evaluations vis à vis political considerations, especially in relation to ethics and socioeconomics.

While numerous surveys on Novel Foods and cell-based meat focus on consumer acceptance and behaviour, the abovementioned survey specifically addressed regulatory aspects, a topic that remained underexplored in existing literature.

The present contribution reflects upon several findings from the survey, centring on the following research questions:

1. To what extent are Italian consumers familiar with the current EU legislative framework on Novel Foods and its main characteristics?
2. What is the level of knowledge regarding the regulatory landscape surrounding cell-based meat in Italy?
3. What are citizen-consumer preferences concerning the regulatory approaches on Novel Foods and, more specifically, cell-based meat? In particular, which institutions do consumers believe should be responsible or empowered in this regulatory process?
4. What role is attributed to science and which aspects should be properly considered when assessing possible risks associated with Novel Foods in general and cell-based meat more specifically?

Ultimately, this analysis seeks to offer valuable '*Novel* food for thought' and insights for both private and public actors, helping to evaluate citizen-consumer knowledge, preferred regulatory solutions, and trust regarding Novel Foods within the EU. These findings could inform legislative and policy initiatives aimed at improving regulatory procedures—especially with regards to which entities should be involved in the risk assessment and risk management phases during the authorisation process at the EU level—while also enhancing trust

Research; Project Code PE00000003, Ministerial Decree No. 1550 of 11 October 2022 granting the funding, project title: 'ON Foods—Research and innovation network on food and nutrition Sustainability, Safety and Security—Working ON Foods'.

16 Alongside the authors of this chapter, the following scholars contributed to the design and development of the survey: Nicola Bergamaschi, Maria Chiara Errigo, Maria Cecilia Mancini, Simeon Benedict Rolla, and Lucia Scaffardi.

in Novel Foods and identifying which concerns (eg human health, environment, animal welfare) are most salient to consumers.

Accordingly, Section 2 of this chapter reviews the current state of EU Novel Foods legislation, with specific attention to the peculiar debate surrounding the marketing of cell-based meat. The Section serves as a foundation for understanding the methodological choices characterising the survey as well as the questions elaborated and included in the analysis, as detailed in Section 3. The empirical evidence collected is explained and evaluated in Section 4. The chapter concludes by offering critical perspectives and suggestions for future regulatory developments and stakeholder engagement rooted in the survey's results.

2 The Novel Foods Discipline in the European Union and the Regulatory Debate on Cell-Based Meat

As anticipated, the marketing of Novel Foods in the EU is governed by Reg. (EU) 2015/2283. Entered into force in January 1, 2018, it defines as 'novel' those food products that meet both of the following criteria: a) they have not been consumed to a significant degree by humans within the EU prior to May 15, 1997 (the date the first EU regulation on Novel Foods entered into force)[17] and b) they fall under one of the ten categories listed in Article 3 of the Regulation, among which 'food consisting of, isolated from, or produced from material of mineral origin'; 'foods consisting of, isolated from, or produced from cell cultures or tissue derived from animals, plants, microorganisms, fungi, or algae'; and traditional foods coming from third countries are included.[18]

Therefore, according to this legislative framework, the vast Novel Foods list includes, on the one hand, foods that are innovative per se—either due to new processing methods or unconventional sources—and, on the other hand, foods considered 'new' from a strictly European perspective, based on geographical and temporal criteria.

---

17 Regulation (EC) 258/97 of the European Parliament and of the Council of 27 January 1997 concerning Novel Foods and Novel Food ingredients [1997] OJ L43/1.

18 Article 3, para 2, lett b). See Lucia Scaffardi, 'A Peculiar Category of Novel Foods: Traditional Foods Coming from Third Countries and the Regulatory Issues Involving Sustainability, Food Security, Food Safety, and the Free Circulation of Goods' in Lucia Scaffardi and Giulia Formici (eds), *Novel Foods and Edible Insects in the European Union* (Springer 2022); Hanna Schebesta and Kai Purnhagen, *EU Food Law* (OUP 2024).

Foods falling within the scope of this Regulation are subject to a complex pre-market authorisation procedure, aimed at ensuring not only the smooth functioning of the internal market but also a high level of protection of human health and consumer interests (Article 1, para 2). In fact, Novel Foods can be legitimately marketed only if they do not pose safety risks to human health, on the basis of the scientific evidence available (Article 7, lett a).[19] Consequently, in the absence of authorisation, the commercialisation of the Novel Food is prohibited across the EU.

The authorisation procedure established by the Novel Foods Regulation is long and complex. Operators wishing to commercialise a Novel Food have to initiate a centralised and fully harmonised procedure with the European Commission.[20] The Commission receives the application and carries out a preliminary 'formal' validity check (Article 11, para 1). Crucially, it is the responsibility of the applicant to prepare a scientific dossier, providing 'scientific evidence that the Novel Food does not pose a risk to human health' (Article 10, para 2, lett e).

The application is then transferred to the European Food Safety Authority (EFSA), an independent EU authority which is tasked with conducting a risk assessment to evaluate the product's food safety.

Nevertheless, EFSA's opinion does not mark the conclusion of the authorisation process, nor does it constitute the sole factor determining the final decision. Rather, EFSA evaluation is followed by a separate risk management phase, involving different actors and a broader range of considerations. In fact, the Commission is responsible for drafting a proposed implementing act, authorising (or rejecting) the Novel Food (Article 12). This act must take into account not only EFSA's scientific food safety assessment—which is non-binding—but also relevant provisions of EU law, 'including the precautionary principle' (Article 12, para 1, lett b) as well as 'any other legitimate factors' (Article 12, para 1, lett d). Although the Regulation does not define these 'other legitimate factors' in detail, it is important to note that while 'irrational fears or purely

19 Other conditions are: 'b) the food's intended use does not mislead the consumer, especially when the food is intended to replace another food and there is a significant change in the nutritional value; c) where the food is intended to replace another food, it does not differ from that food in such a way that its normal consumption would be nutritionally disadvantageous for the consumer'.

20 The authorisation 'shall start either on the Commission's initiative or following an application to the Commission by an applicant', art 10.

emotional reactions ... cannot be considered legitimate factors',[21] certain non-scientific considerations may indeed be relevant during the risk management phase. These can include economic, social, ethical, and environmental considerations, as acknowledged in Recital 19 of Reg. (EC) 178/2002.[22]

Finally, the Commission's proposed implementing act must be voted on by a qualified majority in the Standing Committee on Plants, Animals, Food, and Feed (commonly referred to as the PAFF Committee), which involves Member States' representatives. Once approved, the authorised Novel Food is included in the public Union List, together with any specific requirements regarding labelling, conditions of use, or post-market monitoring obligations (Article 9).

It is worth highlighting that this Regulation—unlike others, such as the one concerning cultivation of Genetically Modified Organisms—fully covers the procedural aspects, thereby excluding national legislators from intervening in this domain.[23] This interpretation is reinforced by the exclusion from the current legal framework of the flexibility clause included in the previous 1997 Regulation (Article 12), which allowed Member States to restrict or suspend the marketing of an authorised Novel Food within their national territory in the event of emerging health or environmental risks. As will be discussed later in relation to cell-based meat, the strong, centralised approach adopted in the

21 Annalisa Volpato, 'Novel Foods in the EU Integrated Administrative Space: An Institutional Perspective' in Lucia Scaffardi and Giulia Formici (eds), *Novel Foods and Edible Insects in the European Union* (Springer 2022).

22 Regulation (EC) 178/2002 of the European Parliament and of the Council of 28 January 2002 laying down the general principles and requirements of food law, establishing the European Food Safety Authority and laying down procedures in matters of food safety [2002] OJ L31/1, better known as General Food Law Regulation; Recital 19 states: 'It is recognised that scientific risk assessment alone cannot, in some cases, provide all the information on which a risk management decision should be based, and that other factors relevant to the matter under consideration should legitimately be taken into account including societal, economic, traditional, ethical, and environmental factors and the feasibility of controls'.

23 Discussion should include the possibility of invoking arts 53–54 of Regulation (EC) 178/2002 of the European Parliament and of the Council of 28 January 2002 laying down the general principles and requirements of food law, establishing the European Food Safety Authority and laying down procedures in matters of food safety [2002] OJ L31/1. On this point Giulia Formici, 'Meating the Future: alcune riflessioni sulla necessità di promuovere un attento dibattito regolatorio in materia di c.d. carne sintetica' (2023) 2 Forum di Quaderni Costituzionali 15, 18; Guido Bellenghi and Luca Knuth, 'EU Food Law and the Politics of the Internal Market: The Challenge of Cultivated Meat' (2024) 17(3–4) Review of European Administrative Law 39; Vito Rubino and Francesco Rossi Dal Pozzo, 'The Regulatory Framework for the Authorisation to Produce and Market Cultured Meat in the EU' (2024) 19 European Food and Feed Law Review 199.

2015 legislation has significant implications for assessing the compatibility between certain unilateral national actions and EU law.

In conclusion, the 2015 Regulation's innovative structure and relative success—despite some weaknesses and areas for improvement[24]—can be attributed in part to the dual-phase process it establishes. This process separates risk assessment and risk management, assigning them to distinct institutional actors. At the same time, the procedure maintains a meaningful role for Member States through their participation in the PAFF Committee, notwithstanding the centralised nature of the authorisation pathway. Furthermore, the explicit inclusion of decision-making criteria beyond food safety allows for broader considerations (eg economic, social, ethical, and environmental) which are particularly relevant when evaluating highly innovative food products. These aspects have undoubtedly helped to prevent—at least thus far—major tensions between EU-level decisionmakers (particularly the Commission and Member State representatives), as well as between scientific risk assessments and subsequent risk management decisions, which have so far consistently aligned with EFSA's opinions.[25]

Nonetheless, this trend now appears to be at a critical juncture. Attempts by some Member States to deviate from the full harmonisation imposed by Reg. (EU) 2015/2283 are multiplying, particularly in relation to sensitive and potentially divisive Novel Foods, such as insect-based products for human consumption[26] and cell-based meat.

Particularly on the latter category of Novel Foods, the EU is currently experiencing a lively and complex regulatory debate. To date, cultured meat has neither been authorised nor marketed following the abovementioned procedure. Recently, two applications were submitted to the European Commission concerning cultivated duck meat (*foie gras*) and cultivated beef fat.[27] Although these authorisation procedures are still in their very early stages, political and legislative discussions around the effectiveness and suitability of the existing Novel Foods legal framework have intensified, giving rise to fragmented national approaches which potentially create conflicts between the supranational and national regulatory levels.

---

24 Martin Holle, 'Pre-market Approval and its Impact on Food Innovation: The Novel Foods Example' in Harry Bremmers and Kai Purnhagen (eds), *Regulating and Managing Food Safety in the EU* (Springer 2018).

25 Volpato (n 21).

26 Paganizza (n 13) 814.

27 Lucia Scaffardi and Giulia Formici, 'Cell-Based Meat' in Luigi Costato, Ferdinando Albisinni, and Theodore Georgopoulos (eds), *European and Global Food Law* (3rd edn, Wolters Kluwer 2025).

In particular, Italy has adopted national legislation banning the production and marketing of cell-based foods deriving from vertebrate animals.[28] France, Romania, and Hungary are attempting to follow suit, with legislative proposals under discussion in their national Parliaments.[29] These 'centrifugal forces' have prompted a crucial dialogue (and in some cases confrontation) with the European Commission, within the framework of the TRIS Directive procedure.[30] In Hungary's case, the Commission, supported by several Member States, declared in its opinion about the compliance of the proposed national ban with the EU law, that such provisions are incompatible with the Novel Foods Regulation.[31] Whether this clear stance will ultimately halt these unprecedented national attempts to circumvent the centralised authorisation procedure established by Reg. (EU) 2015/2283 remains to be seen.

What clearly emerges from these attempted or already in place national legislations are the multiple and delicate questions surrounding cell-based meat and concerning not only food safety but also environmental sustainability, socioeconomic implications, animal welfare, and ethical considerations—including compliance with religious dietary rules—, and the protection of cultural identity.[32] These concerns are mirrored in the regulatory discourse, with several Member States questioning the adequacy of the existing legal framework and its ability to fully address such multifaceted and complex challenges. Scientific uncertainties still characterising various aspects of cell-based meat

28 Law 172 of 1 December 2023, *Disposizioni in materia di divieto di produzione e di immissione sul mercato di alimenti e mangimi costituiti, isolati o prodotti a partire da colture cellulari o di tessuti derivanti da animali vertebrati nonche' di divieto della denominazione di carne per prodotti trasformati contenenti proteine vegetali* (Official Gazzette General Series 281 of 1 December 2023).

29 Maria Giulia Corazza and Giulia Formici, 'Cell-Based Meat in the European Union—A Regulatory Crossroads' in Giulia Formici, Maria Cecilia Mancini, and Lucia Scaffardi (eds), *Cell-Based Meat in the European Union and Beyond. An Interdisciplinary Study* (Springer 2025).

30 Directive (EU) 2015/1535 of the European Parliament and of the Council of 9 September 2015 laying down a procedure for the provision of information in the field of technical regulations and of rules on Information Society services [2015] OJ L241/1; Diana Cerini, ''From farm to fork' vs. 'from factory to lab': riflessioni su sostenibilità sociale e benessere animale a partire dalla L. 172/2023 in materia di alimenti e mangimi da colture cellulari' (2025) Rivista di Diritto Alimentare 76.

31 Notification 2024/0394/HU—Draft act prohibiting the production and placing on the market of laboratory-grown meat ('a laboratóriumi hús')—Delivery of a detailed opinion pursuant to Art. 6(2) of Directive (EU)2015/1535, <https://technical-regulation-information-system.ec.europa.eu/en/notification/26066> accessed 10 April 2025.

32 Giulia Formici, Maria Cecilia Mancini and Lucia Scaffardi (eds), *Cell-Based Meat in the European Union and Beyond. An Interdisciplinary Study* (Springer 2025); Carlos Ricardo Soccol and others (eds), *Cultivated Meat. Technologies, Commercialization and Challenges* (Springer 2024).

production and consumption[33] have in fact led a group of Member States to advocate for an EU-wide moratorium, along with the development of specific, *ad hoc* supranational legislation.[34]

The described highly polarised political and regulatory debate has, in many cases, fostered confusion and disinformation within civil society.

Accurate knowledge on the EU legislative framework is therefore crucial for reorienting the debate within proper, science-based boundaries, free from ideologically-driven distortions that can mislead public opinion. Such knowledge is the indispensable starting point for a much-needed dialogue among civil society (including citizens-consumers but also food business operators), policymakers, lawmakers, and the academic community. This discussion is essential for shaping future regulatory approaches and potential reforms, which will significantly influence how innovation, food safety, and food security are governed and balanced.

Building on these premises, the idea emerged to conduct a survey exploring citizens' or consumers' awareness as well as their regulatory perceptions and preferences.

3 The Methodological Approach and Survey Structure

To analyse both the awareness of current EU regulations on Novel Foods and individuals' preferences regarding how such regulations should ideally be shaped, we used original data collected through online surveys. The dataset includes a sample of 2,102 individuals representative of the adult Italian population in terms of gender, age, and macro-geographical area of residence (North-West, North-East, Center, and South).

---

33 Numerous documents, among which FAO and WHO, *Food Safety Aspects of Cell-Based Food* (Rome 2023), underline the need for further research in this innovative field in order to better understand lights and shadows, potentialities and risks in terms of food safety but also environmental sustainability and potential socio-economic effects. Hanna Tuomisto and Tony Ryynänen, 'Environmental Impacts of Cultivated Meat' in Carlos Ricardo Soccol and others (eds), *Cultivated Meat. Technologies, Commercialization and Challenges* (Springer 2024); Davide Lanzoni and others 'Biotechnological and Technical Challenges Related to Cultured Meat Production' (2022) 12(13) Applied Sciences 6771; Maria Cecilia Mancini and Federico Antonioli, 'The Future of Cultured Meat Between Sustainability Expectations and Socio-Economics Challenges' in Rajeev Bhat (ed), *Future Foods. Global Trends, Opportunities, and Sustainability Challenges* (Academic Press 2021).

34 *CAP's role in safeguarding high-quality and primary farm-based food production—Note from the Austrian, French and Italian Delegations*, 5469/2024-REV1 <https://data.consilium.europa.eu/doc/document/ST-5469-2024-REV-1/en/pdf> accessed 10 April 2025.

3.1 *Awareness of the Regulatory Framework*

Awareness of the regulatory framework and its various dimensions was assessed through a set of targeted questions.

The first question aimed to gauge basic knowledge of whether any EU regulation on Novel Foods exists: 'To the best of your knowledge, is there a regulation governing the placing on the market of Novel Foods in the European Union?' (Possible responses: yes; no; or I don't know).

A second question explored familiarity with the existence of a pre-market authorisation process: 'To the best of your knowledge, is there a pre-market approval process for Novel Foods in the European Union?' (Possible responses: yes; no; or I don't know). For respondents answering affirmatively, a follow-up question was asked: 'To the best of your knowledge, at what level does this pre-market approval take place?' (Possible responses: at the EU level; at the level of individual Member States; at both levels; I don't know).

The final general question investigated respondents' knowledge of EFSA's role in this context: 'To the best of your knowledge, is there an independent body in the European Union responsible for the scientific risk assessment of the food safety of Novel Foods?' (Possible responses: yes; no; or I don't know).

In addition, we included two questions specifically addressing cell-based meat, as a particular category of Novel Foods: 'To the best of your knowledge, has the European Union adopted specific legislation regulating the placing on the market of cell-based meat?' *and* 'To the best of your knowledge, has Italy adopted specific legislation regulating the placing on the market of cell-based meat?' (Possible responses: yes; no; or I don't know for both).

3.2 *Preferences for Regulatory Approaches*

Preferences regarding how the regulation of Novel Foods should be designed were explored through a series of questions targeting different aspects of the regulatory process.

First, we aimed to understand which institutions respondents consider most appropriate to be involved in the authorisation procedure for Novel Foods, and what roles they should play. To this end, participants were asked to indicate which institutions they would like to see involved in a hypothetical EU-level authorisation process:

> 'If you were to imagine an EU-level (European Union) authorisation procedure for Novel Foods, which institutions would you like to see involved? You may select more than one answer'. (Possible answers: European Parliament; European Commission; independent agency composed of experts; Member States; other).

We then examined which of these institutions respondents believed should have final decision-making power. The question was:

> 'Among the following institutions, which one do you think should have final say in authorising a Novel Food across the entire European Union?' (Possible answers: European Parliament; European Commission; independent agency composed of experts; unanimous agreement of Member States; majority vote of Member States).

Along the same lines, we investigated public attitudes toward the degree of autonomy and discretionary power individual countries should have within this regulatory framework. Respondents were presented with the following scenario:

> 'Imagine the following scenario: the commercialisation of a Novel Food has been authorised by the European Union. This authorisation, valid throughout the EU, was approved by a majority of Member States' representatives following a favourable scientific opinion from an expert agency. In this case, would you want individual Member States to have the power to autonomously prohibit the commercialisation of this Novel Food within their own national borders?'(Possible answers: yes; no; I don't know).

If the answer was 'yes', respondents were then asked to explain their reasoning by responding to the following questions:

- 'Would food safety for Novel Foods be better guaranteed?' (Possible answers: yes; no)
- 'Would the economic interests of those operating in the agrifood sector be better protected?' (Possible answers: yes; no)
- 'Would environmental sustainability be better safeguarded?' (Possible answers: yes; no)
- Respondents could also provide a narrative response providing additional thoughts.

We also investigated preferences regarding the role independent expert agencies should play in the authorisation process. First, we asked whether the scientific assessments made by such bodies should be considered binding or non-binding:

> 'Imagine that, as part of an EU-level authorisation procedure for Novel Foods, an independent agency composed of experts is tasked with

> assessing the food safety of the product for consumer health. In your opinion, what should be the value of this scientific opinion?' (Possible answers: Binding—EU institutions must follow this opinion; Non-binding—EU institutions may decide otherwise, also considering other interests such as environmental impact, economic considerations, or animal welfare.)

Next, we asked which areas respondents believe should fall under the responsibility of an independent scientific agency. Respondents were asked to state how interested they were in the technical-scientific opinion of the independent agency regarding: i) safety of the Novel Food for consumer health; ii) environmental sustainability; and iii) impact on animal welfare. (Possible answers: 1 = I am not interested in the opinion; 2 = I am somewhat interested in the opinion; 3 = I am very interested in the opinion.)

Finally, to specifically explore attitudes toward the regulation of cell-based meat, as a particularly interesting category of Novel Foods, we included two scenario-based questions. The first asked:

> 'Imagine the following scenario: the commercialisation of cell-based meat has been authorised by the European Union. This authorisation, valid throughout the EU, was approved by a majority of Member States' representatives following a favourable scientific opinion from an expert agency. In this case, would you want individual Member States to have the power to autonomously prohibit the commercialisation of this Novel Food within their own national borders?' (Possible answers: yes; no; I don't know.)

If respondents chose 'yes', they were asked to specify their reasons by choosing among the following:

- I would not trust the scientific opinion of the independent agency regarding the food safety.
- I am concerned that cell-based meat could have a negative environmental impact.
- I am concerned that this product could negatively affect animal welfare.
- I am concerned that this product could have a negative economic impact.
- Other (please specify).

The second question presented a different decision-making scenario:

> 'Imagine the following scenario: an independent European agency composed of experts has issued a favourable opinion regarding the food safety

of cell-based meat for consumers' health. Now the European Union must decide whether to authorise its commercialisation. What should it do?

- It should authorise its commercialisation across the entire EU.
- It should authorise its commercialisation across the EU, but allow individual Member States to ban its sale within their borders.
- It could ban its commercialisation across the EU, considering other factors besides food safety for consumers' health (eg, environmental impact, economic impact, animal welfare).
- It could still ban its commercialisation across the EU.

3.3 *Survey Structure*

As further detailed below, the survey was organized into six Parts and respondents were divided into two groups. Questions assessing respondents' awareness of current EU regulations (described in Section 3.1 of this chapter) were included in Part 3 of the questionnaire and were asked to all survey participants. Conversely, questions about individuals' preferences regarding how such regulations should be designed (Section 3.2 above) were included in Part 5 of the survey and administered only to half of the sample.

In fact, for half of the sample, the questionnaire included—between Parts 3 and 4—detailed information about the EU marketing authorisation process. This information was provided in order to analyse its potential effects on attitudes toward Novel Foods. For respondents who received this information, we did not ask how they would design the regulation; instead, we asked for their evaluation of the existing regulatory framework, about which they had just been informed.

As a result, when analysing awareness of the EU Regulation on Novel Foods, we considered the entire sample of 2,102 individuals. In contrast, when analysing preferences regarding the characteristics of the Regulation and, consequently, of the authorisation process, we focused only on the half of the sample that had not received the background information about this topic (ie Part 3a of the survey). It is worth noting that this sub-sample is also representative of the adult Italian population in terms of age group, gender, and macro-geographical area of residence—just like the full sample and the other sub-sample that received the authorisation process background information. Moreover, to increase comparability between the two sets of questions, in the next Section of this Chapter, we discuss what the data revealed about the awareness of the Regulation, both considering the full sample of subjects and the sub-sample of respondents who also answered the questions on preferences for regulatory approach (Group A).

TABLE 5.1 Survey structure

Part of survey	Type of questions/content	Groups completing	# of participants completing
1	Socio-demographic information	All	2,102
2	Respondents' attitudes and behaviours, including aspects such as risk preferences and impatience; trust in science, scientific research, and various institutions; political orientation; dietary habits; and levels of concern about environmental issues, health risks related to food, animal welfare, and rising prices of food and basic necessities	All	2,102
3	Definitions and background information on the concept of Novel Foods as defined by the European Union legal framework; participants' perceptions of Novel Foods and their awareness of the EU legal framework	All	2,102
3a	Detailed background information about the EU marketing authorisation process	Group B only	1,051
4	Respondents' attitudes and perceptions toward two specific and highly debated categories of Novel Foods: cell-based meat and insect-based flour products	All	2,102
5	Questions on how respondents would design the regulatory framework for marketing authorisation of Novel Foods	Group A only	1,051
5	Respondents' evaluation of the current regulatory system governing marketing authorisation of Novel Foods	Group B only	1,051
6	Respondents' views on the clarity of the information provided about Novel Foods and whether they perceive any political bias in the survey	All	2,102

As already underlined and in accordance with the abovementioned research questions, this Chapter does not focus on the effects of the additional background information that was shared with Group B.

The general contents of the survey's six Parts were as follows:

- Part 1 collected socio-demographic information.
- Part 2 focused on respondents' attitudes and behaviours, including aspects such as risk preferences and impatience; trust in science, scientific research, and various institutions; political orientation; dietary habits; and levels of concern about environmental issues, health risks related to food, animal welfare, and rising prices of food and basic necessities.
- Part 3 began with definitions and background information on the concept of Novel Foods as defined by the European Union legal framework. It then explored participants' perceptions of Novel Foods and their awareness of the EU legal framework, as described earlier.
- Part 3a provided detailed background information about the EU marketing authorisation process but was only shown to half the respondents.
- Part 4 examined respondents' attitudes and perceptions toward two specific and highly debated categories of Novel Foods: cell-based meat and insect-based flour products.
- Part 5 varied depending on whether respondents received information about the EU regulatory process for the marketing authorisation of Novel Foods, as previously discussed (Part 3a). For those who did not receive this information, the Part included questions on how they would design the regulatory framework. For those who did receive it, the part asks for their evaluation of the current regulatory system.
- Part 6 contained two questions assessing respondents' views on the clarity of the information provided about Novel Foods and whether they perceived any political bias in the survey.

4 Empirical Evidence

In this Section, we present the empirical evidence gathered from the survey results, focusing on both the respondents' awareness of current EU Regulation on Novel Foods and their opinions on how such a regulation should be shaped according to their preferences.

In particular, we analyse the frequency of the different response options selected for each question.

4.1 *Respondents' Awareness of Current EU Novel Foods Regulation*

The first key finding regarding regulatory awareness is that an absolute majority of respondents (51.33%) stated that they did not know whether an EU Regulation governing the marketing of Novel Foods existed. Meanwhile, 38.77% believed that such a Regulation did exist, while 9.90% stated that, to the best of their knowledge, no such Regulation exists.

When the same question was asked specifically about cell-based meat, the share of respondents who were unsure increased to 57.90%. Similarly, the proportion of negative responses rose to 12.84%, while the percentage of positive responses decreased to 29.26%. With specific reference to the existence of a legal framework adopted by Italy concerning cell-based meat, the responses showed a similar pattern: 25.07% believed such a regulation existed, 19.70% believed it did not, and 55.23% reported not knowing.

Knowledge about the existence of a pre-market approval process for Novel Foods in the EU was slightly higher: 40.82% of respondents believed that such a process existed, compared to 10.23% who believed it did not, and 48.95% who were unsure. Among those who correctly believed that a pre-market approval process exists, nearly half (45.69% of the total sample) thought that it takes place both at the EU level and the Member State level. Meanwhile, 24.94% believed it occurs only at the EU level, 15.03% only at the Member State level, with 14.34% who reported not knowing.

Finally, only 33.44% of respondents were aware that an independent body responsible for the scientific assessment of the food safety of Novel Foods exists in the European Union. Meanwhile, 11.56% believed that no such body exists, and 55.00% were unsure.

Overall, only 321 out of 2,102 respondents (15.27%) demonstrated an accurate understanding of the current EU Regulation on Novel Foods. For the purposes of this analysis, with respect to the question concerning the pre-market approval process, responses were considered correct if participants identified the pre-market approval process as taking place either 'only at the EU level' or 'both at the EU level and at the level of individual Member States'.

Figure 5.1 summarises data about regulation awareness as it emerges from the questions previously analysed.

The previous percentages refer to the full sample of 2,102 respondents, with no missing values for any of the questions. When the analysis is broken down by the two sub-samples of 1,051 respondents each—one group that answered questions about preferences regarding how the regulation should be shaped, and one that did not according to what is discussed in the previous

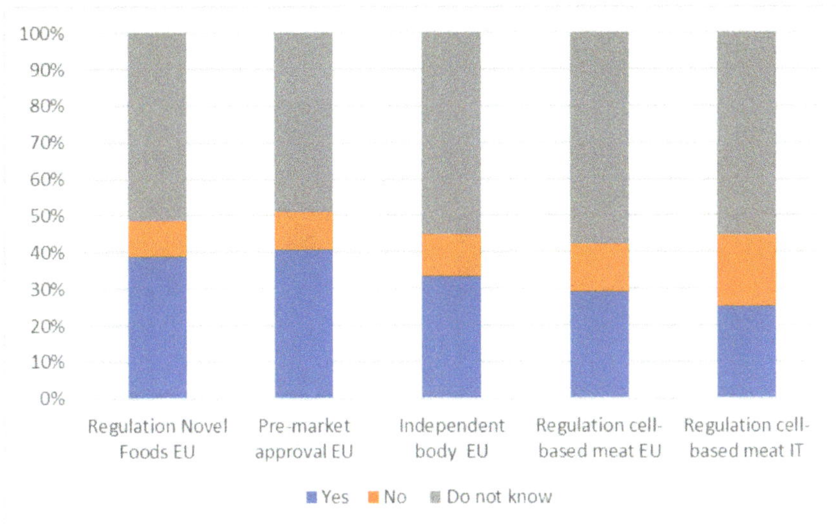

FIGURE 5.1 Regulation awareness

Section—we find that the response distributions are very similar across both groups.[35]

4.2 *Preferences on How Novel Foods Regulation Should Be Shaped*

With regard to the institution(s) to be involved in the authorisation procedure for Novel Foods, respondents—who could select more than one option—tended to favour an independent agency composed of experts (50.80%), followed by the European Commission (40.15%). The European Parliament and individual Member States were selected with the same frequency (38.77%) (Figure 5.2).

When focusing on preferences concerning the involvement of multiple institutions and considering only those explicitly listed in the response options (European Parliament, European Commission, independent agency composed

35 Only in the case of the question concerning the existence of an independent body responsible for the scientific assessment of the food safety of Novel Foods does the distribution of responses differ significantly (Two-sample Wilcoxon rank-sum [Mann-Whitney] test, Prob > |z| = 0.0133). In this case, a higher percentage of respondents in the sub-sample that was also asked about regulatory preferences declared that such an authority exists (35.97% vs. 30.92%). This difference is almost entirely offset by a lower percentage of respondents in that same group who were unsure about the existence of such an authority (52.52% vs. 57.45%).

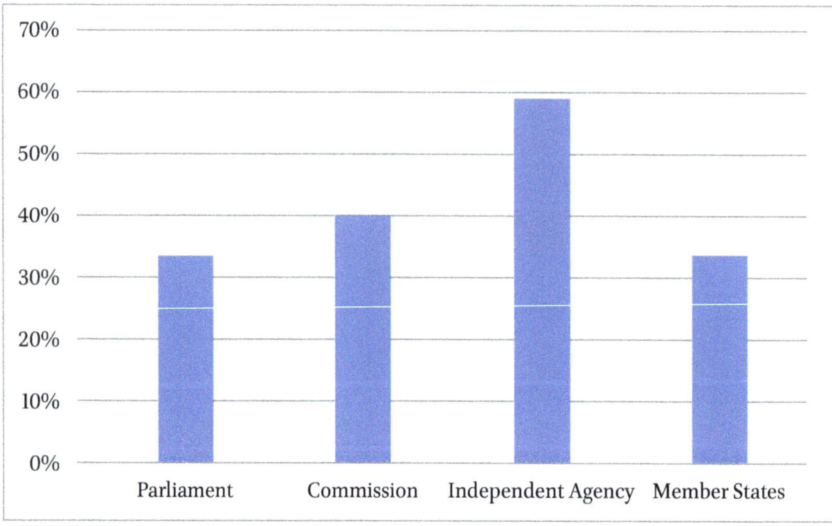

FIGURE 5.2 Preference for the involvement of EU institutions in the approval of Novel Foods (Multiple answers allowed)

of experts, Member States), 8.56% of respondents indicated a preference for the involvement of all these institutions in the authorisation process. Among those favouring a centralised procedure at the EU level, 18.55% of respondents opted for a procedure involving at least both the European Commission and the European Parliament, while 4.95% selected *only* these two institutions. 20.46% of respondents favored a procedure involving both the European Commission and an independent agency. Looking at exclusive preferences for a single institution, 6.76% of respondents favoured solely the European Parliament, 9.51% selected only the European Commission, 25.98% chose only an independent agency, and 6.76% preferred only the Member States.

Regarding the institution that should have the final say in authorising a Novel Foods across the entire EU, respondents' preferences once again leaned toward an independent agency composed of experts, selected by a relative majority (33.78%). This is followed by the requirement of unanimous agreement among Member States (21.50%), a majority vote among Member States (15.79%), the European Commission (15.41%), and the European Parliament (13.51%).

The roles of Member States and independent agencies were further explored through specific questions. Concerning Member States, an absolute majority of respondents (51.28%) expressed the view that individual Member States should have the authority to unilaterally prohibit the commercialisation of Novel Foods within their own national borders, even when an

FIGURE 5.3 Aspects you would like the independent agency to express technical-scientific opinion

EU-wide authorisation has been granted by a majority of Member States' representatives based on a favourable scientific opinion from an expert agency. Specifically, respondents believe that such power at the national level would better ensure food safety (according to 84.23% of those supporting this position), better protect the economic interests of stakeholders in the agrifood sector (80.52%), and better safeguard environmental sustainability (71.61%). Conversely, 21.50% of respondents oppose granting such authority to individual Member States, while 27.21% expressed no opinion.

As for the role of an independent authority providing EU-wide assessments, 65.94% of respondents would prefer the agency's assessment of product safety for consumer health be binding in the context of the EU-level authorization procedure for Novel Foods, compared to 34.06% who favor a non-binding role. Furthermore, when asked which issues should be evaluated by an independent panel of experts, respondents expressed higher approval of the option for technical scientific opinions regarding the food safety of Novel Foods for consumer health over opinions regarding environmental sustainability or the impact on animal welfare. These were also considered relevant but to a lesser extent, as reflected in respondents' answers shown in Figure 5.3.

Finally, we address two questions that allowed us to broaden our analysis concerning cell-based meat. The first question appears to confirm the importance that respondents attribute to independent scientific agencies, while also highlighting the role of individual Member States. Specifically, respondents were asked what the EU should do in a hypothetical scenario where an independent European agency composed of experts issued a favourable opinion regarding the safety of cell-based meat for consumers.

In this context, a relative majority of respondents (49.95%) believed that the EU should authorise the commercialisation of cell-based meat across the Union, while allowing individual Member States to ban its sale within their own borders. A significantly smaller proportion of respondents believe that the EU should authorise commercialisation across the entire Union without exceptions (19.52%); ban commercialisation altogether based on considerations beyond food safety (eg environmental impact, economic consequences, animal welfare) (18.10%); or simply ban commercialisation throughout the EU (15.43%).

As was the case with Novel Foods more generally, an absolute majority of respondents (53.62%) believed that individual Member States should retain the authority to unilaterally ban the commercialisation of cell-based meat within their national borders, even when an EU-wide authorisation has been granted based on a favourable scientific opinion from an expert agency. Those who held this view justified their position by stating that they would not trust the scientific opinion of the independent agency regarding the product's safety (33.39%)—a finding that somewhat contradicts the importance attributed to such agencies in other parts of the survey. Others cited concerns about the potential negative economic impact (26.82%), environmental impact (14.03%), or effects on animal welfare (12.26%).

5 Unpacking the Survey: Civil Society and the Future of Novel Foods Regulation

Based on the empirical evidence examined, several key conclusions can be drawn.

First of all, the survey clearly reveals limited awareness of the current EU Novel Foods Regulation among the average citizen-consumer. This emerges from both the respondents' lack of knowledge about the existence of this specific EU legislation and the incorrect belief that such a legislative framework exists at all. These findings highlight the need for lawmakers and policymakers to implement targeted information strategies and public communications campaigns to increase awareness and to correct misunderstandings about the regulatory solutions currently in place. If the EU, national governments, and food business operators want to encourage public participation and stimulate debate concerning reform of the Novel Foods discipline, adequate public education is a crucial prerequisite. The observed lack of awareness of regulatory aspects can also offer useful insights for companies interested in the production and marketing of Novel Foods, helping them to design communications strategies aimed at enhancing consumer acceptance through greater knowledge and transparency about the regulatory process.

When it comes to cell-based meat, the awareness gap becomes even more evident, with regard not only to EU legislation but also to national solutions. Considering the highly polarised debate already underway in different Member States, a limited level of knowledge and understanding of the regulatory framework currently in place could ultimately foster fear, misinformation, and the spread of fake news. Moreover, it is worth underlining that the public's scant awareness does not only concern the Novel Foods Regulation but also the role of EFSA, whose existence (and, consequently, function and purpose) appears to be surrounded by uncertainty.

Secondly, if we consider the authorisation process and how it should be shaped, the empirical evidence interestingly underscores two main findings:

a) A significant share of respondents recognised the central role played by independent experts and, consequently, scientific evaluations. This may prompt reflection on the need to reform the existing risk assessment process by expanding it beyond food safety considerations and analysis. In fact, one potential legislative reform and intervention is the integration into the current authorisation process of not only independent evaluations of food safety, but also assessments of other key aspects, such as environmental effects and animal welfare impacts.

b) A noteworthy segment of respondents identified the European Commission and independent agencies as legitimate actors in the authorisation process, thus suggesting widespread acceptance of the current multilevel, biphasic governance structure. In other words, when given multiple choices, respondents mainly expressed their preference for shared decision-making. Nonetheless, another aspect is worth examining: differently from what the current Novel Foods Regulation establishes, a large proportion of respondents supported the possibility for Member States to exercise individual powers to ban or restrict the marketing of new foods within their national borders, even if these products are already authorised at the EU level. This dynamic surprisingly holds true when cell-based meat is investigated as well: a total opposition—in the form of an outright ban—to this innovative food is supported by a minor number of respondents. Nonetheless, a relative majority expressed preference for

EU-level authorisation with Member State discretion to limit the sale in their territory; in this case, the reasons behind this choice indicate less clear-cut confidence in the independent agencies' scrutiny.

In conclusion, what we can infer from this evidence is, on the one hand, the important role accorded to science—by also potentially recognising scientific opinions expressed during the regulatory process as binding for risk managers. On the other hand, the role of Member States is reaffirmed, reinforcing the importance of national risk governance. Although only apparently contradictory, these findings perfectly reflect the constant tension that emerges when innovation enters the regulatory domain. In this case, while the need to affirm and reinforce scientific, independent assessments clearly emerges from respondents' positions, the demand for a final political decision—also at the national level—was simultaneously expressed. This could represent the perceived necessity to counterbalance the attribution of powers to independent authorities that lie outside the framework of democratic legitimacy, and therefore to mitigate potential technocratic drifts.[36] This duality concretely illustrates the complex regulatory choices and emerging trends that arise when innovation must be governed, thus revealing the pressing challenge of defining a balance point between 'politicisation of science' and 'scientification' of political decision-making.[37] Such complex challenges impose serious and profound reflection on democratic representation and, in a broad sense, public involvement in sensitive decision-making processes.

Ultimately, this survey highlights the complexity of regulating innovation. It emphasises the crucial role of knowledge in reducing polarisation and rebuilding credibility in both regulatory processes and scientific evaluations. At the same time, it points to the need to effectively integrate scientific assessments with political considerations: this could lead to a reconfiguration of the roles played by different actors and a rethinking of the governance of emerging technological advancements in a way that ensures solutions and decisions are both scientifically sound and socially acceptable and grounded in political considerations.

36 Laura Salvi, 'Agri-Food Law and Innovation through the Lenses of Better Regulation' in AIDA-IFLA (ed), *Innovation in Agri-Food Law Between Technology and Comparison* (Wolters Kluwer 2019), 28.

37 Guido Bellenghi and Luca Knuth (n 22).

Bibliography

AIDA-IFLA (ed), *Innovation in Agri-Food Law Between Technology and Comparison* (Wolters Kluwer 2019).

Bellenghi G and Knuth L, 'EU Food Law and the Politics of the Internal Market: The Challenge of Cultivated Meat' (2024) 17(3–4) Review of European Administrative Law 39.

Cerini D, "From farm to fork' vs. 'from factory to lab': Riflessioni su sostenibilità sociale e benessere animale a partire dalla l. 172/2023 in materia di alimenti e mangimi da colture cellulari' (2025) Rivista di Diritto Alimentare 76.

Corazza MG and Formici G, 'Cell-Based Meat in the European Union—A Regulatory Crossroads' in Giulia Formici, Maria Cecilia Mancini and Lucia Scaffardi (eds), *Cell-Based Meat in the European Union and Beyond. An Interdisciplinary Study* (Springer 2025).

Costato L, Albisinni F and Georgopoulos T (eds), *European and Global Food Law* (3rd edn, Wolters Kluwer 2025).

Formici G, 'Meating the Future: alcune riflessioni sulla necessita di promuovere un attento dibattito regolatorio in materia di c.d. carne sintetica' (2023) 2 Forum di Quaderni Costituzionali 15.

Formici G, Mancini MC and Scaffardi L (eds), *Cell-Based Meat in the European Union and Beyond. An Interdisciplinary Study* (Springer 2025).

Holle M, 'Pre-market Approval and its Impact on Food Innovation: The Novel Foods Example' in Harry Bremmers and Kai Purnhagen (eds), *Regulating and Managing Food Safety in the EU* (Springer 2018).

Lanzoni D and others, 'Biotechnological and Technical Challenges Related to Cultured Meat Production' (2022) 12(13) Applied Sciences 6771.

Mancini MC and Antonioli F, 'The Future of Cultured Meat Between Sustainability Expectations and Socio-Economics Challenges' in Rajeev Bhat (ed), *Future Foods. Global Trends, Opportunities, and Sustainability Challenges* (Academic Press 2021).

Monaco A, 'Data Protection under the Novel Food Regulation: Valuable Instrument or Barrier to Innovation? Insights from the Insect Sector' (2023) 18 European Food and Feed Law Review 172.

Paganizza V, 'Artificial Intelligence in the Food Sector' in Luigi Costato, Ferdinando Albisinni and Theodore Georgopoulos (eds), *European and Global Food Law* (3rd edn, Wolters Kluwer 2025).

Paganizza V, 'I nuovi alimenti ("Novel Foods")' in Paolo Borghi, Irene Canfora, Alessandra Di Lauro and Luigi Russo (eds), *Trattato di diritto alimentare italiano e dell'Unione europea* (2nd edn, Giuffrè 2024).

Pisanello D and Caruso G, *Novel Foods in the European Union* (Springer 2018).

Pitto S, *La rilevanza costituzionale e globale della sicurezza alimentare. Una lettura olistica e comparata della food security* (Editoriale Scientifica 2024).

Rossi Dal Pozzo F and Rubino V (eds), *La sicurezza alimentare tra crisi internazionali e nuovi modelli economici* (Cacucci 2023).

Rubino V and Rossi Dal Pozzo F, 'The Regulatory Framework for the Authorisation to Produce and Market Cultured Meat in the EU' (2024) 19 European Food and Feed Law Review 199.

Salvi L, 'Agri-Food Law and Innovation through the Lenses of Better Regulation' in AIDA-IFLA (ed), *Innovation in Agri-Food Law Between Technology and Comparison* (Wolters Kluwer 2019).

Scaffardi L and Formici G, 'Cell-Based Meat' in Luigi Costato, Ferdinando Albisinni and Theodore Georgopoulos (eds), *European and Global Food Law* (3rd edn, Wolters Kluwer 2025).

Scaffardi L and Formici G, 'A Peculiar Category of Novel Foods: Traditional Foods Coming from Third Countries and the Regulatory Issues Involving Sustainability, Food Security, Food Safety, and the Free Circulation of Goods', in Lucia Scaffardi and Giulia Formici (eds), *Novel Foods and Edible Insects in the European Union* (Springer 2022).

Schebesta H and Purnhagen K, *EU Food Law* (OUP 2024).

Sforza S, 'Food (In)Security: The Role of Novel Foods on Sustainability' in Lucia Scaffardi and Giulia Formici (eds), *Novel Foods and Edible Insects in the European Union* (Springer 2022).

Soccol CR and others (eds), *Cultivated Meat. Technologies, Commercialization and Challenges* (Springer 2024).

Tuomisto H and Ryynänen T, 'Environmental Impacts of Cultivated Meat' in Carlos Ricardo Soccol and others (eds), *Cultivated Meat. Technologies, Commercialization and Challenges* (Springer 2024).

Van Der Meulen B, *Reconciling Food Law to Competitiveness. Report on the regulatory environment of the European Food and dairy sector* (Wageningen Academic Publisher 2009).

Volpato A, 'Novel Foods in the EU Integrated Administrative Space: An Institutional Perspective' in Lucia Scaffardi and Giulia Formici (eds), *Novel Foods and Edible Insects in the European Union* (Springer 2022).

Webster E, Gupta A and Ambros R (eds), *Transnational Food Security* (Routledge 2020).

CHAPTER 6

The Internet of Farming and Agriculture 4.0: Regulatory Perspectives on the Fourth Industrial Revolution in Agriculture

Maria Giulia Corazza

Summary

1 Introduction

The advent of the Fourth Industrial Revolution, also known as Industry 4.0 or the digital transition, has impacted nearly every economic sector,[1] recently extending its influence on agriculture, giving rise to the phenomenon known as 'Agriculture 4.0'.

The Smart Agrifood Observatory[2] defines Agriculture 4.0 as the evolution of precision farming achieved through the automatic collection, integration, and analysis of field data, from sensors or other third-party sources. The integration of digital technology into farming has facilitated the generation of data which can empower farmers to make more informed decisions regarding their own operations and their interactions with other actors in the supply chain.

1 For a general overview of the development of new technological paradigms and the emergence of a true Digital Age, Gianpaolo Neri, *L'impresa nell'Era Digitale. Tecnologie informatiche e rivoluzione digitale al servizio dell'impresa* (3rd edn, Guaraldi 2015).

2 Smart Agrifood Observatory, 'Agricoltura 4.0 la trasformazione digitale del settore primario' (2018) <https://www.osservatori.net/report/smart-agrifood/agricoltura-4-0-trasformazione-digitale-settore-primario/> accessed 27 February 2025.

This, in turn, has the potential to transcend conventional boundaries of individual enterprises. The overarching objective of this paradigm shift, as will be elaborated upon in the subsequent sections, is to enhance the profitability, economic viability, environmental sustainability, and social responsibility of agricultural practices.

This new phase of technological innovation in the agrifood sector is characterised by the integration of the Internet of Things (IoT) into agriculture, also known as the 'Internet of Farming', the main feature of which is a previously-unparalleled level of digitalisation that is profoundly impacting a substantial segment of conventional agricultural practices. By leveraging advanced technologies such as smart sensors, robotics, drones, and big data, farmers can optimise the management of data collected directly from the field, enhancing resource efficiency and increasing productivity while reducing environmental impact.

Agriculture 4.0 is therefore considered to be a cross-cutting phenomenon that has the potential to exert a positive effect on the entire agrifood supply chain, from production methods to market structures.

Undoubtedly, these technologies play a critical role in achieving the food sustainability goals outlined by the European Green Deal[3] and the Farm to Fork strategy.[4] Nevertheless, substantial regulatory gaps remain at both the national and European levels, inhibiting the swift and uniform adoption of Agriculture 4.0 tools across different regions and time frames.[5] This regulatory void, likely temporary, is an inherent aspect of the digitalisation process itself, which, by definition, is constantly evolving.

In this context, the issue fits within the broader debate on the relationship between law and techno-scientific innovation, as noted by leading scholars.[6] The legal challenges around Agriculture 4.0 relate to the wide range of regulatory frameworks that need to be updated to accommodate the phenomenon's highly innovative and interdisciplinary nature.

---

3 Commission, *The European Green Deal* COM (2019) 640 final.

4 Commission, *A Farm to fork strategy: for a fair, healthy and environmentally-friendly food system* COM (2020) 381 final.

5 For more on this theme, see Wanda D'Avanzo, 'Smart farming. La quarta rivoluzione industriale e la digitalizzazione nel settore agricolo' [2022] Diritto Agroalimentare 279.

6 Consultation of the following contribution is recommended, among the extensive body of literature on this subject: Ferdinando Albisinni, 'Agricoltura e digitalizzazione: l'impresa agricola nel tempo presente' (2023) 1 Quaderni della Rivista di Diritto Alimentare 92; the subject is also addressed in depth in the present volume, see the chapter by Lorenza Violini.

In order to facilitate a systematic presentation of the main legal problems, this analysis will classify these challenges into two broad groups based on the perspective from which the issues are being analysed.

From an objective perspective, legal issues concerning the data collected through 4.0 technologies[7] will be addressed. A review of the doctrinal debate that has developed in recent years on the subject (starting from the classification and governance of agro-data as either personal or non-personal data), as well as the different regulatory and legislative responses, is presented here.

The subsequent analysis concentrates on agro-data ownership and portability, through a comparison of the new Regulation (EU) 2023/2854 (Data Act) and relevant soft law sources (Codes of Conduct).

From a subjective perspective, the analysis addresses the evolving arena of agriculture, focusing on Agricultural Technology Providers (ATPs), new actors in the agrifood supply chain. The entry into the sector of these new players, who are vendors of Agriculture 4.0 machinery, has important implications for the role of agricultural entrepreneurs (users of such machinery) within the supply chain. This chapter analyses how Agriculture 4.0 technologies will affect the position of agricultural entrepreneurs within the agrifood supply chain in relation to other stakeholders. The barriers that the individual farmer faces in adopting the tools of Agriculture 4.0 will then be outlined, from the digital divide to access to advanced technologies in rural areas to the role of the 2023–2027 Common Agricultural Policy (CAP).

This analysis primarily focuses on the European context, but draws on comparative examples from select non-European countries to highlight soft law developments.

The central objective of this analysis is to present a comprehensive overview of the predominant legal concerns that have emerged during the implementation of Agriculture 4.0's technological advancements. In addition to this, it is hoped that insights derived from this study will be of significant value in informing the development of more harmonised and efficacious regulatory frameworks, designed to facilitate a uniform and effective digital transformation within the agricultural domain.

7 Henceforth referred to as 'agro-data'. For a specific definition and commentary on this particular type of data, taken from the famous *Bayer v Monsanto* (Case M.8084) Commission Decision [2018] OJ C459/10, paras 2453 and following, see Can Atik and Bertin Martens, 'Competition Problems and Governance of Non-personal Agricultural Machine Data: Comparing Voluntary Initiatives in the US and EU' (2021) 12 Jipitec 370, 379.

2 Agriculture 4.0: Potential Positive Outputs of the Digital Revolution in the Agrifood Supply Chain

Agriculture 4.0 is, in every respect, an umbrella term encompassing any tool based on intensive use of IoT technologies that enables real-time analysis of data collected during field operations to make agriculture more precise and adaptable. The so-called Internet of Farming involves a range of operations spanning various phases of the farming process: from soil preparation and seeding, to plant monitoring, treatment, and harvesting. It includes the use of blockchain tools in the distribution process.[8]

These technologies affect the entire agrifood supply chain, from farm to table, with different impacts at each stage. Potential positive externalities will be outlined here, before focusing on the most debated legal issues in the next sections.

2.1 *Sustainability*

Sustainability, understood in its various environmental, economic, and social manifestations, is an essential component in the formulation of agricultural enterprises and agricultural activities, in general.[9] A critical assessment is necessary to determine the extent to which Agriculture 4.0 technologies contribute to the realisation of an 'agricultural sustainability model',[10] with technological innovation regarded as a meaningful indicator of sustainability. The potential for positive environmental impact is clear: starting from the field itself, IoT technologies include sensors that monitor parameters such as soil moisture, air temperature, nutrient levels, and crop health, providing farmers with guidance on optimising irrigation, fertilisation, pesticide application, and the best time for harvest. It is evident that Agriculture 4.0 facilitates a transition from conventional agricultural practices, which utilise substantial amounts of water, fertiliser, and pesticides, to a more sustainable and efficient model. The success of this transition is predicated on a reduction in resource consumption

---

8 For a definition of precision farming, see D'Avanzo (n 5); Pamela Lattanzi, 'L'agricoltura di precisione: fisionomia, quadro strategico di riferimento e implicazioni giuridiche' (2024) 2 Rivista di Diritto Alimentare 19.

9 As argued on several occasions by Antonio Jannarelli 'Agricoltura sostenibile e nuova PAC: problemi e prospettive' [2020] Rivista di Diritto Agrario 23, 'Il diritto agrario del nuovo millennio tra food safety, food security e sustainable agriculture' [2018] Rivista di Diritto Agrario 511 and 'Il divenire del diritto agrario italiano ed europeo tra sviluppi tecnologici e sostenibilità' [2013] Rivista di Diritto Agrario 11.

10 As outlined in Lorenza Paoloni, 'Sostenibilità e innovazione in agricoltura. Dilemma o opportunità?' [2024] Diritto Agroalimentare 569.

and its resulting minimisation of environmental impact.[11] Likewise, it should be noted that there are positive implications for economic and social sustainability arising from the adoption of Agriculture 4.0 methods. From an economic perspective, there is substantial evidence to suggest that farms which invest in digital transformation can achieve considerably higher productivity and product quality, as well as increased competitiveness.[12] Though not investigated in this chapter, positive social externalities from this transition, such as the revitalisation of rural areas due to a flourishing agricultural sector[13] or the emergence of new professional roles that require Agriculture 4.0 expertise,[14] are also becoming increasingly apparent.

2.2 *Food Security*

Meeting increasing demand for food—ie food security and its four dimensions of availability, access, utilisation, and stability—represents a fundamental objective of sustainable practices within the food industry. Digitalisation in agriculture is an essential tool for achieving, among other things, the 'rationality' that must characterise the development of primary production, as stated in Article 39, para 1, letter a) of the Treaty on the Functioning of the EU (TFEU), which outlines the objectives of the CAP.

'Rational development of agricultural production' entails not only an awareness of what is produced and how it is produced, but also of how much of it needs to be produced to meet the ever-increasing demand for food.[15] The need to increase production is thus balanced through an economically sustainable

11 Precision agriculture—one of the most widespread applications of IoT in agriculture—allows inputs to be tailored to the specific needs of each plot, preventing waste, as explained in Irene Canfora, 'Politica Agricola Comune e digitalizzazione del comparto agroalimentare' (2023) 1 Quaderni di Rivista di Diritto Alimentare 11.

12 As stated in Paoloni (n 10) 587. For more about concrete prospects for development and profitability, see Antonio Jannarelli, *Cibo e Diritti. Per un'agricoltura sostenibile* (Giappichelli 2015) and 'I vantaggi dell'Agricoltura 4.0 per le aziende e per i consumatori finali: dalla razionalizzazione delle risorse alla tracciabilità end-to-end. I numeri in Italia e le agevolazioni per le imprese' (ESG 360, 22 August 2024) <https://www.esg360.it/agrifood/agricoltura-4-0-cose-incentivi-e-tecnologie-abilitanti/> accessed 27 February 2025.

13 Comitato consultivo Accademia dei Georgofili, *Le prospettive della digitalizzazione per lo sviluppo sostenibile nel territorio rurale* (Accademia dei Georgofili, 2021) <https://www.georgofili.it/Media?c=f08b0d41-5a47-4aa6-8fa3-a159d90e66ae> accessed 27 February 2025; Beatrice La Porta, *Contributo per una visione contemporanea dell'azienda agricola. Tra sostenibilità e sfide del mondo digitale* (Giappichelli 2023).

14 For an in-depth study on the subject, see Claudia Faleri, 'Transizione ecologica e sostenibilità sociale per un'Agricoltura 4.0' (2022) 36 Lavoro e diritto 449, 457–458.

15 FAO, *How to feed the world in 2050* (Rome 2009).

approach that still ensures food security through 'optimum utilisation of production factors' and 'technical progress'.[16]

2.3 *Traceability and Food Safety*

Traceability is another crucial aspect facilitated by IoT technologies, particularly blockchain technologies applied to distribution. Modern food supply chains are long and complex, and the ability to monitor every stage of production, processing, and distribution is essential not only to ensure food safety, but also to comply with increasingly stringent traceability regulations. For example, agricultural traceability for food safety is mandated both in Article 168, para 5 (public health) and Article 169, para 1 (consumer protection) of the TFEU.

The principle is also implemented in Regulation (EC) 178/2002 (General Food Law),[17] which requires the traceability of food in several provisions,[18] making it a cornerstone of food safety legislation. Certain Agriculture 4.0 methods, such as blockchain and other distributed ledger technologies, can in fact be used to track every food product from its origin to the final consumer, improving the transparency—and, consequently, ensuring the food safety[19]—of the agrifood system.[20]

3 Legal Implications of Agriculture 4.0

As outlined in the preceding section, the benefits of digitalisation in agriculture are indisputable. However, its development is accompanied by increasingly complex legal relationships within the sector. This growing intricacy can be attributed to two primary factors.

16 On the importance of not reducing the concept of sustainability solely to its environmental meaning, see Paolo Borghi, 'L'agricoltura 4.0: il futuro del settore agroalimentare e il filo rosso che lo lega alle origini della PAC' (2023) 1 Quaderni della Rivista di Diritto Alimentare 5.

17 Regulation (EC) 178/2002 of 28 January 2002 lays down the general principles and requirements of food law, establishes the European Food Safety Authority, and lays down procedures in matters of food safety [2002] OJ L31/1.

18 ibid, art 18.

19 About Food Safety Management, see Ettore Battelli, 'Innovazione tecnologica e gestione della filiera agroalimentare' [2024] Diritto Agroalimentare 455, 457.

20 Marta Arisi, 'Coltivare la fiducia? Una prospettiva giuridica su dati, blockchain e tracciabilità lungo la filiera agroalimentare' (2023) 1 Quaderni della Rivista di Diritto Alimentare 56.

First, the innovative nature of the tools themselves introduces a new asset: agro-data.[21] This novel element, the existence and utility of which are contingent on digital machinery, is assuming an increasingly pivotal role within the agrifood chain. Assessing the economic and legal implications of agro-data as a component of the supply chain itself and developing a regulatory framework to ensure its responsible use is imperative. Substantiating agro-data as a genuine instrument used by agricultural operators, with intrinsic market exchange value, would help legitimise data-driven practices as a core component of modern agricultural economics.[22]

Second is the emergence of new, powerful entities that impact the already precarious economic-commercial balance of the supply chain.[23] The advent of these new players, such as ATPs, has introduced additional complexity to an already-complex situation. ATPs are companies that offer digital services to agricultural operators, generating profits from both the provision of services (eg the use of technology-equipped machinery) and, most significantly, agricultural data. The owners of the software exploit this data to enhance their services and expand their market share. Consequently, agricultural operators and farms are assuming a more passive role, reduced to being mere data collectors. This evolution signifies a shift in the role of the farmer, who is increasingly becoming a 'supporting actor' in the digital transformation process.[24]

3.1 *Agricultural Data: New 'Assets' in the Agrifood Supply Chain*

One of the main legal issues arising from Agriculture 4.0 concerns the nature, governance, and ownership of data generated during farming operations as a new 'product'.[25] Modern agricultural technologies produce large amounts

---

21 See Atik and Martens (n 7) 379–380; Paolo Guarda, 'Riflessioni in merito alla natura giuridica dei dati nell'agricoltura di precisione' (2023) 1 Quaderni della Rivista di Diritto Alimentare 20, 21–22; Matteo Ferrari, 'Digitalizzazione e innovazione nell'attività delle imprese agricole' in Mario Mauro (ed), *Start-up e PMI innovative in agricoltura. Le imprese agricole fra innovazione e sostenibilità* (Wolters Kluwer 2024).

22 See Matteo Ferrari, *Fattori di produzione, innovazione e distribuzione di valore nella filiera agroalimentare* (Ledizioni 2023).

23 See Roberto Caso, 'Capitalismo dei monopoli intellettuali, pseudo-proprietà intellettuale e dati nel settore dell'agricoltura di precisione e dello smart farming' (2023) 1 Quaderni della Rivista di Diritto Alimentare 36; Matteo Ferrari, 'Digitalizzazione e strutture agricole. Rivista di diritto alimentare' (2023) 1 Quaderni della Rivista di Diritto Alimentare 46.

24 See Atik and Martens (n 7), 371; Guarda (n 21), 22.

25 In this context, the term '(agricultural) product' is not interpreted in accordance with its strict definition, eg as outlined in art 4, para 2 letter a) of Regulation (EU) 2021/2115 of the European Parliament and of the Council of 2 December 2021 establishing rules supporting the development of strategic plans by Member States under the common agricultural

of data that can be used to improve productivity and optimise resources. However, the collection and use of this so-called agro-data raises complex questions about who owns the data and how it can be commercially exploited. Defining the legal status of this data, starting with the definition of its nature, is crucial to applying the correct legal regime. A lack of clarity in the current legal framework regarding the ownership of this data poses the potential to harm the farmers creating it.[26]

In Europe, the law distinguishes between natural persons—human individuals—and legal persons, such as companies or organisations. The General Data Protection Regulation (GDPR) protects the personal data[27] of natural persons only, defining it broadly in Article 4(1) as any information relating to an identifiable individual. This scope may extend to agricultural data: while agro-data typically concerns goods (eg crops, soil, or livestock), its use can influence the decisions of natural persons—such as individual farmers—especially when processed through Agriculture 4.0 tools that recommend actions like fertiliser use.

By contrast, data relating solely to legal persons[28] falls outside the GDPR's scope. Yet in practice, especially in agriculture—where a large share of businesses are sole proprietorships (82.1% in Italy as of 2020)[29]—the line

---

policy (CAP Strategic Plans) and financed by the European Agricultural Guarantee Fund (EAGF) and by the European Agricultural Fund for Rural Development (EAFRD) and repealing Regulations (EU) 2013/1305 and (EU) 2013/1307 [2021] OJ L435/1. Rather, it is understood in atechnical sense, signifying an element that is produced as a by-product of the agrifood chain.

26 The discourse surrounding the doctrine on the nature and circulation of data from the agricultural sector is a particularly fruitful one. See Guarda (n 21); Ferrari (n 22), 98; Giuseppe Versaci, 'La regolazione dei dati per l'agricoltura di precisione tra questioni generali ed esigenze settoriali' [2024] Diritto Agroalimentare 619; Can Atik, 'Understanding the role of agricultural data on market power in the emerging Digital Agriculture sector: a critical analysis of the Bayer/Monsanto decision' in David Bosco and Michal S Gal (eds), *Challenges to Assumptions in Competition Law*, (Edward Elgar 2021); Matteo Ferrari, 'Agricoltura di precisione: proprietà o accesso?' in Eloisa Cristiani, Alessandra Di Lauro and Eleonora Sirsi (eds), *Agricoltura e Costituzione. Una Costituzione per l'Agricoltura, in onore di Carlo Goldoni* (Pisa University Press 2018).

27 Regulated by Regulation (EU) 2016/679 of the European Parliament and of the Council of 27 April 2016 on the protection of natural persons with regard to the processing of personal data and on the free movement of such data, and repealing Directive 95/46/EC [2016] OJ L119/1 (General Data Protection Regulation).

28 Regulated by Regulation (EU) 2018/1807 of the European Parliament and of the Council of 14 November 2018 on a framework for the free flow of non-personal data in the European Union [2018] OJ L303/1.

29 ISTAT, *Le imprese agricole in Italia nel Registro Asia* (2020) (15 December 2022) <https://www.istat.it/tavole-di-dati/le-imprese-agricole-in-italia-nel-registro-asia-anno-2020

between legal and natural persons blurs. Regulation (EU) 2018/1807 clarifies that non-personal data includes anonymised datasets or precision farming data used to optimise pesticide or water use. However, if such data becomes re-identifiable through technological means, the GDPR applies. This legal uncertainty reveals a regulatory gap when agro-data affects individual behaviour but is not clearly personal data under current definitions.

Understandably, the classification of any kind of data as personal has significant implications on its governance, collection, and circulation. To balance personal data protection with the need to ensure the free flow of data within the EU, the GDPR establishes stringent legal mechanisms. Of note among these is the lawfulness of data processing based on the data subject's consent or the necessity for the performance of a contract to which the data subject is a party. However, these forms of protection are lacking for non-personal data, which is defined as a residual category and into which most mechanically-generated agricultural data would fall.[30]

Regulation (EU) 2018/1807 addresses three key data privacy issues with the main objective of promoting the free flow of non-personal data within the EU: the prohibition of mandatory data requirements (except in cases of public security and in compliance with the principle of proportionality); access to non-personal data by authorities (only in the exercise of official functions); and the development of Codes of Conduct, which are private-sector tools to regulate the governance of non-personal data between the parties involved.[31]

Currently, there is no specific legal framework establishing the jurisdictional nature or ownership of data generated by IoT technologies in agriculture.[32]

/#:~:text=Nel%202020%2C%20sono%20oltre%20401mila,è%20costituito%20da%20imprese%20individuali> accessed 27 February 2025.

30 The reference is to Recital 9 Regulation (EU) 2018/1807, which expressly provides: 'Specific examples of non-personal data include aggregate and anonymised datasets used for big data analytics, data on precision farming that can help to monitor and optimise the use of pesticides and water, or data on maintenance needs for industrial machines. If technological developments make it possible to turn anonymised data into personal data, such data are to be treated as personal data, and Regulation (EU) 2016/679 is to apply accordingly'. It is therefore evident that the interpretation of the nature of the data remains open and must be determined on a case-by-case basis.

31 See Ferrari (n 22).

32 On the potential legal frameworks applicable to agro-data, it is worth noting that in certain jurisdictions, a broad interpretation of the legal definition of 'agricultural activity' may apply to the subject matter of this study. See, in particular, the interpretation of Article 2135 of the Italian Civil Code—as amended in 2001—as discussed in Ferdinando Albisinni, 'Pratiche commerciali sleali e beni immateriali nella filiera agroalimentare: novità e possibili letture', SSM Scuola Superiore Magistratura, (Giuffrè 2025), *in press*.

This regulatory gap creates uncertainties for both sector operators, the farmers whose activities generate the data, and ATPs who provide the devices and platforms for data management.[33] This unregulated 'market' for agricultural data results in a free business-to-business (B2B) market between farms and ATPs, governed only by bilateral contracts between the parties. These are often characterised by a significant imbalance in bargaining power, to the detriment of the farms. The risk is that the farm loses control of its own data and becomes dependent on technology service providers to access the information it needs to run its business, creating a digital lock-in.[34]

The debate has thus shifted from the legal nature of agro-data to the consideration of the potential rights that may be associated with these innovative elements.[35]

In this context, the Data Act[36] has precipitated a paradigm shift in the manner of analysis, with the new approach being predicated on the concept of free access to data as opposed to the granting of exclusive rights over them. This represents a departure from the 'property' paradigm, with the right of access to data being viewed as more in need of protection than the ownership of data.[37] The new measures complement the Data Governance Act,[38] the first outcome of the European Data Strategy,[39] which establishes processes and structures for voluntary data sharing, while the Data Act clarifies who can create value from data and under what conditions. Together, these two acts facilitate reliable and secure access to data, promoting its use in key economic sectors and areas of public interest and establishing a unified data market in the EU.

The incorporation of agro-data within this regulatory framework[40] gives rise to a model of protection predicated on consent, which seeks to legitimise

33 See Caso (n 23).

34 See Guarda (n 21).

35 See Can Atik, 'Towards Comprehensives European Agricultural Data Governance: moving beyond the "Data Ownership" Debate' (2022) 53 International Review of Intellectual Property and Competition Law 701.

36 Regulation (EU) 2023/2854 of the European Parliament and of the Council of 13 December 2023 on harmonised rules on fair access to and use of data and amending Regulation (EU) 2017/2394 and Directive (EU) 2020/1828 [2023] OJ L2854/1 (Data Act).

37 See Versaci (n 26).

38 Regulation (EU) 2022/868 of the European Parliament and of the Council of 30 May 2022 on European data governance and amending Regulation (EU) 2018/1724 OJ L152/1 (Data Governance Act).

39 Commission, *A European Strategy for Data* COM (2020) 66 final (European Data Strategy).

40 Precision agriculture is precisely highlighted as an example in the explanatory page of the new European Data Law, see <https://digital-strategy.ec.europa.eu/it/policies/data-act> accessed 27 February 2025.

the factual utilisation of data. This is facilitated by the obligations imposed upon the data holder (defined as the individual who wields factual control over the data, such as the ATPs) to grant access to other parties, including data recipients, to the data over which they have control.

It is important to note that the relationship between subjects is governed by contracts between the data holder and data recipient (as defined in Art 2 of the Data Act). This raises the potential for abuse of power, due to the greater contractual weight often held by data holders. This phenomenon is particularly evident in the agricultural sector, where small and medium-sized agricultural enterprises (data recipients) frequently interact with large multinational corporations that manufacture the requisite equipment for the digital transition (data holders).

Examples of specific regulatory responses to address this potential to date include soft law instruments, specifically self-regulation, that are dedicated to the agricultural sector and do not distinguish between personal and non-personal data—ie in the European context, the EU Code of Conduct on Agricultural Data Sharing by Contractual Agreement (2020)[41] and at the international level, the U.S. Privacy and Security Principles for Farm Data (2016).[42] Both instruments are based on the centrality of contracts in regulating the circulation of agricultural data and attribute data ownership[43] to the farmer who has the right to make use of it as they see fit through contractual arrangements. Beyond the element of consent regarding data collection and storage, these instruments emphasise the right to data portability, ensuring system openness and allowing farmers to switch service providers freely, avoiding the risk of digital lock-in. The principles underpinning the regulation of the two codes draw considerable inspiration from the provisions for the protection of personal data outlined in the GDPR. This approach directly correlates the rights pertaining to original data and agricultural operators. The use of such Codes of Conduct, while addressing the need for a more specific regulation of agro-data, nonetheless encounters two fundamental issues. The first, of a substantive nature, relates to the absence of a clearly defined entity that can serve as an anchor for these rights. The second, of a formal nature, concerns the legal

41 COPA-COGECA and others, *EU Code of conduct on agricultural data sharing by contractual agreement* (2018) <https://cema-agri.org/images/publications/brochures/EU_Code_of_conduct_on_agricultural_data_sharing_by_contractual_agreement_update_2019.pdf> accessed 27 February 2025.

42 Fb. Org., *Privacy and Security Principles for Farm Data* (2014) <https://www.agdatatransparent.com/principles> accessed 27 February 2025.

43 There are notable discrepancies in the nuances of property rights between the systems of the US and the EU, see Versaci (n 26).

design of such instruments: their soft law nature cannot counterbalance market dynamics and power asymmetries in contractual negotiations, ultimately leading to their non-application and reducing them to mere programmatic declarations.[44]

3.2 *New Actors in Agriculture, Technological Barriers, and the (Non) Role of the European Common Agricultural Policy*

The digital transformation of agriculture demands an evolution of not only the tools used but also the operators in the sector. Digitisation processes are changing the players and mechanisms of the agrifood supply chain, beginning with the emergence of ATPs.[45]

This redefinition of relationships in the agricultural sector—which encompasses a plurality of actors from farmers to ATPs—and the perceived absence of protection against multinational giants consequently contribute to agricultural operators lacking the confidence to approach suppliers of technological machinery.[46] The sense of insecurity felt by agricultural operators can, in the most extreme cases, result in their perceiving innovation as a malevolent force. This can create a divide within the sector and hinder the pursuit of homogeneous transition, which is essential for the uniform distribution of technology. This, in effect, would empower agricultural enterprises to interact collectively with service providers, thereby rebalancing their bargaining power against these newly dominant actors.

---

44 See Atik and Martens (n 7), 389; Mark Ryan and others, 'The future of agricultural data-sharing policy in Europe: stakeholder insights on the EU Code of Conduct' (2024) 11 Humanities & Social Sciences Communications 1197.

45 On the role and mechanisms of this monopolistic phenomenon, see Atik and Martens (n 7), 374.

46 See Versaci (n 26), 631, from which footnote 55 is taken to point out Wiseman's contribution in doctrine: Leanne Wiseman and others, 'Farmers and their data: an examination of farmers' reluctance to share their data through the lens of the laws impacting smart farming' (2019) 90–91 NJAS—Wageningen Journal of Life Sciences 100301; Leanne Wiseman and Jay Sanderson, 'Empowering farmers by resolving the trust and legal issues emerging from precision farming' in John V Stafford (ed), *Precision agriculture '19* (Wageningen Academic Publishers 2019). In addition, the US case law reported in the discussion is of interest. This case law concerns the use of data by an agricultural statistics company with the aim of reducing the fees of farmers to whom the data related. The conduct of the company was later challenged under competition law and unfair trade practices. See *Haff Poultry Inc. et al. V. Tyson Foods, Inc. et al.*, Case No 6:17-CV-00033 (E.D. Okla. 2017). It would be a worthwhile endeavour to assess the scope of a similar case in the EU, where Directive (EU) 2019/633 of the European Parliament and of the Council of 17 April 2019 concerning unfair business-to-business commercial practices in the agricultural and food supply chain does not provide for protection against services providers [2019] OJ L111/59.

Another significant obstacle to achieving a homogeneous digital transition is of a factual nature, namely the digital divide that afflicts many rural areas in Europe. The term 'digital divide' refers to the disparity in access to digital technologies, including high-speed internet and connected devices, which are essential for implementing IoT technologies in agricultural operations.[47] While urban areas are reaping the benefits of advanced infrastructure, many regions, particularly those situated in more remote areas, lack access to broadband internet or other basic digital infrastructure. This has led to uneven development across Europe, wherein those engaged in agricultural activities in more developed areas or those with more favourable access to technology may enjoy enhanced benefits from Agriculture 4.0, while those in less connected locations are at a disadvantage.[48]

The digital divide can be categorised into three phases: infrastructural, relating to actual access to the internet; applicative, where access to services is lacking even in the presence of infrastructure; and formative, reflecting the inability of potential users to access services. Clearly, this is a phenomenon that is not only technological, but also social. The digital skills of farmers and agricultural workers represent an additional challenge: without adequate training and support, even agricultural entrepreneurs who have access to digital infrastructure may struggle to adopt and effectively use new technologies.

To address these issues, the EU has allocated significant investment towards improving access to digital technologies in rural areas through funds such as NextGenerationEU and the Broadband Plan. The objective of these programmes is to facilitate the integration of rural communities into the digital age by providing financial support for the construction of internet infrastructure and the promotion of digital literacy. However, the implementation of these policies is still slow and requires more effective coordination between national governments and local authorities.[49]

Meanwhile, the CAP, which has historically focused on supporting agricultural production and rural development, has not yet fully adapted to the needs of the digital revolution in agriculture.[50] CAP regulations need to be revised to ensure support not only for sustainable production, but also for technological innovation. For instance, Regulation (EU) 2021/2115, which redefines the

---

47 See D'Avanzo (n 5).

48 See Canfora (n 11).

49 See Arisi (n 20).

50 See Canfora (n 11); Borghi (n 16); Silvia Rolandi, 'Il ruolo attribuito alla digitalizzazione nella strategia Farm to Fork dell'Unione Europea, tra riferimenti espliciti e nascosti. Quali interventi legislativi in quattro anni?' [2023] Rivista di Diritto Agrario 636.

concept of 'modernisation of agricultural structures' within the CAP, stipulates that the specific objectives of national strategic plans must integrate the CAP's cross-cutting goal of modernising agriculture and rural areas. This modernisation is to be achieved through the promotion, sharing, and use of knowledge, innovation, and digitalisation in the agricultural and rural sectors, facilitating access to research, innovation, and training for farmers.

Under Article 114 of Regulation (EU) 2021/2115, Member States must provide a dedicated section on CAP modernisation, which includes two main aspects. The first (a) is the definition of the general framework for the actions that the state intends to implement to pursue the cross-cutting objective of modernisation, with priority given to digital innovation. This point connects to the organisational structure of AKIS (Agricultural Knowledge and Innovation Systems) and the provision of advisory services to agricultural enterprises, facilitating the transfer of knowledge suited to the use of new technologies in the agricultural sector.

The second aspect (b) concerns the strategy for the development and use of digital technologies in agriculture and rural areas. This element not only applies to agricultural production but also to improving services for rural populations, with the aim of supporting the development of innovative infrastructure and services. Agritech companies, for example, could play an expanding role, contributing to the spread of technological innovation in rural areas.[51]

In this context, Regulation (EU) 2021/2115 requires Member States to adopt appropriate tools to enable agricultural enterprises to acquire the necessary skills to manage and integrate technological innovation into their operations. This involves an adaptation on the part of the economic actors involved, who must collaborate in an ecosystem where technology and innovation are central not only to the development of individual farms but also to the agricultural sector and rural communities more broadly.[52]

To address these gaps, it is therefore essential to develop a unified regulatory framework at the European and national levels that provides clear and consistent guidelines for the adoption of digital technologies by the agriculture industry. This is also of pivotal significance when taking into consideration the

---

51 As stated in Canfora (n 11).

52 The problematic practical side, characterised by complexity of application and overbureaucratisation of CAP practices, aimed at achieving environmental sustainability without protecting farms, is well highlighted in Camillo Zaccarini Bonelli, 'L'UE scommetta sulla PAC come arma geopolitica' <https://terraevita.edagricole.it/featured/lue-scommetta-sulla-pac-come-arma-geopolitica/> (Terraevita, 19 April 2024) accessed 25 June 2025.

considerable decline in the number of farms and farmers within the EU.[53] Due to the limited and indirect effect of the CAP on agricultural structures, there is a necessity to reconsider the distribution of funds, so that they are no longer exclusively based on farm performance,[54] to facilitate widespread support with a view to ensuring that all farms are able to participate in the digital transition.

4 Conclusion: towards an Inclusive and Innovative Regulatory Framework for Agriculture 4.0

Agriculture 4.0 offers an unprecedented opportunity to revolutionise the agricultural sector, merging technological innovation with environmental sustainability to create a more efficient and productive farming model. The introduction of advanced tools such as IoT technologies, blockchain, big data, and precision agriculture represents a fundamental shift in how farming is conducted, enabling more precise management of resources and greater transparency across the entire agrifood supply chain. However, the realisation of the full potential of this digital transformation is contingent upon overcoming significant regulatory, infrastructural, and social challenges that currently hinder its widespread implementation.

The management of such issues is crucial to mitigating the adverse effects of 'creative destruction',[55] which is intrinsic to the very concept of innovation, and to accompany the sector and its operators towards the 'Twin Transitions'[56] in which the farmer remains the primary agent of change.

One of the most pressing challenges is the fragmentation of regulations across different levels of governance. Agriculture 4.0 technologies operate in a complex legal landscape, where different regulatory frameworks for data protection, intellectual property, and agricultural policies intersect.

---

53 European Parliament, *The Future of the European Farming Model: Socio-economic and territorial implications of the decline in the number of farm and farmers in the EU*, Study requested by the AGRI Committee, policy department for structural and cohesion policies, PE 699.620 (April 2022).

54 See Paoloni (n 10), 580–581.

55 According to Schumpeter, the 'gale of creative destruction' is defined as 'the process of industrial mutation that incessantly revolutionises the economic structure from within, relentlessly destroying the old one and always creating a new one' in Joseph A Schumpeter, *Capitalism, Socialism and Democracy* (first published 1942, Routledge 1994), 82–83.

56 The term 'Twin Transitions' is used to denote the simultaneous digital and ecological transitions, see Ursula Von Der Leyen, President of the European Commission, 'Move Fast, Build to Last: Europe's New Generation' (Brussels 7 May 2020).

This can create confusion and inconsistency, particularly for small and medium-sized farms that lack the resources to navigate these complexities. A unified European regulatory framework is essential to harmonise rules and provide clear guidelines for the adoption and use of digital technologies in agriculture. This framework should address key issues such as data ownership, access to technology, and the rights and responsibilities of different actors in the agrifood supply chain.

Importantly, the regulation must be flexible and adaptive, capable of evolving alongside technological advancements to avoid becoming obsolete in the face of rapid innovation.

A central goal of this regulatory framework should be to prevent the digital lock-in of farmers, ensuring that they maintain control over their operations and data, rather than becoming overly dependent on technology providers. This can be achieved by promoting open systems,[57] supporting data portability, and ensuring that farmers can freely choose and switch between service providers without losing access to essential data.[58]

Finally, it is important to recognise that Agriculture 4.0 is not merely a technological shift, but a transformational change that will reshape the relationships, structures, and dynamics within the agricultural sector. The role of the agricultural entrepreneur is evolving, as is the nature of the agricultural supply chain, which is becoming increasingly interconnected and data driven.

It is the opinion of the author that two principles emerge as fundamental in shaping the regulatory framework within which the future of agriculture will be able to grow: agricultural exceptionalism and innovation. These principles have, in recent years, been almost obscured by the relentless pursuit of sustainability, which, in its environmental sense, has overridden the economic and social needs of the entire sector.

The principle of agricultural exceptionalism must be considered by the legislator to ensure that the agricultural sector is treated in an appropriately distinctive manner. The sector has invariably been subject to exceptional or ad-hoc regulations that are designed to ensure its effective functioning, for example to address its vulnerability to extreme weather. This arises from its unique organisational structures and the need for specific regulatory frameworks that can

57 AgriDataSpace, for example, is an EU-funded project that aims to create 'a European Data Space for Agriculture that facilitates the sharing, processing, and analysis of data in a secure, trustworthy, transparent, and responsible way, creating new opportunities for monitoring and optimising the use of natural resources and stimulating data-driven innovation' <https://agridataspace-csa.eu> accessed 27 February 2025.

58 See Lattanzi (n 8).

effectively balance its legal relationships. In practice, therefore, the general rule must be followed by a special rule, tailored to the agricultural sector and its needs.[59]

Secondly, and more broadly, the 'newborn' principle of innovation is regarded as an inspiring principle in legislative policies, though it is not legally binding.[60] This principle, in its inspirational capacity, necessitates the pursuit of specific policies by virtue of their innovative purpose, thereby effecting a Copernican revolution in the understanding of innovation. Innovation, no longer regarded as a mere means, but as an end, has the potential to serve as the driving force that would position the agricultural entrepreneur at the centre, thus facilitating a genuine evolution of the subjects within the agricultural domain, and, by extension, the sector itself.[61]

Bibliography

Albisinni F, 'Agricoltura e digitalizzazione: l'impresa agricola nel tempo presente' (2023) 1 Quaderni Rivista di Diritto Alimentare 92.

Albisinni F, 'Pratiche commerciali sleali e beni immateriali nella filiera agroalimentare: novità e possibili letture', SSM Scuola Superiore Magistratura, (Giuffrè 2025), *in press*.

Arisi M, 'Coltivare la fiducia? Una prospettiva giuridica su dati, blockchain e tracciabilità lungo la filiera agroalimentare' (2023) 1 Quaderni della Rivista di Diritto Alimentare 56.

Atik C, 'Understanding the role of agricultural data on market power in the emerging Digital Agriculture sector: a critical analysis of the Bayer/Monsanto decision' in Bosco D and Gal MS (eds), *Challenges to Assumptions in Competition Law* (Edward Elgar 2021).

Atik C, 'Towards Comprehensive European Agricultural data Governance: moving beyond the "Data Ownership" Debate' (2022) International Review of Intellectual Property and Competition Law 701.

59 The notion of 'agricultural exceptionalism' is further elaborated by Versaci (n 26), who in general points to Antonio Jannarelli, *Profili giuridici del sistema agro-alimentare e agro-industriale. Soggetti e concorrenza* (2nd edn, Cacucci 2018).

60 This subject is likewise explored extensively in the current volume, see the chapter by Nicola Bergamaschi.

61 Evidence suggests that this dynamic is emerging at the European level, see Commission, *A Vision for Agriculture and Food Shaping together an attractive farming and agrifood sector for future generations*, COM 2025 (75) final.

Atik C and Martens B, 'Competition Problems and Governance of Non-personal Agricultural Machine Data: Comparing Voluntary Initiatives in the US and EU' (2021) 12 Jipitec 370.

Battelli E, 'Innovazione tecnologica e gestione della filiera agroalimentare' [2024] Diritto Agroalimentare 455.

Borghi P, 'L'agricoltura 4.0: il futuro del settore agroalimentare e il filo rosso che lo lega alle origini della PAC' (2023) 1 Quaderni della Rivista di Diritto Alimentare 5.

Canfora I, 'Politica Agricola Comune e digitalizzazione del comparto agroalimentare' (2023) 1 Quaderni della Rivista di Diritto Alimentare 11.

Caso R, 'Capitalismo dei monopoli intellettuali, pseudo-proprietà intellettuale e dati nel settore dell'agricoltura di precisione e dello smart farming' (2023) 1 Quaderni della Rivista di Diritto Alimentare 36.

D'Avanzo W, 'Smart farming. La quarta rivoluzione industriale e la digitalizzazione nel settore agricolo' [2022] Diritto Agroalimentare 279.

Faleri C, 'Transizione ecologica e sostenibilità sociale per un'Agricoltura 4.0' (2022) 2 Lavoro e diritto 449.

Ferrari M, 'Agricoltura di precisione: proprietà o accesso?' in Cristiani E, Di Lauro A, Sirsi E (eds), *Agricoltura e Costituzione. Una Costituzione per l'Agricoltura, in onore di Carlo Goldoni* (Pisa University Press 2018).

Ferrari M, 'Digitalizzazione e strutture agricole. Rivista di diritto alimentare' (2023) 1 Quaderni della Rivista di Diritto Alimentare 46.

Ferrari M, *Fattori di produzione, innovazione e distribuzione di valore nella filiera agroalimentare* (Ledizioni 2023).

Ferrari M, 'Digitalizzazione e innovazione nell'attività delle imprese agricole' in Mario Mauro (eds), *Start-up e PMI innovative in agricoltura. Le imprese agricole fra innovazione e sostenibilità* (Wolters Kluwer 2024).

Guarda P, 'Riflessioni in merito alla natura giuridica dei dati nell'agricoltura di precisione' (2023) 1 Quaderni della Rivista di Diritto Alimentare 20.

Jannarelli A, 'Il divenire del diritto agrario italiano ed europeo tra sviluppi tecnologici e sostenibilità' [2013] Rivista di Diritto Agrario 11.

Jannarelli A, *Cibo e Diritti. Per un'agricoltura sostenibile* (Giappichelli 2015).

Jannarelli A, 'Il diritto agrario del nuovo millennio tra food safety, food security e sustainable agriculture' [2018] Rivista di Diritto Agrario 511.

Jannarelli A, *Profili giuridici del sistema agro-alimentare e agro-industriale. Soggetti e concorrenza* (2nd edn, Cacucci 2018).

Jannarelli A, 'Agricoltura sostenibile e nuova PAC: problemi e prospettive' [2020] Rivista di Diritto Agrario 23.

La Porta B, *Contributo per una visione contemporanea dell'azienda agricola. Tra sostenibilità e sfide del mondo digitale* (Giappichelli 2023).

Lattanzi P, 'L'agricoltura di precisione: fisionomia, quadro strategico di riferimento e implicazioni giuridiche' (2024) 2 Rivista di Diritto Alimentare 19.

Neri G, *L'impresa nell'Era Digitale, Tecnologie informatiche e rivoluzione digitale al servizio dell'impresa* (3rd edn, Guaraldi 2015).

Paoloni L, 'Sostenibilità e innovazione in agricoltura. Dilemma o opportunità?' [2024] Diritto Agroalimentare 569.

Rolandi S, 'Il ruolo attribuito alla digitalizzazione nella strategia Farm to Fork dell'Unione Europea, tra riferimenti espliciti e nascosti. Quali interventi legislativi in quattro anni?' [2023] Rivista di Diritto Agroalimentare 636.

Ryan M, Atik C, Rijswijk K, Bogaardt MJ, Maes E, and Deroo E, 'The future of agricultural data-sharing policy in Europe: stakeholder insights on the EU Code of Conduct' (2024) 11 Humanities & Social Sciences Communications 1197.

Schumpeter JA, *Capitalism, Socialism and Democracy* (first published 1942, Routledge 1994) 82–83.

Versaci G, 'La regolazione dei dati per l'agricoltura di precisione tra questioni generali ed esigenze settoriali' (2024) 3 Diritto Agroalimentare 619.

Wiseman L and Sanderson J, 'Empowering farmers by resolving the trust and legal issues emerging from precision farming' in Stafford JV (ed), *Precision agriculture '19* (Wageningen Academic Publishers 2019).

Wiseman L, Zhang A, and Jakku E, 'Farmers and their data: an examination of farmers' reluctance to share their data through the lens of the laws impacting smart farming' (2019) 90–91 NJAS 100301.

CHAPTER 7

Vertical Farming: Regulatory Perspectives and Sustainability Implications

Simone Pitto

Summary

1 Introduction

In the current so-called Anthropocene era, the connection between food and sustainability has become increasingly vital. The food industry plays a significant role in climate change, accounting for approximately a quarter of global greenhouse gas emissions as well as extensive land and water use.[1] This reality is intensified by global population growth, estimated to reach 9.5 billion by 2050, along with urban expansion and increasing urbanisation.[2]

Further compounding this are adverse impacts from food production such as land consumption, which also contribute to climate change.[3]

1 Ritchie Hannah, Rosado Pablo, and Roser Max 'Environmental Impacts of Food Production' (*OurWorldinData.org* 2022) <https://ourworldindata.org/environmental-impacts-of-food> accessed 18 June 2025.

2 Bernd Van Der Meulen and Bart Wernaart, 'Comparative Food Law' in Michael T Roberts (ed), *Research Handbook on International Food Law* (Edward Elgar 2023) 13; Francesco Bruno, *Il Diritto Alimentare. Sviluppo Sostenibile e Tutela della Salute* (Wolters Kluwer 2022) 204. It should be noted that although in early 2024 the International Commission on Stratigraphy ruled out the Anthropocene as a true geological era, this did not diminish the conceptual relevance of this concept to identify the present historical moment and the impact of human activities on the environment, climate, and biodiversity. See International Union of Geological Sciences, 'The Anthropocene'. (IUGS 2024) <www.iugs.org/_files/ugd/f1fc07_40d1a7ed58de458c9f8f24de5e739663.pdf?index=true> accessed 18 June 2025.

3 See Marta Antonelli, Simona Castaldi and Riccardo Valentini, 'Cambiamento Climatico e Cibo' (2020) 1 Equilibri 36.

© 2026 THE AUTHOR(S) | HTTPS://DOI.ORG/10.1163/9789004740907-009

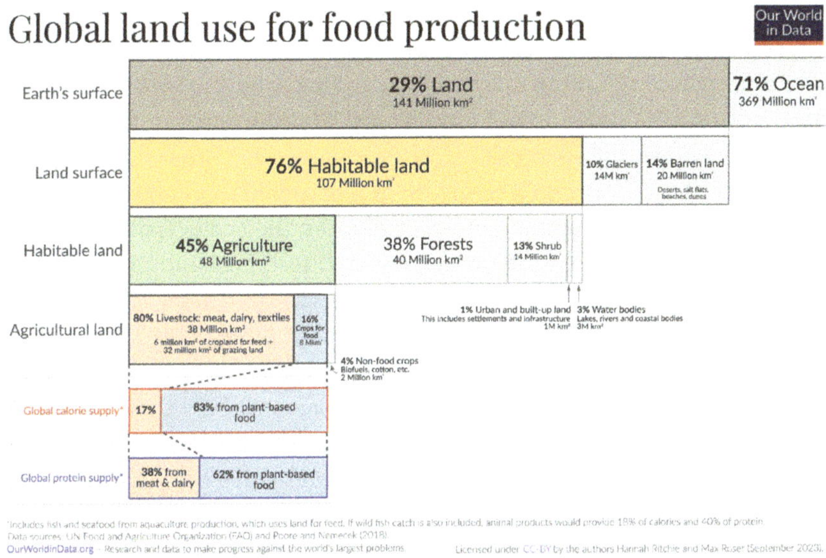

FIGURE 7.1 Global Land Use for Food Production
Note: Hannah Ritchie and Max Roser 'Half of the world's habitable land is used for agriculture', (*OurWorldinData.org* 2024) <https://ourworldindata.org/global-land-for-agriculture> accessed 18 June 2025. Licensed under CC-BY by the authors Hannah Ritchie and Max Roser (September 2023)

Indeed, as shown by Figure 7.1 below, agriculture and livestock farming occupy nearly half of Earth's available land, accelerating climate change. This happens in two main ways: by altering ecosystems, such as through deforestation, and by reducing the soil's ability to absorb greenhouse gases. Agriculture and livestock farming also consume around 70% of the world's available fresh water.[4]

Global population growth is expected to lead to increasing demand for food and a consequent need to increase food production. Currently, this growth can only be met by using more land for farming and livestock, which runs the risk of further exacerbating this cycle.[5] Population growth, however, is not an entirely

4 Ritchie, Rosado and Roser, 'Environmental Impacts of Food Production' (n 1).

5 Other relevant data in this context concern the reduction of food waste, which makes it possible to increase the amount of available food without augmenting production and, thus, addresses related climatic and environmental effects. On this subject see Lucia Scaffardi, 'La Sicurezza Alimentare ovvero come Il Diritto a Togliere la Fame Evolve in un Mondo che Cambia', (2023) 2 DPCE Online 59; Tomaso Ferrando, Valentina De Gregorio, Sara Lorenzini and Lidia Mahillon 'The Right to Food in Italy between Present and Future' (2018) 11 and Chiara Cerbone, 'Pratiche Virtuose Contro lo Spreco Alimentare in Italia: Alcune Note a Partire dalle Recenti Proposte di Legge sulla c.d. Doggy Bag' (2024) 24 federalismi.it 78.

homogeneous phenomenon as it goes hand in hand with increasing urbanisation, affecting metropolitan and industrial areas to a greater extent. Proceeding at the current rate, it is estimated that by 2050 almost 90% of the world's population will reside in urban areas.[6] This raises further concerns, as food demand and supply chains will increasingly focus on larger and more densely populated cities, where ensuring food security will become more complex.

In response to the aforementioned challenges, the ecological transition in the food sector has led to the development of technical and organisational solutions. These include, inter alia, ensuring sufficient food for a growing population while reducing environmental impact, minimising food systems' contribution to climate change, and protecting biodiversity. It is no surprise, therefore, that many recent technological innovations share these goals. One can cite the rise of Novel Foods[7] designed to reduce the environmental and climate footprint of food production, such as alternative protein sources and cultured meat.[8]

It is within this sphere, of shifts affecting the food sector and food law,[9] that we can also place so-called vertical farming, or vertical agriculture (hereafter VF),[10] an example of a 'vehicle for institutional innovation'.[11] VF encompasses a 'kaleidoscope' of innovative (and rather heterogeneous) cultivation methods, including growing a variety of crops, while sharing the common characteristic of being cultivated in multiple stacked layers within controlled environments, often integrating other techniques such as hydroponics, aeroponics, or aquaponics to reduce the use of water and other resources.[12] Additionally, VF can be applied in different contexts such as greenhouses, warehouses,

6 See Galan S 'Urbanization rate of the population worldwide, by regional development 1950–2050. Percentage of Population Living in Urban Areas Worldwide from 1950 to 2050' (2018) Statista, <https://www.statista.com/statistics/671366/change-in-urbanization-of-countries-worldwide-by-regional-development/> accessed 14 September 2024. Available via campus license (University of Genova, 2024).

7 For more, see Lucia Scaffardi and Giulia Formici (eds.), *Novel Foods and Edible Insects in the European Union: An Interdisciplinary Analysis* (Springer 2022).

8 See Giulia Formici and others, 'Cultured Meat in the European Union: Legislative Context and Food Safety Issues' (2024) 8 Current Research in Food Science 1.

9 For a general reconstruction, see Margherita Ramajoli, 'Quale Futuro per la Regolazione Alimentare' (2021) 2 Milan Law Review.

10 It should be noted, for the sake of completeness, that certain types of vertical cultivation were also used in the past. References to similar practices are found with regard to the gardens of Babylon and forms of cultivation by Aztec populations.

11 Ferdinando Albisinni, 'La Sicurezza Alimentare Veicolo di Innovazione Istituzionale' (2009) 4 Rivista di Diritto Alimentare 15.

12 As it will be discussed below, in order to assess the actual suitability of VF, the energy source used by vertical farms must be taken into account.

buildings, and even skyscrapers or containers, presenting possible opportunities for advancing food sustainability. In fact, VF is also an emerging market with substantial growth potential, marked by increasing competition among major players in Europe, the US, and Asia.[13]

Like all innovations in the agrifood sector, VF, particularly in its early stages of adoption, requires a well-defined regulatory framework and presents significant legal, regulatory, and social challenges. Establishing clear regulations for VF is crucial to develop its full potential to contribute to food sustainability and address the needs of stakeholders and businesses by filling numerous gaps and absences found in existing regulatory frameworks.

However, the ability of VF to effectively address these challenges of food law remains debated. Indeed, the sector is currently characterised by several economic and productive challenges, primarily associated with the high energy costs and substantial initial investments necessary to establish a vertical farm.

Against this backdrop, this chapter examines the main legal challenges pertaining to VF, following a brief analysis of its advantages and limitations. This chapter focuses on the regulatory approach adopted by the EU, with brief references to the distinct agricultural policy choices implemented in other geographical areas that are relevant to the VF sector. Finally, the chapter provides a more in-depth analysis of the Italian legal framework, highlighting open legal questions and recent developments within Italian regional legislation.

2 Possibilities and Challenges

For the purposes of this chapter, the term 'vertical farming' (VF) is used to describe a diverse set of cultivation techniques organised at multiple levels in a controlled environment, applicable in multiple contexts, such as greenhouses, warehouses, roofs, public and private buildings, and even skyscrapers.[14] VF uses a variety of techniques (hydroponics, aeroponics, and aquaponics being

13 Mahsa Shahbandeh 'Projected Vertical Farming Market Worldwide from 2022 to 2032' (*Statista 2023*) <https://www.statista.com/statistics/487666/projection-vertical-farming-market-worldwide/> accessed 18 June 2025.

14 The term 'vertical farming' originates from the research of Professor Dickson Despommier of Columbia University in the 2000s. Despommier argued for the need to bring farming practices back into urban spaces by developing them vertically in controlled modules in order to reduce the environmental impact of intensive farming practices. See Dickson Despommier, *The Vertical Farm: Feeding the World in the 21st Century* (Thomas Dunne Books 2010); Dickson Despommier, 'The Rise of Vertical Farms' (2009) 301(5) Scientific American 80–87.

the most common) to cultivate plants without the use of soil, saving resources such as water, fertilisers and, above all, using less space than traditional agriculture.

The relevance of this phenomenon can be appreciated by considering its environmental potential and process efficiency: cultivation without soil can reduce water use by 90% when compared with traditional cultivation.[15] In addition, the use of a controlled environment with artificial light, humidity, and constant microclimatic conditions makes it possible to grow crops in any season, at any latitude, and in any climatic condition, ensuring greater product uniformity.[16]

VF systems are typically designed to minimise waste by supplying plants exclusively with the specific nutrients essential for their growth, while significantly reducing, if not eliminating, the use of pesticides.[17] The possibility to cultivate crops within vertical modules, some of which may be removable, provides flexibility in selecting locations for vertical farms. Even a standard shipping container can be redesigned to accommodate a vertical farm (a practice known as 'container farming'), thus enabling the reuse of decommissioned containers for the cultivation of crops such as basil or lettuce.[18]

From the point of view of climate risk mitigation, VF seems to represent (at least prima facie) a valuable alternative to traditional agriculture, given the latter's vulnerability to extreme climatic events, which are becoming increasingly more frequent.

Furthermore, VF's potential extends to the world of urban agriculture,[19] an emerging frontier of food systems according to the FAO.[20] Decommissioned

---

15 See Laura Carotti and others 'Improving water use efficiency in vertical farming: Effects of growing systems, far-red radiation and planting density on lettuce cultivation' (2023) 285 Agricultural Water Management. Additional benefits of VF include the reduction of demand for new soil, the use of which has potentially harmful consequences such as increased desertification, erosion, and reduced biodiversity.

16 This aspect also supports waste reduction as many agricultural products are discarded from the market or disposed of due mainly to aesthetic defects.

17 Some of the largest companies in VF worldwide can be found in Singapore, eg Sky Greens, the US, eg Aerofarms and Farm.one, and in the EU, eg Infarm. In Italy, too, small and medium-sized companies are present in the sector, such as Planet Farms and Zerofarm (Zero s.r.l.).

18 Cf. Carrasco, Gilda, Fernando Fuentes-Peñailillo, Paula Manríquez, Pabla Rebolledo, Ricardo Vega, Karen Gutter, and Miguel Urrestarazu, 'Enhancing Leafy Greens' Production: Nutrient Film Technique Systems and Automation in Container-Based Vertical Farming' (2024) 14(9) Agronomy 1932. https://doi.org/10.3390/agronomy14091932.

19 See Élodie Valette and others, *Evaluating Sustainable Food System Innovations: A Global Toolkit for Cities* (Routledge 2023).

20 Cf. FAO, Rikolto, RUAF, *Urban and Peri-Urban Agriculture Sourcebook from Production to Food Systems* (2022).

industrial sites or abandoned and unused buildings are well-suited to housing vertical urban farms, offering a potential means of productive reutilisation. Moreover, they can contribute to enhancing urban food availability, shortening supply chains, and consequently reducing the environmental and climatic impact associated with food transportation.[21] The possibilities for developing VF even extend to 'domestic agriculture' which would enable families to grow food indoors, right in their own homes.[22]

Currently, however, VF also faces serious challenges to its development which help explain the aforementioned crises experienced by large VF companies across geographies. The main current challenge concerns cost. Not all crops are suitable for VF which will remain a limiting factor until the sector grows through broader adoption and scale-up.[23] Additionally, compared to traditional farming, VF demands significant initial investments for the materials necessary to establish the infrastructure, as well as ongoing fixed expenses for securing extensive space and hiring a highly specialised workforce.[24]

Another major challenge, and a significant source of cost compared to traditional agriculture, is related to energy dependency. Continuous energy consumption is required to maintain proper lighting and stable micro-climatic conditions in vertical farms. This raises two additional regulatory aspects worth considering.

First is the competition between traditional and VF. While traditional farms generally have lower labour specialisation and energy costs, vertical farms face higher costs in these areas and, at least for the moment, lower productivity.[25] In other words, traditional agriculture is currently more cost competitive than VF.[26]

The strategic setup, therefore, of a vertical farm, including crop selection and revenue generation, represents a critical point. This is also the reason why many vertical farms are focusing on high-value products such as medicinal herbs or saffron to offset costs with higher revenues.[27]

---

21 See Sander H. Van Delden and others, 'Current Status and Future Challenges in Implementing and Upscaling Vertical Farming Systems' (2021) 2 Nature food 944.

22 See Gary Nissembaum, 'Legal Aspects of Implementing Vertical Farming Solutions' (2021) <gdnlaw.com>, accessed 1 March 2025.

23 Sander, Van Delden and others (n 22) 946.

24 Sander, Van Delden and others (n 22) 946.

25 The energy crisis following Russia's invasion of Ukraine and the resulting increase in energy costs has undoubtedly contributed to the financial difficulties of some VF groups, especially in Europe.

26 Traditional agriculture also undoubtedly requires relevant initial investments in machinery, operations, fertilisers, plant protection products, and irrigation systems.

27 Andrew M. Beacham, Laura H. Vickers and James M. Monaghan, 'Vertical Farming: a Summary of Approaches to Growing Skywards' (2019) 94(3) Journal of Horticultural

Second, the energy consumption of vertical farms is crucial in evaluating their environmental and climate benefits and impact. To achieve a real reduction in greenhouse gas emissions, for instance, the source of energy used must be considered. If non-renewable energy sources are utilised, the higher energy demand of VF risks merely shifting pollution upstream in the chain, rather than reducing overall emissions, thus reducing the sustainability benefits of this technology.

For this reason, some vertical farms are complex and integrated structures combining agricultural production with other activities, including life-cycle development (eg aquaculture). Some facilities are connected to photovoltaic power plants, wind farms, or other non-fossil energy sources in order to include renewable energy in their production cycle and reduce external energy supply costs.[28]

3 The Legal Dimensions of Vertical Farming

In addition to the above-mentioned issues, one might question the role of law and legislators concerning VF. First of all, the need for clear regulatory frameworks in this sector has already been established.[29]

The areas of potential regulatory intervention are numerous, ranging from medium-and long-term strategic planning, support for scientific research, inclusion of VF in agricultural normative policies and integration with urban agriculture and smart city policies.[30]

However, several gaps remain in the current legislation, such as the absence of specific legal definitions and uncertainties in determining applicable regulations for vertical farms. While, generally, these aspects stem from the

Science and Biotechnology 277. VF also prevents environmental contamination which is essential in medicinal herb production. Several companies have begun sourcing from the premium crop market because of its product quality, such as the American brand Oishii, which produces strawberries for high-end cuisine.

28 This may also help reduce the final cost of products from vertical agriculture, making it more competitive with traditional agriculture. See Kurt Benke and Bruce Tomkins, 'Future food-production systems: Vertical farming and controlled-environment agriculture' (2017) 13 Sustainability: Science, Practice and Policy 13, 16.

29 See Thijs Van Gerrewey, Nico Boon, Danny Geelen,'Vertical Farming: The Only Way is Up?' (2021) 12(1) Agronomy 7; Sander, Van Delden and others (n 21) 953–955, arguing that 'To realise the full potential of vertical farming for addressing these food supply-chain challenges, policy blind spots and ambiguities must be addressed'.

30 See Filippo Orsini, 'Food Vertigo. Processi e Dispositive per la Resilienza Alimentare Metropolitana' (2022) 23 Techne 104–116.

difficulty in precisely framing a phenomenon linked to a variety of regulatory frameworks, in the case of VF, one key regulatory gap, inter alia, is interpretative doubt in identifying which set of rules apply to companies in the VF sector. Other uncertainties relate to corporate structure, compatibility with urban planning regulations, applicability of agricultural legislation, and the application of pertinent intellectual property provisions to VF materials, processes, and products. Additionally, a central regulatory issue is whether products from VF can be considered organic, which is closely linked to labelling.

Finally, one of the most pressing demands from stakeholders and operators concerns the clarification of which tax and fiscal regulations apply to vertical farms, as well as the possibility of accessing incentives and a taxation framework that thoroughly assesses all traits of the sector.[31] In the Italian legal context, the question of whether the rules on agricultural enterprises also apply to vertical farms is of particular concern, as will be discussed below.

4 Vertical Agriculture and EU Policies

Moving onto a more specific analysis of regulations relevant to VF, a first domain of interest is EU law. At the EU level, however, the interest of EU institutions in VF is mainly focused on supporting scientific research. Several European VF projects are funded this way, and some of the largest companies active in the sector in Europe (such as the German company Infarm) are established in connection with research projects and 'spin-offs' financed by EU programmes.[32]

Although investment in research in this field has increased significantly in recent years, it must be noted that VF is not yet fully integrated into the EU's main agricultural and climate policy, nor has it been addressed through dedicated support measures.[33]

The EU supports initiatives related to VF indirectly through specific initiatives financed by the European Regional Development Fund (ERDF) and the

31 On this point, see Maurizio Interdonato, 'Le Colture Fuori Suolo nel Reddito Agrario, tra l'Indispensabile Presenza del Fondo e la Difficile Trasposizione delle Conoscenze Tecniche di tali Colture su quelle Tradizionali ai Fini della Valutazione dei Limiti dell'Agrarietà', (2022) Rivista di Diritto Tributario.

32 See <https://eic.ec.europa.eu/success-stories/urban-farming_en> accessed 19 June 2025. See also the project PLANET FARMS LIFE, reference: LIFE19 ENV/IT/000142 <https://webgate.ec.europa.eu/life/publicWebsite/index.cfm?fuseaction=search.dspPage&n_proj_id=759> accessed 19 June 2025.

33 On this point, see Nera Kuljanic, *What if We Grew Plants Vertically?* (EPRS, 2022), arguing that VF 'is not covered by EU agricultural and climate policies'.

European Agricultural Fund for Rural Development (EAFRD).[34] However, VF is not expressly mentioned in the strategic plans of the Common Agricultural Policy nor within the European Green Deal, despite the latter acknowledging the need to reinforce urban agriculture.

In Communication COM (2020) 381 of May 2020, the European Commission introduced the 'Farm to Fork' (F2F) strategy for a fair, healthy, and environmentally sustainable food system, as part of the European Green Deal.[35] The F2F strategy also seeks to promote a new paradigm of food sustainability, viewing the environmental transition not only as an economic opportunity, but also as a catalyst for enhancing food quality standards. Yet, even the F2F strategy[36] lacks explicit references to VF, despite the interest shown about 'urban food systems'.[37]

It is precisely with regard to urban agriculture that the main spaces for VF at EU level, apart from the aforementioned support of scientific research, can currently be found.[38]

The transversal nature of VF and its tendency to intersect with different types of EU policies and competences (including at the crossroads between rural and urban agriculture) partly explain the absence of explicit references to VF within the EU's main agricultural policy documents. An omission that, however, remains somewhat surprising in the context of plans that strongly

---

34 See Kuljanic (n 33) 2, referring to the project 'GROWX 2.0 Robotic vertical farm' financed by the ERDF and another project of VF developed in the Canary Islands and financed by the EAFRD. <https://ec.europa.eu/enrd/sites/default/files/project/attachments/gp_es_greenfodderproduction_web_fin_0.pdf> accessed 19 June 2025.

35 Antonietta Lupo, 'Diritto al Cibo e Cambiamenti Climatici: Quale Futuro per la Sicurezza Alimentare Globale?' (2022) 1 Rivista di Diritto Alimentare 54.

36 Communication from the Commission to the European Parliament, the Council, the European Economic and Social Committee and the Committee of the Regions: '*A farm-to-fork Strategy for a Fair, Healthy and Environmentally Friendly Food System*', COM/2020/381.

37 See Enrico Mezzacapo, 'Mind the Gap: Assessing Member States' Implementation of Farm-to-Fork Targets within the 2023–2027 Common Agricultural Policy' (2024) 15(2) European Journal of Risk Regulation 265–279.

38 See James McEldowney, *Urban Agriculture in Europe: Patterns, Challenges and Policies* (EPRS, 2017). The report considers VF as a form of urban agriculture. See, in this regard, the reply E-001084/2022(ASW) to the related parliamentary question: <https://www.europarl.europa.eu/doceo/document/E-9-2022-001084-ASW_EN.html>, in which the Commission 'considers urban agriculture (UA), including controlled environment agriculture (CEA), a part of Europe's food production landscape'. Notably, the answer also focuses on supporting research and innovation, pointing out that 'The EU's Farm to Fork Strategy has identified urban food systems as a key area for research and innovation as part of the research and innovation programme Horizon Europe.'

incentivise the use of innovative, environmentally sustainable farming methods aimed at strengthening urban agriculture, reducing the use of substances, such as pesticides, and shortening supply chains.[39] Arguably, this may be explained by admitting that VF is included in broader regulatory areas such as general agriculture (despite the differences highlighted with traditional cultivation) or urban agriculture (despite the fact that vertical farms may also be raised outside of urban areas), which have benefited from broader attention by EU institutions.[40]

Other positions taken by EU institutions should also be considered. According to EU law and EU institutions, products derived from VF do not qualify for certification as organic. This was clarified by the European Commission itself in its answer to a question for written answer to the Commission raised by Social Democrat MEP Christel Schaldemose in 2022.[41] The response provided by the Commissioner for Agriculture, Polish Wojciechowski, asserted that vertical farms using hydroponics (the majority) cannot be certified as organic the reason being the lack of soil and the need for external inputs to enable plant growth. In the Commissioner's response, in particular, reference is made to Article 5 of Regulation 2018/848 (EU),[42] which includes, among the principles of organic farming: the responsible use of energy and natural resources such as water, soil, and air (Art 5 para c); the adoption of methods that 'practice soil-related crop cultivation and land-related livestock production, or practice aquaculture which complies with the principle of the sustainable exploitation of aquatic resources' (Art 5 para f (ii)); and the limited use of external inputs (Art 5 para g).

Based on this normative framework, hydroponic production used in a vertical farm to cultivate without soil using nutrient solutions is considered

---

39 In the same vein, see Kuljanic (n 33) 2, according to whom VF should be further integrated into European policies.

40 Indeed, although small vertical farms are technologically feasible, such small-scale configurations are generally not economically optimal due to the relatively high initial investment required. Larger installations, typically a minimum of 500 square metres, may offer quicker returns on investment, which appears to be the prevailing trend. However, this also poses challenges for the integration of vertical farms into urban environments. See <https://ifarm.fi/> accessed 19 June 2025.

41 European Parliament, question and answer E-002588/2022 to the Commission. <https://www.europarl.europa.eu/doceo/document/E-9-2022-002588_EN.html> (question) and <https://www.europarl.europa.eu/doceo/document/E-9-2022-002588-ASW_EN.html> (answer) both accessed 19 June 2025.

42 Regulation (EU) 2018/848 of the European Parliament and of the Council of 30 May 2018 on organic production and labelling of organic products and repeal of Council Regulation (EC) No 834/2007 (2018) OJ L 150/1 (EU).

incompatible with organic farming.[43] This situation does not seem likely to change, at least in the short term: the response added that it is not in the Commission's interest to further adapt the EU organic legislation to include VF.

From a strictly legal point of view, however, the interpretation adopted does not appear to be the only one possible. Indeed, there are arguments that justify a more nuanced reading. With regard to the limit on inputs, it should be noted that Article 5 allows the use of external inputs where appropriate management practices and methods do not exist, specifying that external inputs, in such cases, must however be limited to 'i) inputs from organic production … ; ii) natural substances or substances derived from natural substances; [or] iii) low solubility mineral fertilisers'. Indeed, these attributes are often found in the external inputs used to support the natural cycle of vertical farms, where it is common to prioritise nutrients of natural or organic origin and to reuse natural biological residues to minimise waste. The Commission's strict stance on this point appears to underestimate the possibility that a vertical farm might cultivate its products using external inputs that meet the criteria outlined in Article 5, such as the use of natural substances and select mineral fertilisers.[44]

However, beyond the general characteristics and aims of organic farming regulation, the main legal obstacle to the compatibility between VF and organic certification in the EU lies in the connection with soil. This connection, as will be discussed in the Italian context, is open to different interpretations. While it can generally be understood in both a physical and functional sense, the EU regulation seems to require a strong physical link with the soil.[45] In this regard, there may still be a margin (although strict) for interpretation that allows, in certain circumstances, the inclusion of products derived from VF within the scope of the Regulation 2018/848 (EU). A questionable case, for instance, could be that of aquaponics, which is not mentioned in the relevant recital or any other provision of the Regulation 2018/848 (EU). Indeed,

43 This is subject to limited exceptions for some specific crops, including the special derogation granted to Finland, Sweden, and Denmark until 2031.

44 In countries where organic certification has been granted to production from vertical agriculture, on the other hand, the use of specific nutrients and inputs of natural origin is usually required.

45 This is particularly evident from recital 28 of the Regulation 2018/848 (EU), according to which 'As organic plant production is based on nourishing the plants primarily through the soil ecosystem, plants should be produced on and in living soil in connection with the subsoil and bedrock. Consequently, hydroponic production should not be allowed, nor growing plants in containers, bags, or beds where the roots are not in contact with the living soil'.

aquaponics integrates aquaculture with plant production and is already used in some vertical farms to enhance the efficiency of the production cycle.[46]

5 Brief Comparative Notes

A similar situation with respect to the EU regulatory approach to VF is also found in the post-Brexit United Kingdom (UK). In addition to prohibiting the organic certification of hydroponic products, again due to the absence of soil in VF, UK legislation makes no explicit reference to vertical agriculture in key, public, multi-year programming plans, such as the Agricultural Transition Plan 2021–2024[47] and the Long-Term Plan for Towns,[48] despite the availability of public funding for field research or the number of companies operating in the sector.[49] Notably, as discussed before regarding the EU approach, the lack of an explicit reference does not preclude the possibility of providing public support to VF within those measures generally directed towards agriculture and farms.[50]

In general terms, however, the regulation of VF in Europe differs from the approach taken in other regions. For the purposes of this chapter, it seems appropriate to focus on legal systems where VF is the most developed and publicly supported.

---

46 It should be noted that aquaponics generally does not use soil. Plants develop roots in specially established environments such as layers of solid and semi-solid substances or within nutrient-rich water-based suspensions from the breeding of aquatic organisms. Despite the non-exclusion of aquaponics, explicitly, compatibility with the regulation would remain doubtful even in this case.

47 Department for Environment, Food & Rural Affairs (UK), *The Path to Sustainable Farming: An Agricultural Transition Plan 2021 to 2024* (2020) <https://www.gov.uk/government/publications/agricultural-transition-plan-2021-to-2024> accessed 19 June 2025.

48 Department for Levelling Up, Housing and Communities (DLUHC), *Our Long-Term Plan for Towns* (September 2023) <https://www.gov.uk/government/publications/our-long-term-plan-for-towns>.

49 On the connection between *urban agriculture* and the promotion of food sustainability and *food security* more generally, see Bethan R Mead and others, 'Does Urban Agriculture Contribute to Food Security, and How Might This Be Achieved?' (2024) 83 Proceedings of the Nutrition Society 195.

50 See for instance Section 2.2 of the Agricultural Transition Plan 2021 to 2024 (n 47), 12 which refers to general measures aimed at improving farm prosperity.

For example, the US has long pursued a different general approach.[51] In addition to supporting scientific research on urban and vertical agriculture,[52] the US has specifically included vertical agriculture in federal agricultural policy since 2018, as part of a broader, legally-relevant category of Controlled Environment Agriculture (CEA).[53] Specific institutions have also been established to promote and support innovative agricultural practices, including VF. These encompass the Federal Advisory Committee for Urban Agriculture and Innovative Production and the Office of Urban Agriculture and Innovative Production, the latter of which plays a key role in coordinating initiatives to promote urban agriculture.[54]

The regulatory approach in the US regarding compatibility with organic certification also appears to be quite different. After some initial fluctuations and uncertainty, products from hydroponic-based VF can now be certified as organic by authorised third-party certifiers, as long as they meet the additional requirements set out by the National Organic Program (NOP) and the Organic Foods Production Act.[55] As a result, in the US market, VF entrepreneurs can benefit from the higher revenues associated with organic certification.

A similar situation exists in Singapore regarding organic certification, where vertical farms have been able to apply for and obtain the organic label for several years.[56]

In Asia, the case of China is of particular interest where strategic rural development plans include forms of urban agriculture that can be applied to VF. This aligns with their long-standing policy aimed at increasing food production.[57]

---

51 Michael Martinez, 'Vertical Farming: A Bottom-Up Approach' (2023) 2 *Seattle Journal of Technology*, Environmental, & Innovation Law, 1–19.

52 This support is mainly due to funding programmes and grants from the USDA—Agricultural Research Service (U.S. Department of Agriculture). See USDA—Agricultural Research Service (US), *Urban, Indoor, and Other Emerging Agricultural Production Research, Education, and Extension Initiative*, 7 USC 5925g.

53 See the Agriculture Improvement Act of 2018 and Kelly J. Walters and others, 'Historical, Current, and Future Perspectives for Controlled Environment Hydroponic Food Crop Production in the United States' (2020) 55(6) HortScience 758–767.

54 On this topic, see Congressional Research Service (US), *Controlled Environment Agriculture (CEA) Production* (31 August 2023).

55 Organic Foods Production Act of 1990, amended by Law 109-97 (10 November 2005).

56 The company Sky Greens was among the first in the world, in June 2019, to obtain organic certification (Singapore Standard 632 SS 632) for its hydroponics-based VF products. See Ann J. Diehl and others, 'Feeding Cities: Singapore's Approach to Land Use Planning for Urban Agriculture' (2020) 26 Global Food Security 100377.

57 See Ina Vîrtosu and Chen Li, 'Vertical Farming Perspective and Challenges: A Comparative Review between China and the EU' (CEEeGov 2024) 13 in Central and Eastern European eDem and eGov Days 2024 1.

Incentives for vertical agriculture are also common, with the sector experiencing significant growth in the country, despite a regulatory framework that lacks specific regulations on the subject.[58]

Finally, the case of Japan presents some peculiar characteristics. Although already developed in the country, VF gained momentum after the Fukushima nuclear disaster, when government support and incentives for alternative forms of agriculture (including VF) contributed to the partial recovery of agricultural production losses within one decade.[59]

6 Vertical Farming in the Italian Legal System

In Italy, the legal issues currently related to VF are diverse and multidisciplinary. The central question is whether a vertical farmer can be classified as an agricultural entrepreneur under Italian law. The classification of VF as an agricultural enterprise has significant legal and operational implications, including the applicability of rules regarding the jurisdiction of agricultural sections of tribunals; the possibility of claiming a lien under Article 2751-bis (4) of the Civil Code; as well as the relevant insolvency regulations and tax regime applicable to vertical farms.[60]

While, traditionally, the rules on agricultural enterprise have been conceived and interpreted to address economic activities closely linked to the land, the definition of an agricultural entrepreneur under Article 2135 of the Italian Civil Code was later the subject of a profound reform under Legislative Decree No. 228/2001.[61] The intent of the reform was, among other factors, to extend the scope of Article 2135 of the Civil Code to include innovative agricultural activities, whose organisational structures differ from traditional agriculture.[62]

---

58 See He Zhang, Ashish Asutosh and Hu Wei, 'Implementing Vertical Farming at University Scale to Promote Sustainable Communities: A Feasibility Analysis' (2018) 10(12) Sustainability 1.

59 See Daniela De Lorenzo, 'Food from Fukushima: Restoring Trusts Using AgriTech' <https://www.forbes.com/sites/danieladelorenzo/2023/07/24/food-from-fukushima--restoring-trusts-using-agritech/> accessed 19 June 2025.

60 See Interdonato (n 31).

61 On the reform see Luigi Costato, 'La nuova versione dell'articolo 2135 cod. civ. e la Corte di cassazione' (2004) 1(I) Rivista di Diritto Agrario 3–12.

62 Irene Canfora, 'Art. 2135 c.c.', in Giovanni Bonilini, Massimo Confortini and Carlo Granelli (eds.), *Codice Civile Commentato* (Utet, 2012). The author argues that the reform entailed a substantial extension of the scope of the agricultural enterprise, where agrarianism and connection with the land are replaced by the care of a biological cycle or a phase thereof. See also Luigi Costato, *Corso di Diritto Agrario*, (Giuffré, 2004) 106.

This is precisely the approach envisaged in the revised version of Article 2135 of the Civil Code, which, following the reform, defines an agricultural entrepreneur as anyone engaged in activities 'aimed at the care and development of a biological cycle or a necessary phase thereof, of a plant or animal nature, that uses or may use the land, forest, or fresh or marine waters'.[63] The fact that, according to Article 2135 Civil Code, the use of land is not strictly necessary ('may use the land') thus leading to certain types of soilless cultivation (including VF) being considered agricultural enterprises.[64] Scholars have emphasised that this interpretation of Article 2135 Civil Code supports the conclusion that vertical farming falls within the normative category of agricultural enterprise, given that land use is no longer strictly necessary under Italian civil law.[65]

Italian jurisprudence has also gradually adopted a broader interpretation of connection to the soil, moving away from a previously restrictive approach.[66]

The Italian Supreme Court of Cassation more recently affirmed that by referring to activities directed to the care and development of a biological cycle, the Italian legislator:

> [C]learly intended to include among complementary activities even those that do not present a necessary connection between production and use of the land, being, instead, sufficient that there is a mere functional and instrumental connection with the land, outside of a strict real connection.[67]

Additionally, the relevant organisation of personnel, resources, and investment required for a vertical farm does not appear to be an obstacle to its classification as an agricultural enterprise. Italian jurisprudence has clarified that Article 2135 of the Civil Code imposes no limits on the economic scale, size, or technical complexity of agricultural enterprises.[68]

---

63 See Alberto Germanò, Eva Rook Basile, 'Impresa agricola', in Rodolfo Sacco (ed.), *Digesto delle Discipline Privatistiche* (Utet, 2012).

64 Court of Cassation, I, 5 December 2002, No. 17251, according to which 'the legislative amendment considers the "possibility", and no longer the "necessity", of using the fund, relegating such use to a merely potential fact'.

65 See Camilla della Giustina, 'La Transizione Ecologica Attraverso l'agricoltura: Prime Riflessioni in Tema di "Vertical Farming". Il Modello ESG di Agricoltura nella "Smart City"?' (2022) 1 Il diritto dell'agricoltura 60.

66 This approach was motivated mainly by an intent to limit the number of exceptions from insolvency procedures granted to ordinary commercial enterprises.

67 Court of Cassation, IV, 7 March 2018, No. 5391.

68 Court of Appeal Naples, Decree, 16/01/2003, (2003) 2 Diritto Fallimentare 948.

Furthermore, this broad interpretation of the Civil Code, which includes vertical farms within the scope of agricultural enterprises, could find additional support in the case law of the Constitutional Court. The Court has recognised the agricultural nature of businesses engaged in aquaculture, an activity that, as mentioned, can be integrated with vertical farms and combined with hydroponics (so-called aquaponics).[69]

Remaining in the constitutional context, in seeking a proper interpretation of Article 2135 of the Italian Civil Code, it seems relevant to consider the recent reform introduced by Constitutional Law No. 1 from February 2022, which amended Articles 9 and 41 of the Italian Constitution (Cost).[70] The constitutional amendment of Article 41 Cost requires economic initiatives to respect environmental sustainability, thus providing a constitutional framework to protect the environment, biodiversity, and ecosystems, keeping in mind future generations. In this regard, a constitutionally-oriented interpretation of Article 2135 of the Italian Civil Code could therefore highlight the capacity for certain types of cultivation, possibly including VF, to benefit the environment and support climate action, thus justifying the assignment of the advantages reserved for agricultural enterprises to VF.[71] A reading in these terms would then justify a broad interpretation of Article 2135 Civil Code to include, within the agricultural enterprise, those activities offering environmental benefits.

However, as stated above, verifying the concrete environmental and climate benefits of this type of cultivation is essential. For VF, this involves considering factors such as energy sources and assessing the overall environmental impact, including upstream and downstream emissions, while evaluating the benefits for the legal interests protected by Article 9 of the Constitution.[72]

Other recent developments in the Italian legal system may also enable a favourable environment for the growth of VF. Section 224 of Decree-Law No. 34/2020, converted with amendments into Law No. 17 July 2020, established

---

69 See Constitutional Court. nos. 104/2012 and 190/2001. Particularly, in the decision No. 104/2012, the Italian Court stated that 'On the other hand, the circumstance that aquaculture, typically carried out by the fish farmer, can be traced back to an agricultural entrepreneurial activity is a fact that has long been established in the case law of this Court'.

70 See Domenico Amirante, *Costituzionalismo Ambientale* (Il Mulino 2022) 110; Stefano Grassi, 'La Cultura dell'Ambiente nell'Evoluzione Costituzionale' (2023) 3 *Rivista AIC* 219–254; Paolo Dell'Anno, *Diritto dell'Ambiente* (Giuffrè 2022).

71 Cf. Camilla Della Giustina, 'La Transizione Ecologica' (n 65) 61.

72 Article 9 Cost. states that 'The Republic promotes the development of culture and scientific and technical research. It protects the Nation's landscape and historical and artistic heritage. It protects the environment, biodiversity and ecosystems, including in the interest of future generations. The law of the State regulates the ways and forms of animal protection'.

an updated definition of a specific classification for activities frequently related to VF such as hydroponic and aquaponic farming for the purpose of assigning an ATECO code (ie a code used for fiscal classification of economic activities).[73] According to this piece of legislation, the new classification was justified by the increased development of 'new soilless cultivation practices applied to hydroponic and aquaponic crops, for which valorisation and promotion is necessary'.[74]

7 The 'Avant-Garde' of Vertical Farming Regulation: Regional Legislation

While interpretative uncertainties persist regarding the regulatory framework for vertical farms at the national level, partly due to the lack of a clear legal definition, some significant developments have emerged at the regional level, where the Italian Constitution establishes legislative powers for regions in certain matters.

Based on regional authority over agriculture envisaged by Article 117(4) Cost., the Lombardy Region approved Italy's first dedicated legislation on VF in 2021.[75] This piece of legislation also included the first legally-relevant definition of the phenomenon in Italy.

According to Article 2 of the regional law, 'vertical farming' or 'vertical agriculture' refers to a:

> [S]ystem of agricultural cultivation in closed growth chambers with total environmental control, in the absence of soil, above ground, or even in the absence of natural light, developed on overlapping vertical modules,

73 Decree-Law No. 34/2020, converted with amendments by Law No. 77 of 17 July 2020.

74 The ATECO code classification was finally updated in 2021 with the inclusion of new corresponding sub-codes in section A, related to Agricultural Activities.

75 Regional Law of Lombardia No 21 of 8 November 2021 on 'Urban, peri-urban, and metropolitan agriculture'. On the legislative power of Italian regions over agriculture, see Constitutional Court No. 12/2004, which endorsed a broad reading of regional legislative power in agricultural matters, stating that the activity relating to the production of plants and animals belongs at the heart of agriculture (and therefore belongs under the authority of the regions according to Italian Constitution). See Luca Antonini 'Art. 117 Cost.' in Raffaele Bifulco, Alfonso Celotto, and Marco Olivetti (eds.), *Commentario alla Costituzione* (Vol. III, UTET 2006).

exploiting a combination of techniques such as aquaponics, hydroponics, or aeroponics.[76]

The regional law seems to consider VF as an agricultural activity rather than a commercial one, as can be appreciated from the reference to 'cultivation', the explicit use of the expression 'vertical agriculture', and also from Article 2(2) of the Lombardy law,[77] which specifies that the provisions of Legislative Decrees 18 May 2001, No. 228 and 29 March 2004, No. 99[78] apply to the entrepreneur carrying out VF activities. This clearly indicates that vertical farms are considered agricultural enterprises.

Another key provision, Article 3(3), envisages the establishment of vertical farms in areas designated for agriculture under Lombardy Regional Law 12/2005. The illustrative report for the Regional Law highlights the direct link between VF and environmental and climate preservation objectives, as well as the alignment with the 'Green Revolution and Ecological Transition' mission of the Italian Recovery Plan ('PNRR').[79]

In this regard, the regional legislative measure aims to support both conventional and innovative agricultural production that contributes to greater environmental and climatic sustainability, while promoting the growth of the 'zero-kilometre' food supply. From this point of view, therefore, the regional law also affirms the connection between vertical agriculture, sustainability, and food security, with special attention paid to urban areas. In this way, Regional Law 21/2021 closely links vertical agriculture with urban regeneration and smart cities.[80]

Furthermore, in Lombardy vertical farms can also be built by renovating existing facilities, a testimony to the comprehensive regulatory approach the

76 Vertical farms are also defined as facilities where the cultivation systems referred to in Article 2(1)(a) are implemented.

77 Cf. Camilla Della Giustina 'La Transizione Ecologica' (n 65) 49. Lombardia approved this piece of legislation invoking the legislative authority of Regions over agriculture pursuant to Article 117(4) Cost. It is worth noting that the Government did not challenge the Lombardia law before the Constitutional Court arguing a conflict of legislative powers.

78 'Provisions on subjects and activities, corporate integrity, and administrative simplification'.

79 See the Illustrative Report to Project of regional Law No. 192 of 21 October 2021, Lombardia Region, Regional Council.

80 On this topic, see Giuseppe F Ferrari (ed.), *Smart Cities. L'Evoluzione di un'Idea* (Mimesis 2020).

Regional Law has taken towards this legal phenomenon.[81] Indeed, alongside clarifications on the definition and applicable regime, the law includes support measures related to urban planning[82] and tax regulations,[83] as well as coordination provisions aimed at aligning the interventions of Regional Law 21/2021 with the region's urban food policy projects (Article 4).

8 Conclusions

Vertical farming is an emerging phenomenon with significant potential, though it also presents certain limitations.

VF may contribute to the sustainability of agrifood systems while also creating opportunities for urban regeneration, smart city development, and metropolitan food security.

This chapter presents analysis to support the idea that a clear and coherent regulatory framework is essential to enable the development of VF. This is especially important given the initial challenges faced by many businesses related to efficiency and cost, which have often fuelled scepticism towards these agricultural practices. Strengthening collaboration between economic operators, policymakers, and the research and innovation sectors will be crucial to foster the development of VF under a regulatory point of view.

In this regard, this chapter highlighted that a key legal challenge in regulating VF lies in its cross-disciplinary nature. Indeed, vertical farms operate at the intersection of several fields, including agricultural policy, urban planning, ecological transition, and the regulation of innovative enterprises. This underscores the need for effective regulatory mechanisms and a comprehensive framework to connect and coordinate different sectors.

Legislators must also consider the consequences that overly rigid regulation—especially if motivated by ends other than the pursuit of effective protection of fundamental needs such as nutrition and public health—may

81 It is worth underlining that vertical farms co-located in existing buildings and urban areas pose further regulatory issues with respect to elements such as noise emissions, the adaptability of existing spaces, and construction materials.

82 Including the possibility of establishing vertical farms in buildings intended for residential use.

83 Such as the extension of urban regeneration incentives regulated by Lombardia Regional Law No. 12/2005 to the renovation of existing buildings for the construction of vertical farms.

have on European companies.[84] The global VF market is currently quite polarised, with Asia and North America representing the two main geographies where it has flourished. As noted above, despite a diverse and heterogeneous landscape, specific regulatory attention to VF and controlled environment agriculture in other jurisdictions appears to be more developed than in the EU, where VF could benefit from the measures provided to support general and urban agriculture.

In this regard, certain features of the Italian legal system could offer promising opportunities for the development of vertical farms. Italy benefits from a geographical context known for its world-class food production, a strong manufacturing sector that can support technological advancements, abundant renewable energy sources, and robust support networks for agricultural businesses. The Italian legal context also offers potentially favourable elements, including recent regulatory and judicial trends aimed at extending the legal and economic benefits of agricultural enterprises to soilless activities. This is compounded by incentives and legal developments at the regional level. Lombardy's regional law represents the first comprehensive regulatory framework for VF, advancing a promotional regulatory model that other Italian regions may soon follow. In Veneto, a region where several VF companies are already active, the Regional Council is currently discussing a proposal for a regional law aimed at introducing 'support measures for vertical farming'.[85]

The regional legislative powers in agriculture envisaged by the Italian Constitution could allow other regions to adopt additional measures, especially given the lack of clarity on this topic found in the current national and European regulatory frameworks. Indeed, such regional initiatives could provide valuable regulatory support for operators and stakeholders in this emerging sector, which faces both regulatory gaps and economic difficulties such as high initial investment costs and scarcity of a specialised workforce.

---

84 In this regard, it is worth mentioning EFSA's Technical report of 18.5.2021 (https://doi.org/10.2903/sp.efsa.2021.EM-6658) <https://www.efsa.europa.eu/en/supporting/pub/en-6808> accessed 19 June 2025. In this technical opinion related to the authorisation procedure of two traditional foods from third countries pursuant to Article 14 of EU Regulation 2015/2283, EFSA stated that, although VF was a different production process from the one traditionally used to grow plants, the fact that the production process had taken place by means of VF techniques did not raise concerns regarding food safety.

85 Veneto Region, proposal of regional law No. 160/2023. A further proposal of regional law under discussion aims to introduce 'Provisions for urban and peri-urban agriculture' (Veneto Region, proposal of regional law No. 162/2023).

Yet, a national intervention on the subject also appears appropriate to avoid a 'mosaic' of different regional legislations. Moreover, a national framework on innovative agriculture and VF would help coordinate these activities with the relevant missions of the Italian National Recovery and Resilience Plan (PNRR), clarify the legal status of enterprises in this sector, and address the limits of regional legislative powers. Indeed, based on a different possible interpretation, the classification of vertical farmers as agricultural entrepreneurs under the Italian Civil Code can also be considered as a matter of civil law, thus falling within the exclusive legislative authority of the State under Article 117(2)(l) of the Italian Constitution concerning civil law (*ordinamento civile*).

Finally, national legislation would clearly help to define the applicable tax regime, including incentives and benefits, and prevent regulatory discrepancies between different regions.[86]

Bibliography

Albisinni F, 'La sicurezza alimentare veicolo di innovazione istituzionale' (2009) 4 *Rivista di diritto alimentare* 15.

Antonelli M, Castaldi S and Valentini R, 'Cambiamento climatico e cibo' (2020) 1 *Equilibri* 36.

Beacham AM, Vickers LH and Monaghan JM, 'Vertical Farming: a Summary of Approaches to Growing Skywards' (2019) 94(3) *Journal of Horticultural Science and Biotechnology* 277–283.

Benke K and Tomkins B, 'Future food-production systems: Vertical farming and controlled-environment agriculture' (2017) 13 Sustainability: Science, Practice and Policy 13–26.

Bruno F, *Il diritto alimentare. Sviluppo sostenibile e tutela della salute* (Wolters Kluwer 2022).

Canfora I, 'Art. 2135 c.c.' in Bonilini G, Confortini M and Granelli C (eds), *Codice Civile Commentato* (Utet 2012).

Carotti L, Pistillo, Ilaria Zauli, Davide Meneghello, Michael Martin, Giuseppina Pennisi, Giorgio Gianquinto, Francesco Orsini, 'Improving Efficiency In Vertical Farming: Effects Of Growing Systems, Far-Red Radiation And Planting Density On Lettuce Cultivation, (2023) 285 *Agricultural Water Management* 108365.

Cerbone C, 'Pratiche virtuose contro lo spreco alimentare in Italia: alcune note a partire dalle recenti proposte di legge sulla c.d. doggy bag' (2024) 24 *federalismi.it* 78.

86 Cf. Interdonato (n 31).

Costato L, *Corso di diritto agrario* (Giuffré 2004).

Costato L 'La nuova versione dell'articolo 2135 cod. civ. e la Corte di cassazione' (2004) 1 *Rivista di Diritto Agrario*.

Della Giustina C, 'La transizione ecologica attraverso l'agricoltura: prime riflessioni in tema di "vertical farming". Il modello ESG di agricoltura nella "smart city"?' (2022) 1 *Il diritto dell'agricoltura* 60.

Dell'Anno P, *Diritto dell'ambiente* (Giuffrè 2022).

Despommier D, *The Vertical Farm: Feeding the World in the 21st Century* (Thomas Dunne Books 2010).

Diehl AJ, Sweeney E, Wong B, Sia CS, Yao H, Prabhudesai M, 'Feeding Cities: Singapore's Approach to Land Use Planning for Urban Agriculture' (2020) 26 Global Food Security.

Ferrando T and De Gregorio V, *The Right to Food in Italy between Present and Future* (2018) 11.

Formici G, Violini L, Lanzoni D, Rebucci R, Cheli F, Sundaram T.S., 'Cultured Meat in the European Union: Legislative Context and Food Safety Issues' (2024) 8 *Current Research in Food Science* 1.

Galan S 'Urbanization rate of the population worldwide, by regional development 1950–2050. Percentage of Population Living in Urban Areas Worldwide from 1950 to 2050' (2018) *Statista*,

Germanò A and Rook Basile E, 'Impresa agricola' in Sacco R (ed), *Digesto delle Discipline Privatistiche* (Utet 2012).

Grassi S, 'La cultura dell'ambiente nell'evoluzione costituzionale' (2023) 3 *Rivista AIC*.

Interdonato M, 'Le colture fuori suolo nel reddito agrario, tra l'indispensabile presenza del fondo e la difficile trasposizione delle conoscenze tecniche di tali colture su quelle tradizionali ai fini della valutazione dei limiti dell'agrarietà' (17 May 2022) *Rivista di Diritto Tributario*.

Kuljanic Npa, *What if We Grew Plants Vertically?* (EPRS, Bruxelles 2022).

Lupo A, 'Diritto al cibo e cambiamenti climatici: quale futuro per la sicurezza alimentare globale?' (2022) 1 *Rivista di Diritto Alimentare* 54.

Martinez M, 'Vertical Farming: A Bottom-Up Approach' (2023) 2 *Seattle Journal of Technology, Environmental, & Innovation Law* 1–19.

McEldowney J, *Urban Agriculture in Europe: Patterns, Challenges and Policies* (EPRS, Brussels 2017).

Mezzacapo E, 'Mind the Gap: Assessing Member States' Implementation of Farm-to-Fork Targets within the 2023–2027 Common Agricultural Policy' (2024) 15(2) *European Journal of Risk Regulation* 265–279.

Orsini F, 'Food Vertigo. Processi e dispositive per la resilienza alimentare metropolitana' (2022) 23 *Techne* 104–116.

Ramajoli M, 'Quale futuro per la regolazione alimentare' (2021) 2 *Milan Law Review*.

Scaffardi L, 'La sicurezza alimentare ovvero come il "diritto a togliersi la fame" evolve in un mondo che cambia' (2023) 2 *DPCE Online* 59.

Scaffardi L and Formici G (eds), *Novel Foods and Edible Insects in the European Union: An Interdisciplinary Analysis* (Springer 2022).

Shabandeh M, 'Projected Vertical Farming Market Worldwide from 2022 to 2032' (2023) *Statista*.

United Nations General Assembly, *Transforming Our World: The 2030 Agenda for Sustainable Development* UNGA Res 70/1, UN Doc A/RES/70/1 (25 September 2015).

Valette É, Blay-Palmer A, Intoppa B, Di Battista A, Roudelle O, Chaboud G, *Evaluating Sustainable Food System Innovations: A Global Toolkit for Cities* (Routledge 2023).

Van Der Meulen B and Wernaart B, 'Comparative Food Law' in Roberts M T (ed), *Research Handbook on International Food Law* (Edward Elgar Publishing 2023).

Van Delden SH, SharathKumar, M., Butturini,Graamans, L.J.A., Heuvelink, E., Kacira, M., Kaiser, E., Klamer, R.S., Klerkx, L., Kootstra, G., Loeber, A., Schouten, R.E., Stanghellini, C., Van Ieperen, W., Verdonk, J.C., Vialet-Chabrand, S., Woltering, E.J., Van de Zedde, R., Zhang, Y., Marcelis, L.F.M., 'Current Status and Future Challenges in Implementing and Upscaling Vertical Farming Systems' (2021) 2 *Nature Food*.

Van Gerrewey T, Boon N and Geelen D, 'Vertical Farming: The Only Way is Up?' (2021) 12(1) *Agronomy* 7.

Vîrtosu I and Li C, 'Vertical Farming Perspective and Challenges: A Comparative Review between China and the EU' (CEEeGov 2024) 13 *Central and Eastern European eDem and eGov Days 2024* 1–12.

Whitfield S and Marshall A, 'Defining and Delivering "Sustainable" Agriculture in the UK After Brexit: Interdisciplinary Lessons from Experiences of Agricultural Reform' (2017) 15(5) *International Journal of Agricultural Sustainability* 501–513.

Zhang H, Asutosh A and Wei H, 'Implementing Vertical Farming at University Scale to Promote Sustainable Communities: A Feasibility Analysis' (2018) 10(12) *Sustainability* 1–18.

CHAPTER 8

The Regulation of Agrifood Biotechnology: from GMOs to New Genomic Techniques

Maria Chiara Errigo

Summary

1 From Innovation to Sustainability: a Brief Introduction

Agriculture's environmental footprint is particularly impactful: it is one of the main sources of greenhouse gas emissions and, therefore, influences climate change trends which, in turn, affect agriculture itself.[1] The development of a more efficient agricultural sector, capable of supporting the ever-increasing need for food through a resilient ecosystem and biodiversity-conscious production, appears to be a necessary building block in the pursuit of global sustainability goals.

To achieve this challenge, scientific and technological innovation offer new possibilities to develop a more sustainable agrifood system (eg one that is resistant to certain climatic conditions, has lower water and soil use, and can store more food). Biotechnology, in particular, could be a significant tool to improve the sustainability of the agrifood sector. New techniques make it possible to modify the genetic makeup of plant species so they better respond to current environmental and volume demands. While such genetic manipulation may appear 'unnatural', it must be remembered that many of the foods we consume today are the result of artificial selections that have been made on

1 Antonietta Lupo, 'Il diritto al cibo nella crisi climatica tra sicurezza e "sostenibilità" alimentare' [2023] (2) Biolaw Journal 277 <https://teseo.unitn.it/biolaw/article/view/2710> accessed 19 February 2025.

HTTPS://DOI.ORG/10.1163/9789004740907-010

a continuous basis by human beings over time in an effort to adapt different plant species to our own needs.

Thanks to important scientific and technological developments, genetic breeding techniques have progressively become more sophisticated. Since the development of Genetically Modified Organisms (GMOs), the scientific debate has now turned to New Genomic Techniques (NGTs) that carry out modifications more precisely than traditional GMOs, similar to what occurs spontaneously in nature.

However, the use of biotechnology in the agrifood sector also poses ethical and legal challenges related to safety standards, food quality and 'authenticity', consumer and environment health, and labeling. Despite these challenges, biotechnology also represents an opportunity in terms of food security as a possible remedy for malnutrition[2] and to safeguard indigenous foods.[3]

The regulation of biotechnology, therefore, appears to be a crucial issue to address as it can help achieve sustainability in the agrifood sector. This chapter explores this topic, focusing specifically on the regulation of GMOs and NGTs at the EU and national levels.

---

2 See the case of Golden Rice, a variety of rice that has been genetically modified in order to contain a sufficient component of beta-carotene and counteract the intake of vitamin A-deficient foods that has serious impacts on people's health (eg blindness, diminished brain development, etc.). The history of Golden Rice is rather troubled: although it is not patented and can be grown freely, it has still met with strong scepticism. In 2021, the Philippines had started the commercialisation of the edited plant, which, however, was soon blocked by a Court of Appeals, due to the lack of scientific consensus about its safety. Bangladesh also appeared on the cusp of starting to plant Golden Rice crops, but planting approval has been under review since 2017. On the Golden Rice case, see Ingo Potrykus, 'The "Golden Rice" tale' (2001) 37 in Vitro Cellular Development Biology-Plant 93; Dennis Normile 'What a Philippine Court Ruling Means for Transgenic Golden Rice, one hailed as a dietary breakthrough' (*Science*, 3 May 2024) <https://www.science.org/content/article/what-philippine-court-ruling-means-transgenic-golden-rice-once-hailed-dietary> accessed on 23 February 2025; Amanda C. Palmer 'Golden Rice: a quarter-century of innovation, challenges, and the promise of better nutrition' (2025, July 2) The Journal of Nutrition.

3 See the case of Hawaii Papaya. Particularly, papaya crops are affected by the PRSV (Papaya RingSpot Virus), a fast-moving, incurable disease. The case of Hawaii is worth noting: to counter the virus and safeguard papaya production, an indigenous food, researchers focused on the possibility of creating a genetically-modified papaya resistant to this virus. The research activity was funded by the US Department of Agriculture (USDA) and yielded very positive results. The introduction of genetically modified papaya has saved the production of the non-transgenic one; traditional papaya fields are often surrounded by a few rows of genetically modified papaya so as to defend them from the virus. On this matter, see Dario Bressanini, *OGM tra leggende e realtà* (Zanichelli 2018).

2 The Regulation of Biotechnology: the Case of Genetically Modified Organisms (GMOs)

The use of biotechnology in the agrifood sector is regulated by a multilevel system of governance: global (including intervention by international organisations such as WTO, WHO, and FAO), 'regional', national, and sub-state.[4] This presents particular complexity because of the plurality of legal topics (eg health, environment, trade, and agriculture) and thematic fields (eg juridical, scientific, ethical, social, and economic) it touches or is touched by. This intertwining of regulatory levels and thematic areas have made it difficult to develop recognised legislation in the field, beginning since the rise of GMOs.

It is important to highlight that EU law provides a foundational regulatory framework for the whole region, guiding the creation of national policies. In this context, the regulation of food biotechnology has been informed by the precautionary principle[5] and the prioritisation of food safety through specific authorisation procedures and oversight by the European Food Safety Authority (EFSA).[6] However, the precautionary approach—marked by lengthy and complex approval procedures—has led to an impasse with respect to the use of biotechnology in the agrifood sector.

4 Mariasole Porpora 'Gli OGM e la frammentazione della Governance nel settore alimentare' [2015] (6) Rivista italiana di Diritto Pubblico Comunitario 1661.

5 Directive 2001/18/EC of the European Parliament and of the Council of 12 March 2001 on the deliberate release into the environment of genetically modified organisms and repealing Council Directive 90/220/EEC [2001] OJ L106, Art 1 states: 'In accordance with the precautionary principle, the objective of this Directive is to approximate the laws, regulations and administrative provisions of Member States and to protect human health and the environment when: carrying out the deliberate release into the environment of genetically modified organisms for any other purposes than placing on the market within the Community; placing on the market genetically modified organisms as or in products within the Community'. More generally, with regard to precautionary principle, see Commission, 'On the Precautionary Principle' COM (2000) 1 final; Cass Sunstein, *Law of Fear: Beyond the Precautionary Principle* (CUP 2005).

6 Particularly, see Regulation (EC) 178/2002 of the European Parliament and of the Council of 28 January 2002 laying down the general principles and requirements of food law, establishing the European Food Safety Authority, and laying down procedures in matters of food safety [2002] OJ L31. See also Simone Gabbi, *L'Autorità Europea per la sicurezza alimentare. Genesi, aspetti problematici e prospettive di riforma* (Giuffrè 2009); Alberto Alemanno and Simone Gabbi (eds), *Foundations of EU Food Law and Policy. Ten Years of the European Food Safety Authority* (Routledge 2016).

More specifically with regard to GMOs, Directive 2001/18/EC represents the key instrument within the EU legal framework.[7] The Directive defines a GMO and provides the procedural steps that must necessarily be followed in order to the release the organism into the environment or place it on the market of GMOs not intended for human or animal consumption. The Directive defines a GMO as 'an organism, other than a human being, whose genetic material has been altered in a way that does not occur naturally by mating and/or natural genetic recombination'.[8]

The notion of GMOs outlined in this definition seems to be an almost legal one, only partially covering the scientific idea. Indeed, it considers a GMO to be any organism that has undergone mutation at the genetic level, whatever the technique used. The European definition, instead, in determining whether a certain organism is a GMO, looks less at the product as a whole than at the process used to obtain it.[9] Agrifood varieties developed through the application of specific genetic engineering techniques are, therefore, framed as GMOs and treated with specific procedures that are characterised by numerous controls and a tangled system of authorisations between EU bodies and national authorities.

It should be noted that Directive 2001/18 was amended by Directive 2015/412 which introduced the possibility for Member States to limit or ban the cultivation of GMOs in their territory.[10] The difficulties that exist among Member States in adopting common rules on this issue make it complicated to reach a consensus on the decision-making process for GMOs. To overcome this stalemate, the EU has introduced the option for Member States to maintain an independent position, enabling the exclusion of GMO cultivation from their territory (totally or partially).

The regulatory framework on GMOs also includes Regulation 1829/2003 that specifically regards the authorisation of market placement of genetically modified food and feed, as well as Regulation 1830/2003 on traceability and labeling systems, as a guarantee to protect consumers' freedom of choice. With regard

7 Angelo Rinella and Concetta Pungitore, *Organismi geneticamente modificati. Profili di diritto comparato ed europeo* (Filodiritto 2015).

8 Directive 2001/18/EC, art 2; for further specifications and exclusions, see Annexes A and B of the Directive.

9 Dario Bressanini (n 3); Roberto Defez, *Il caso OGM. Il dibattito sugli organismi geneticamente modificati* (Carocci 2016).

10 Daniela Corona, *'L'attuazione della Direttiva UE 2015/412: un nuovo capitolo nell'intricata saga dell'autorizzazione degli OGM nell'Unione Europea'* in Ginevra Cerrina Feroni and others (eds), *Ambiente, energia, alimentazione. Modelli giuridici comparati per lo sviluppo sostenibile*, vol 1, II (Cesifin 2016).

to the latter, within the EU, it is mandatory to mark genetically modified products with appropriate labeling. This requirement applies to all food or feed that contains, consists of, or is produced by GMOs with the exception of products where the genetically modified material represents less than 0.9 percent of the total and is contained 'incidentally' or its inclusion is 'technically unavoidable'. That being said, the total absence of GMOs is very difficult to ensure given that trace amounts can be difficult to detect—making it possible that some GMOs remain present, albeit in a very slight quantity. For this reason, there are several doubts regarding so-called negative labeling, such as 'GMO-free', which may not be entirely accurate, representing only partial, and perhaps even misleading, information.[11]

3 The New Genomic Techniques: a Regulatory Challenge

Recently, the development of sophisticated new biotechnologies that can enable targeted genetic modifications in plant life has become the focus of intense scholarly debate regarding their regulatory governance. These so-called New Genomic Techniques (NGTs) perform more circumscribed actions that can directly modify the DNA sequence concerned (this is called gene editing, the most promising technique of which is CRISPR)[12] or transfer genes from one species to another, on the condition that they are 'sexually compatible' (this is the case of cisgenesis). These are techniques with a lower degree of invasiveness: the modifications occur either 'internally' or by introducing genes belonging to varieties of the same or similar species, such that the modifications made could also occur through spontaneous crosses. The new techniques thus differ from transgenesis, used in the case of GMOs, in which the transfer targets a gene belonging to a different species with which any crosses in nature would not be possible.

Despite these differences, the regulatory framework governing GMOs initially also covered products obtained using the most recent, more sophisticated NGTs. This occurred as a result of a landmark decision by the EU Court

11 Francesco Rossi Dal Pozzo, 'Profili recenti in tema di organismi geneticamente modificati nel settore agroalimentare fra procedure di comitato e tutela giurisdizionale' [2014] Il diritto del commercio internazionale 339.

12 Jennifer Doudna and Samuel Sternberg, *Il futuro della vita* (Mondadori 2022); see also Anna Meldolesi, *E l'uomo creò l'uomo. CRISPR e la rivoluzione dell'editing genomico* (Bollati Boringhieri 2017).

of Justice in 2018.[13] The case, filed on behalf of the *Confédération paysanne* (Peasant Confederation) and other environmental associations, questioned the legitimacy of a French regulation that allowed the cultivation of rapeseed varieties produced using new genomic techniques (specifically site-directed mutagenesis). The plaintiff associations argued that products produced by these new techniques should be treated on par with traditional GMOs and, therefore, should be regulated under Directive 2001/18. Article 3, Paragraph 1 (along with Annex I B) of Directive 2001/18 lists mutagenesis among the techniques excluded from the EU regulatory framework; however the Court of Justice emphasised that mutagenesis encompasses various methods of application and that the EU regulatory framework does not specify which of these methods should be excluded. In its ruling, the Court placed considerable importance on Recital 17 of the Directive, stating that the regulation 'should not apply to organisms obtained through certain techniques of genetic modification which have conventionally been used in various applications and have a long safety record'.[14] For this reason, organisms obtained using the most recent mutagenesis techniques cannot be excepted and should be treated as 'traditional' GMOs and subjected to the provisions of Directive 2001/18.[15]

This decision raised strong opposition from relevant members of the scientific community[16] who called for a change and a consequent revision of the current legislation on GMOs. Indeed, biotechnology research offers extraordinary opportunities that could be relevant to the agrifood sector, and the new genomic techniques are more precise and less invasive than traditional GMOs.

On February 7, 2023 the EU Court of Justice ruled again on new genomic techniques, which were questioned once more by the French Council of State. More specifically, discussing the statute of random mutagenesis in vitro, the Court affirmed that,

---

13 Particularly, see the Case C-528/16 *Confédération paysanne and Others v Premier ministre and Ministre de l'Agriculture, de l'Agroalimentaire et de la Forêt* EU:C:2018:583.

14 Rec 17, Directive 1001/18/EC.

15 Serena Mariani, 'New Breeding Techniques e ogm: le innovazioni in agricoltura al vaglio della Corte di Giustizia: il caso della mutagenesi sito-diretta (causa C-528/16)' [2019] (3) Diritto e giurisprudenza agraria, alimentare e dell'ambiente 1 <https://www.rivistadga.it/wp-content/uploads/2019/06/Mariani-New-breeding-techniques-e-OGM.pdf> accessed 23 February 2025; Dario Bevilacqua, 'Le definizioni di OGM, le intenzioni del legislatore e il bilanciamento degli interessi' [2019] Giornale di diritto amministrativo 377.

16 See, eg, the note of the Italian Society of Agricultural Genetics (SIGA), 'Nota sulla situazione normativa delle biotecnologie genetiche in agricoltura' (*SIGA* 2019) <http://old.geneticagraria.it/attachment/SocietaScuolaRicerca/Nota_SIGA.pdf> accessed 23 February 2025.

> [O]rganisms obtained through the application of a technique/method of mutagenesis which is based on the same processes of modification, by the mutagenic agent, of the genetic material of the organism concerned as a technique/method of mutagenesis which has conventionally been used in a number of applications and has a long safety record, but which differs from that second technique/method of mutagenesis by virtue of other characteristics, shall, in principle, be excluded from the exemption laid down in [Article 3, par. 1, Directive 2001/18].

However, with regard to in vitro cultures, the Court also specified that the mere fact that mutagenesis occurs in vitro rather than in vivo cannot be sufficient grounds for exclusion from the exemption under Directive 2001/18.[17] Through this line of reasoning, the Court of Justice determined that, in order to proceed with their release into the environment or placement on the market, organisms obtained through new genomic techniques must still undergo a risk assessment procedure to avoid potential negative effects on human health and the environment. While, in fact, nothing has changed since this ruling regarding the regulation of new genomic techniques, it should be noted that the Court seems to be taking a less rigid stance than it did in 2018. According to the Court, it is not necessary to focus on the method used, but rather on the effects that may result from it. Most likely, this reaction of the Court of Justice is also part of a broader trend that seems to view new techniques with less scepticism.

3.1 *The EU Regulation Proposal*

NGTs continue to be under discussion in Europe due to a current lack of clear legislation on the topic, and a heated debate is ongoing involving the public and EU institutions.[18] The issue of regulation and the 2018 case prompted EU institutions to begin reflecting on the matter, assessing the characteristics of the new techniques and whether the current framework on GMOs should

---

17 'However, the effects inherent in in vitro cultures do not, as such, justify the exclusion from that exemption of organisms obtained by the in vitro application of a technique/method of mutagenesis which has conventionally been used in a number of in vivo applications and has a long safety record with regard to those applications', Case C-688/21 *Confédération paysanne* and Others v *Premier ministre* and *Ministre de l'Agriculture et de l'Alimentation* EU:C:2023:89.

18 Francesco Rossi Dal Pozzo, 'Le nuove tecniche genomiche e il loro impiego nel settore agroalimentare. L'Unione europea alla ricerca di una disciplina giuridica sostenibile' in Lorenza Violini (ed), *One Health, Dal paradigma alle implicazioni giuridiche* (Giappichelli 2022).

be amended. In this context, following an invitation from the Council of the European Union, the European Commission conducted a major study on new genomic techniques, analysing the scientific context and regulatory framework. As a result of the study, the European Commission identified:

> [A] series of challenges relating to the GMO legislation's capacity to keep pace with scientific developments … [T]here are strong indications that it is not fit for purpose for some NGTs and their products, and that it needs to be adapted to scientific and technological progress.[19]

The European Commission then launched a public consultation process, which ended in July 2022 and presented a proposal for a Regulation 'on plants obtained by certain new genomic techniques and their food and feed, and amending Regulation (EU) 2017/625'[20] on July 5, 2023, aimed at introducing a more specific and updated regulation regarding new genomic techniques. The proposal highlights how NGTs can contribute to addressing current challenges in the agrifood sector from climate change and biodiversity loss which demand the development of a more sustainable food chain and more resilient agricultural system.

The proposal divides plants, food, and feed produced by genetic breeding techniques into two categories. The first (the proposal refers to this group as NGT 1) includes plants modified by site-directed mutagenesis or cisgenesis that could also occur spontaneously or be considered as equivalent to those obtained by conventional techniques. In this case, the proposal provides for a more streamlined authorisation process, consisting in a verification procedure. The second (the proposal refers to this group as NGT 2) includes all other plants, foods, or feed resulting from the application of new techniques that do not fall into the first category. Regarding this second group, current GMO regulations would still apply, albeit with some adaptations (eg Article 26b of Directive 2001/18 does not apply with the consequence that Member States would not be able to prohibit, in whole or in part, within their territory, the

---

19 Commission, 'Study on the status of new genomic techniques under Union law and in light of the Court of Justice ruling in Case C-528/16' SWD (2021) 92 final. See also the opinion of EFSA, 'Overview of EFSA and European national authorities' scientific opinions on the risk assessment of plants developed through New Genomic Techniques' (2021) 19 (4) EFSA Journal 6314 <https://www.efsa.europa.eu/en/efsajournal/pub/6314> accessed 23 February 2025.

20 Commission, 'Proposal for a Regulation of the European Parliament and of the Council on plants obtained by certain new genomic techniques and their food and feed, and amending Regulation (EU) 2017/625' COM (2023) 411 final.

cultivation of the new plant species, as, on the contrary, is the case for GMOs).[21] However specific coexistence measures would need to be adopted to avoid possible 'contamination' with conventional and organic crops.[22] Regarding organic cultivation specifically, the EU proposal excludes all NGT plants from this sector (regardless of whether the plant can be qualified as NGT 1 or NGT 2), precluding the possibility of qualifying edited species as organic.[23]

In December 2025, the EU Commission, the EU Parliament, and the EU Council reached an agreement on the provisional text of the regulation.[24] At the end of January 2026, the European Parliament's ENVI Committee also gave

---

21 See Directive 2001/18/EC (as amended by Directive 2015/412) Art 26b, para 3: 'Where no demand was made pursuant to paragraph 1 of this Article, or where the notifier/applicant has confirmed the geographical scope of its initial notification/application, a Member State may adopt measures restricting or prohibiting the cultivation in all or part of its territory of a GMO, or of a group of GMOs defined by crop or trait, once authorised in accordance with Part C of this Directive or with Regulation (EC) No 1829/2003, provided that such measures are in conformity with Union law, reasoned, proportional and non-discriminatory and, in addition, are based on compelling grounds such as those related to: (a) environmental policy objectives; (b) town and country planning; (c) land use; (d) socioeconomic impacts; (e) avoidance of GMO presence in other products without prejudice to Article 26a; (f) agricultural policy objectives; (g) public policy. [...]'. By this provision, States can exclude (totally or partially) the cultivation of GMOs from their territory. For example, Italy, through Legislative Decree 227/2016, has banned cultivation throughout its national territory. With regard to the Italian situation, see Section 4.

22 With regard to GMOs and coexistence measures, see Mario Mauro 'OGM e coesistenza: il punto sulla disciplina europea, alla luce degli orientamenti della Corte di giustizia. Ultimo atto prima di una riforma?' [2023] Rivista di diritto alimentare 71 <https://flore.unifi.it/retrieve/c5333fdd-7732-4749-8fbb-56b79bcbfef5/Ogm%20e%20coesistenza.pdf> accessed 23 February 2025.

23 Particularly, this is specified by Recital 23 of the EU proposal that, after the amendments of EU Parliament, states: 'Regulation (EU) 2018/848 of the European Parliament and the Council on organic production and labelling of organic products and repealing Council Regulation (EC) 834/2007(47) prohibits the use of GMOs and products from and by GMOs in organic production. It defines GMOs for the purposes of that Regulation by reference to Directive 2001/18/EC, excluding from the prohibition GMOs which have been obtained through the techniques of genetic modification listed in Annex 1.B of Directive 2001/18/EC. As a result, category 2 NGT plants will be banned in organic production. However, it is necessary to clarify the status of category 1 NGT plants for the purposes of organic production. Currently, the compatibility of the use of new genomic techniques with the principles of organic production requires further consideration. The use of category 1 NGT plants should therefore be prohibited in organic production, until such further consideration takes place'.

24 See press release, Council of the EU, on December 4th, 2025, <https://www.consilium.europa.eu/en/press/press-releases/2025/12/04/new-genomic-techniques-council-and-parliament-strike-deal-to-boost-the-competitiveness-and-sustainability-of-our-food-systems/pdf/> accessed on February 7th, 2026.

its approval.[25] Although formal approval by the Council and Parliament is still pending, the future outlook appears positive, with a move towards greater openness to innovation in agriculture.

As explicitly outlined by the European Commission in its 2021 study,[26] NGTs are aligned with the goals of the European Green Deal and the 'Farm to Fork Strategy'.[27] Therefore, assuming the field is able to balance the various aspects of agrifood biotechnology, including the protection of human health and the environment, NGTs seem poised to contribute to the EU's broader sustainability objectives.

4 The Italian Scenario

With this background in mind, it is interesting to examine Italy's scenario: although the country has always been opposed to GMOs, it exhibits a more open approach to NGTs.

In Italy, the use of biotechnology in the agrifood sector has been generally perceived with a high degree of scepticism, particularly in the case of GMOs. Beginning with the so-called 'Amato Decree', adopted on August 4, 2000 to block the entry of four GM corn variants into Italian territory, the legislative approach reveals a general closure to new 'biotech' innovations.[28] As of today, Italy prohibits the cultivation of genetically modified organisms across its

---

25 See the Result of roll-call votes on January 28th, 2026 of Committee on Environment, Climate and Food Safety https://www.europarl.europa.eu/cmsdata/302166/2026-01-28%20votes.pdf accessed on February 7th, 2026.

26 See Commission, *Study on the status of new genomic techniques under Union law and in light of the Court of Justice ruling in Case C-528/16*, SWD (2021) 92 final. This document stated that '*several of the plant products obtained from NGTs have the potential to contribute to the objectives of the EU's Green Deal and in particular to the "farm to fork" and biodiversity strategies and the United Nations' sustainable development goals (SDGs) for a more resilient and sustainable agri-food system. Examples include plants more resistant to diseases and environmental conditions or climate change effects in general, improved agronomic or nutritional traits, reduced use of agricultural inputs (including plant protection products) and faster plant breeding*', 2.

27 Commission, *A Farm to Fork Strategy for a fair, healthy and environmentally-friendly food system*, COM (2020) 381 final that stated 'New innovative techniques, including biotechnology and the development of bio-based products, may play a role in increasing sustainability, provided they are safe for consumers and the environment while bringing benefits for society as a whole. They can also accelerate the process of reducing dependency on pesticides'.

28 With regard to the history of Italian regulation on GMOs, see Roberto Defez and others, 'The history of GM crops in Italy: After two decades of a *de facto* ban, the engagement

entire territory, however, it does not prevent the import and marketing of such products from abroad. For example, animal feed represents a large portion of the GMOs imported into Italy for food use and GM products for human consumption from other Member States are available in Italian supermarkets.[29]

With regard to Italian legislation relating to GMOs, Legislative Decree 224/2003 adopted EU Directive 2001/18 in line with the precautionary principle to protect human, animal, and environmental health. Furthermore, following the enactment of Directive 2015/412, which introduced the option for Member States to ban or restrict the cultivation of GMOs, Italy adopted Legislative Decree 227/2016 forbidding the cultivation of GMOs from all of its territory.

Today, the debate on biotechnology is focused on the possible use of NGTs—these more sophisticated tools seem to be viewed in a different light. The need to address the challenge of sustainability for the agrifood field, as well as the impact of climate change, and the more precise nature of these new techniques, have resulted in not only less scepticism but also significant support (from both the scientific and political arenas) for their experimentation.

Italy refers to these new techniques with the expression 'Assisted Evolution Techniques' (TEA).[30] This linguistic choice is due to the fear that the public may connect the term 'genomic' to the term 'genetic' thus evoking the GMO pushback and the feeling that new products resulting from technological processes are unnatural. The new expression instead refers to the idea of a natural evolution and seems to be more comprehensible to the general public and better able to convey a positive image about the new techniques.

With regard to the regulatory framework, initially NGTs fell under the same regulation as GMOs. Later, however, Law Decree 39/2023 (converted to Law 68/2023) introduced an important novelty in this area of research: it consented to the cultivation of organisms produced by genome editing techniques through site-directed mutagenesis or cisgenesis for experimental and scientific purposes.[31] Of particular importance, Law Decree 39/2023 amends Legislative

of farmers and scientists has prompted the Italian government to allow field-testing of NGT/TEA plants again' (2025) 26 EMBO Rep.

29 Bressanini (n 3), 102–103.

30 See the document of Italian Society of Agricultural Genetics (SIGA), *Tecnologie per l'evoluzione assistita—un nuovo nome alle tecnologie, non alle piante* (SIGA 2020) <http://www.geneticagraria.it/SSR_dett.asp?a_pag=7&id=54> accessed 23 February 2025.

31 See Law Decree 39/2023 (converted in Law 68/23), art 9 *bis*. Originally, the deadline to conduct research activities in this field was December 31, 2024, but the term was initially extended by the Law Decree 63/2024 (converted in Law 101/2024) and then also by the 2026 Budget Law (Law 199/2025 that extend the term for all 2026 and 2027). In addition,

Decree 224/2003 on GMOs, introducing this possibility just for these recent techniques. This change represents an interesting inflection point: it constitutes the first autonomous 'opening' of Italy towards agrifood biotechnology which was, in the past, treated with hostility and the total block of its use in agriculture.

It should be noted that this novelty came accompanied by a set of measures addressing the water crisis and an attempt to identify new adaptation strategies from a climate resilience perspective. The new plant species could, thus, represent a part of a 'defense plan' aimed at withstanding environmental and biotic stresses, and contribute to the sustainability of the agrifood supply chain. As already mentioned, the dramatic effects of climate change and the functioning of the agrifood chain are deeply interconnected; for these reasons, scientific innovation could be part of a preservation strategy for the future. NGTs seem to represent one of the tools that can provide a significant contribution in terms of sustainability of production, maintaining high levels of safety, and helping to ensure food security.

For NGTs, the authorisation procedure is expected to last no longer than 65 days and identifies the competent authority in the Ministry of the Environment and Energy Security. In this process, the *Istituto Superiore per la Protezione e la Ricerca Ambientale* (Higher Institute for Environmental Protection and Research) (ISPRA) has a central evaluation role, formulating an appropriate opinion on the application received.

Thanks to this, some applications for experimentation have already been submitted. The first was presented by a research group at the University of Milan to cultivate a rice variety modified by CRISPR to be resistant to a fungus (*Pyricularia oryzae*) that is responsible for the most harmful disease affecting rice plants.[32]

---

it must be considered that Art 82, para 1, of the 2025 Budget Law (Law 207/2024) grants a contribution of 3 million euros for each of the years 2025, 2026, and 2027 to the Council for Agricultural Research and Analysis of Agriculture Economics (CREA), in order to continue research activities on NGTs for experimental and scientific purposes.

32 Particularly, the first field trial of edited crops started in Spring 2024, as a result of the *RIS8ttimo* project, led by Vittoria Brambilla and Fabio Fornara, which aimed to test 'edited' rice seedlings. However, despite the importance of this first experiment (which also has the merit of having 'paved the way' for the submission of further applications), during the night of June 20–21, 2024, the field was devastated by a serious act of vandalism. On this case, see Anna Meldolesi, 'La prima sperimentazione in campo di una pianta editata potrebbe iniziare in primavera' (*Nature Italy* 2024) <https://www.nature.com/articles/d43978-024-00018-1> accessed 23 February 2025; Roberto Defez, 'Gli ecoterroristi responsabili di aver distrutto i campi sperimentali di riso' *Il Foglio* (Milan-Rome, 22 June

In addition to these important opening steps, the Italian Government has expressed a favourable position towards the proposed EU Regulation, considering the act to be necessary to addressing climate change. This opinion is significant, especially because it comes from institutions which have always shown relative scepticism towards innovation in the agrifood sector and a country that is particularly attached to its food traditions, which represent not just nourishment, but a cultural and social heritage to be preserved and handed down. The NGTs do not seem to clash with this idea; on the contrary, they could possibly protect native foods, which could be at risk to adverse climates or diseases.

4 A Crucial Role for the Law: Some Concluding Remarks

Analysis of the complex biotechnology regulatory framework is hard to fully encompass in a few pages. This is due to several reasons already previously outlined (ie the different levels of regulation, the fact that by their nature they touch on different subject areas, and the plurality of constitutionally-relevant values at issue). However, while the debate on GMOs today seems to be stuck in time, the topic of biotechnology in the agrifood sector appears to be opening thanks to the emergence of New Genomic Techniques. The scientific community has long been advocating for a change in terms of regulation (eg the need for a redefinition of the legal notion of 'genetically modified organism', the possibility of carrying out different assessments depending on the technique used, and the context in reference) to promote greater openness to innovation in the agrifood sector.

At the same time, the growing awareness of mankind's manipulative capacity of nature has affirmed the need to strike a new balance, not only from an environmental perspective, but also considering ecosystems and future generations.[33] The precautionary approach should not be completely abandoned, but a greater dialogue between scientists, farmers, and legal scholars is appropriate, as is a more efficient information system, aimed at objectively reporting the scientific facts. This dialogue should keep in mind that modern biotechnology does not aim to supplant traditional practices, rather it can contribute to addressing sustainability-related challenges and, in general, to the enhancement of the agrifood sector.

2024) <https://www.ilfoglio.it/cronaca/2024/06/22/news/gli-ecoterroristi-responsabili-di-aver-distrutto-i-campi-sperimentali-di-riso-tea-non-prevarranno-6674517/>.

33 Antonio D'Aloia, 'Generazioni future', *Enciclopedia del diritto—Annali IX* (2016) 311.

Indeed, with food at the centre of the 2030 Agenda, modern biotechnology represents a key element in the fight against poverty and climate change. From this perspective, the research of alternative methods of production, such as biotechnological innovation seems necessary. Furthermore, in addition to the scientific evolution that has allowed for more refined, less invasive and artificial methods, a 'new' cultural approach has taken root, looking to make more sustainable what was not or is no longer sustainable, in the face of social, natural, scientific, and economic growth—in an attempt to protect the present and the future.

Regulating NGTs therefore emerges as a strategic approach to innovating within agrifood systems, under the driving force of the principle of sustainability and the obvious need to mitigate climate change. In this case, the law is called upon to reformulate the regulatory framework with new definitions that are more responsive to scientific findings, and/or through the modification of existing rules that introduce more appropriate procedures.[34] Obviously, biotechnology techniques are evolving, which demands in-depth evaluation prior to its practical application. Anyway, the law cannot simply accept the scientific facts; it has a more complex role.[35] It must carry out a deeper investigation aimed at understanding social needs and take the measures necessary to manage the uncertainty inherent to this field and seek a balance between the different constitutional values involved.[36]

Bibliography

Albisinni F, 'Scienze della vita, produzione agricola e lawmakers: una relazione incerta' [2018] (5) Rivista italiana di diritto pubblico comunitario 729.

Alemanno A and Gabbi S (eds), *Foundations of EU Food Law and Policy. Ten Years of the European Food Safety Authority* (Routledge 2016).

Bevilacqua D, 'Le definizioni di OGM, le intenzioni del legislatore e il bilanciamento degli interessi' [2019] Giornale di diritto amministrativo 377.

Bressanini D, *OGM tra leggende e realtà* (Zanichelli 2018).

34 Ferdinando Albisinni, 'Scienze della vita, produzione agricola e lawmakers: una relazione incerta' [2018] (5) Rivista italiana di diritto pubblico comunitario 729.

35 Antonio D'Aloia, 'Natura, scienza, diritto: relazione incrociate' (2020) III Rivista di Diritto costituzionale 2611.

36 Lucia Corso, 'Il diritto come mediazione fra saperi distinti. Perché il diritto non ha fatto un passo indietro di fronte alla scienza' [2018] (36) Stato, Chiese e pluralismo confessionale 1 <https://riviste.unimi.it/index.php/statoechiese/article/view/10835> accessed 23 February 2025.

Corona D, *L'attuazione della Direttiva UE 2015/412: un nuovo capitolo nell'intricata saga dell'autorizzazione degli OGM nell'Unione Europea*, in Ginevra Cerrina Feroni, Tommaso Edoardo Frosini, Luca Mezzetti and Pier Luigi Petrillo (eds), *Ambiente, energia, alimentazione. Modelli giuridici comparati per lo sviluppo sostenibile*, vol 1, II (Cesifin 2016).

Corso L, 'Il diritto come mediazione fra saperi distinti. Perché il diritto non ha fatto un passo indietro di fronte alla scienza' (2018) Stato, Chiese e pluralismo confessionale 1.

D'Aloia A, 'Generazioni future' in *Enciclopedia del diritto—Annali* IX (2016) 311.

D'Aloia A, '*Natura, scienza, diritto: relazioni incrociate*' (2020) 3 Rivista di Diritto costituzionale 2611.

Defez R, *Il caso OGM. Il dibattito sugli organismi geneticamente modificati* (Carocci 2016).

Defez R, Errigo MC, Formici G, Scaffardi L, Sirsi E, Fornara F and Brambilla V, 'The history of GM crops in Italy: After two decades of a de facto ban, the engagement of farmers and scientists has prompted the Italian government to allow field-testing of NGT/TEA plants again' (2024) 26 EMBO Rep.

Doudna J and Sternberg S, *Il futuro della vita* (Mondadori 2022).

Gabbi S, *L'Autorità Europea per la sicurezza alimentare. Genesi, aspetti problematici e prospettive di riforma* (Giuffrè 2009).

Lupo A, 'Il diritto al cibo nella crisi climatica tra sicurezza e "sostenibilità" alimentare' [2023] (2) Biolaw Journal 277.

Mariani S, 'New Breeding Techniques e ogm: le innovazioni in agricoltura al vaglio della Corte di Giustizia: il caso della mutagenesi sito-diretta (causa C-528/16)' (2019) 3 Rivista di Diritto e giurisprudenza agraria, alimentare e dell'ambiente 1.

Mauro M, 'OGM e coesistenza: il punto sulla disciplina europea, alla luce degli orientamenti della Corte di giustizia. Ultimo atto prima di una riforma?' [2023] Rivista di diritto alimentare 71.

Meldolesi A, *E l'uomo creò l'uomo. CRISPR e la rivoluzione dell'editing genomico* (Bollati Boringhieri 2017).

Palmer Amanda C, 'Golden Rice: a quarter-century of innovation, challenges, and the promise of better nutrition' (2025, July 2) The Journal of Nutrition.

Porpora M, 'Gli OGM e la frammentazione della Governance nel settore alimentare' [2015] (6) Rivista italiana di Diritto Pubblico Comunitario 1661.

Potrykus I, 'The "Golden Rice" tale' (2001) 37 in Vitro Cellular Development Biology-Plant 93.

Rinella A and Pungitore C, *Organismi geneticamente modificati. Profili di diritto comparato ed europeo* (Filodiritto 2015).

Rossi Dal Pozzo F, 'Profili recenti in tema di organismi geneticamente modificati nel settore agroalimentare fra procedure di comitato e tutela giurisdizionale' [2014] Il diritto del commercio internazionale 339.

Rossi Dal Pozzo F, 'Le nuove tecniche genomiche e il loro impiego nel settore agroalimentare. L'Unione europea alla ricerca di una disciplina giuridica sostenibile' in Lorenza Violini (ed), *One Health, Dal paradigma alle implicazioni giuridiche* (Giappichelli 2022).

Sunstein C, *Law of Fear: Beyond the Precautionary Principle* (CUP 2005).

CHAPTER 9

Technological Innovation for Food Loss and Waste Reduction: An International Law Perspective

Luca Romano

Summary

1 Introduction

Every year since 2020, Member States and specialised agencies of the United Nations (UN) system, together with other international actors, have marked September 29th as 'International Day of Awareness of Food Loss and Waste'. The decision to observe an international day on this matter was made by the UN General Assembly on 19 December 2019, through the adoption of Resolution 74/209.[1] The preamble of this resolution contains an explanation of the reasons for this decision, related to the magnitude of global food loss and waste (FLW) and the 'urgent need to address th[is] issue … worldwide and the risks that this implies for climate change, agriculture sustainability, human livelihoods and food supplies'.[2] As clear as this statement may be in emphasising the seriousness of the problem, it was not the first time that the importance of FLW was mentioned at the international level. Previous high-level political declarations had already underlined the matter,[3] and the objective of reducing

1 UN General Assembly, *International Day of Awareness of Food Loss and Waste,* UN Doc. A/RES/74/209 of 19 December 2019.

2 Ibid, Preamble, thirteenth recital.

3 See the ministerial declaration of the 2018 high-level political forum on sustainable development, UN General Assembly, *Proposed programme budget for 2021,* UN Doc. E/HLS/2018/1

HTTPS://DOI.ORG/10.1163/9789004740907-011

FLW was also included in the widely known 2030 Agenda for Sustainable Development, adopted by the UN General Assembly in 2015.[4]

In recent years, the attention given to FLW—including through initiatives such as the International Day of Awareness—has contributed to a general strengthening of efforts to limit its impact. This can be achieved either by preventing the occurrence of FLW or by reducing its consequences, eg by recovering some of the components of wasted food and redirecting them to other purposes. Technological innovation plays a relevant role in the implementation of these efforts.

The analysis of how and to what extent technological innovations can contribute to addressing FLW has been explored extensively within the ON Foods Project, from which this volume also originates.[5] More specifically, the relationship between innovation and FLW has also been analysed from a legal perspective in other chapters in this volume, focusing on national legal systems.[6] However, given the nature of FLW as a global issue, affecting each State in a variable manner, yet involving concerns common to the entire international community, it seems appropriate to also analyse it from the perspective of international law, which is the one adopted in this chapter.

The main purpose of this chapter is to understand whether, and to what extent, current international instruments promote the use of technological innovation in preventing and reducing FLW. To this end, the analysis is structured as follows. First, it is intended to frame the problem of FLW and, consequently, technological innovation as a possible solution to this issue. As will be discussed, beyond certain undeniably positive aspects, implementation of technological solutions also entails inherent challenges, which must be adequately considered. Second, this chapter will focus on the most relevant international, legally-binding instruments that regulate State conduct with the objective of promoting technology innovation to prevent and reduce FLW.

of 1 August 2018, para 26, which called upon 'all stakeholders to adopt a sustainable food systems approach and to develop effective strategies and innovations to reduce food losses and waste'.

4 UN General Assembly, *Transforming our World: The 2030 Agenda for Sustainable Development*, UN Doc. A/RES/70/1 of 21 October 2015. Target 12.3, in particular, calls on States to halve global per capita food waste at the retail and consumer levels and to reduce food losses along production and supply chains as a means of ensuring sustainable consumption and production patterns by 2030. See ibid, 22.

5 More information on this project can be found at <https://www.onfoods.it/about-onfoods> accessed 24 July 2025.

6 See infra, Chapters 11, 12 and 13.

Finally, attention will be placed on State practice in the adoption of instruments of a non-binding legal nature in this area.

Before moving on to the next sections, it is necessary to stress, at the methodological level, the boundaries within which this study was developed. First, attention is centred on States as primary subjects of international law, although different actors can have an impact on food production and consumption patterns, including private food operators—such as national and multinational companies—and civil society organisations. Second, the focus will be placed on legal instruments with universal scope adopted in the areas of sustainable development and human rights protection, leaving regional instruments outside the scope of analysis.[7] Third, although technological innovation to address FLW is an area of concern also in developed countries, the problem of access to such technology will be considered primarily from the perspective of developing countries. Fourth, this inquiry will mainly cover issues related to 'technological innovation', broadly understood as the development and implementation of new or improved technologies, tools, systems, and processes. While innovation can also occur in political or social spheres—both of which play an essential role in managing the FLW problem[8]—attention will be limited to technical and technological advancements. Finally, issues related to intellectual property rights as barriers to technology use and dissemination will not be addressed, as they are already discussed in another chapter in this volume.[9]

---

7 To mention just a few studies on the topic of FLW within the European Union (EU) framework, see Luis González Vaqué, 'Food Loss and Waste in the European Union: A New Challenge for the Food Law?' (2015) 10 European Food & Feed Law Review 20; Nicola Lucifero, 'Food Loss and Waste in the EU Law between Sustainability of Well-Being and the Implications on Food System and on the Environment' (2016) 8 Agriculture and Agricultural Science Procedia 282; Laura Costantino, *La problematica degli sprechi nella filiera agroalimentare. Profili introduttivi* (Cacucci editore 2018); Beatrice Garske and others, 'Challenges of Food Waste Governance: An Assessment of European Legislation on Food Waste and Recommendations for Improvement by Economic Instruments' (2020) 9 (7) Land 1; David Röttgen and Francesca Allocco, 'Food Waste in EU Food Law' in Cinzia Caporale, Ilja R Pavone and Maria P Ragionieri (eds), *International Food Law: How Food Law Can Balance Health, Environment and Animal Welfare* (Wolters Kluwer 2021), 305.

8 FAO-CIHEAM, *Mediterra 2016. Zero Waste in the Mediterranean. Natural Resources, Food and Knowledge* (Paris 2016), 281.

9 See supra, Chapter 3.

2 Food Loss and Waste and Technological Innovation: Framing the Problem

FLW represents a multifaceted global challenge, often labelled as a 'wicked problem', due to the complexities that arise in the attempt to define, measure, and effectively address it, either by preventing it before it happens or minimising it in the least detrimental way. To establish a coherent understanding of this issue, it is necessary to answer three main questions: what constitutes FLW; why is it significant; and how can it be effectively mitigated. In this context, the role of technological innovation emerges as a critical avenue for addressing this global issue, which, while offering potential solutions, also presents its own set of challenges.

2.1 *Food Loss and Waste as a Complex Global Issue*

The obstacles encountered in tackling FLW worldwide are rooted in the uncertainties that surround this problem, starting with its definition. Indeed, from a scientific point of view, there is no unequivocal, universally accepted definition of 'food waste' and 'food loss'; rather, the two terms are differently understood, depending on the context in which they are used.[10]

Because of this indeterminacy—not only at the scientific level, but even at the intergovernmental level[11]—despite growing international recognition of FLW, no universally agreed-upon definition exists.[12]

10 For example, some scholars, on the one hand, distinguish between food loss and food waste based on the stage of the food supply chain at which the loss or waste of food occurs. Others, however, distinguish based on whether it is 'voluntary' (waste), eg the result of an explicit choice, or not (loss). Still others may adopt yet different approaches. This inevitably limits the possibility of comparing the results of studies conducted on FLW and of reconstructing a sufficiently precise overall picture of its extent: High Level Panel of Experts on Food Security and Nutrition (HLPE), *Food Losses and Waste in the Context of Sustainable Food Systems. A Report by the High Level Panel of Experts on Food Security and Nutrition of the Committee on World Food Security* (Rome 2014), 21–22.

11 Efforts to reach a common definition of FLW have been made at the regional level, with varying approaches. For instance, within the EU system, references to FLW have been subsumed under the general term 'food waste', which reflects the broad category of all food that is wasted, regardless of the step in the supply chain where the waste occurs. In this regard, see Röttgen and Allocco (n 7), 306–307, 336.

12 For an overview of the historical evolution of FLW definitions at the international level, see Monica Delsignore, Margherita Ramajoli and Carola Ricci, 'Defining the Meaning of Food Waste as a Matter of Urgency' in Piergiuseppe Morone, Franka Papendiek and Valentina Elena Tartiu (eds), *Food Waste Reduction and Valorisation: Sustainability Assessment and Policy Analysis* (Springer 2017), 219 ff.

A key reference in this regard is the above-mentioned UN General Assembly's Resolution 74/209, establishing the International Day of Awareness of FLW, that adopted definitions initially proposed by the Food and Agriculture Organisation (FAO).[13] These definitions distinguish between 'food loss', considered to be 'the decrease in the quantity or quality of food resulting from decisions and actions by food suppliers in the chain, excluding retail, food service providers and consumers', and 'food waste', which is 'the decrease in the quantity or quality of food resulting from decisions and actions by retailers, food services and consumers'.[14]

While these distinctions have gained broad acceptance, many ambiguities remain. These include, for instance, whether only edible parts should be classified as lost or wasted and how the notion of 'edible food' should be defined across different cultural contexts.[15] Additionally, the classification of food redirected for non-human uses (eg as biomass or animal feed) and qualitative losses in nutritional value remain unresolved, impeding the establishment of a common understanding of the issue.

In addition to these ambiguities, other aspects of food production and consumption may fall outside the definition of FLW as adopted by FAO and the UN General Assembly. For instance, one could mention food that deteriorates before it is harvested,[16] or the excess consumed due to overnutrition in certain segments of the global population. Such food, if redirected, could contribute to meeting the needs of individuals facing food insecurity and may arguably be considered a form of wasted food.[17] How these uncertainties are addressed largely depends on the context in which FLW is analysed and monitored.

---

13 FAO, *The State of Food and Agriculture 2019. Moving Forward on Food Loss and Waste Reduction* (Rome 2019), 70.

14 UN General Assembly (n 1), Preamble, ninth recital.

15 See Sohyun Jeong and Jeehyun Lee, 'Effects of Cultural Background on Consumer Perception and Acceptability of Foods and Drinks: A Review of Latest Cross-Cultural Studies' (2021) 42 Current Opinion in Food Science 248.

16 See eg Luciana Delgado, Monica Schuster and Maximo Torero, 'Quantity and Quality Food Losses across the Value Chain: A Comparative Analysis' (2021) 98 Food Policy 4, which holds that a standard definition and terminology around FLW is not sufficient 'to identify the underlying causes and potential solutions to food loss and waste or to monitor specific progress on reduction targets. To be most useful, the definition should … include pre-harvest losses'.

17 Zach Conrad and others, 'Relationship Between Food Waste, Diet Quality and Environmental Sustainability' (2018) 13 (4) PLoS ONE 1. Silvio Franco and others, 'Overnutrition Is a Significant Component of Food Waste and Has a Large Environmental Impact' (2022) 12 Scientific Reports 1.

In addition to definitional problems, there is widespread difficulty in measuring FLW, due as much to a lack of adequate instruments for its measurement as the intrinsic complexity of the problem. As for the latter, it is important to note that the drivers of FLW vary significantly across regions and at different stages of the food supply chain. In other words, FLW does not have uniform causes in different parts of the world, with contributing factors ranging from inadequate production and storage infrastructure—usually associated with the first stages of developing country supply chains—to market inefficiencies and consumer misbehaviour, more frequently connected to 'food waste' in developed countries.[18] As regards the former, accurately measuring FLW remains a significant obstacle, with data widely varying across countries. Many developing States also lack comprehensive mechanisms for tracking loss, further complicating global efforts to quantify the problem effectively. Therefore, when it comes to evaluating the extent of FLW at the international level,[19] a critical lack of available data, as highlighted by existing studies, has resulted in aggregate indices that are mainly based on vague and incomplete information.[20]

Despite the above-mentioned difficulties in understanding and measuring FLW, some estimates of its global scope and impact have been made. These statistics, although characterised by technical limitations, contribute significantly to establishing the seriousness of this problem. FLW undermines efforts to develop sustainable food systems, which aim to provide food security and nutrition without compromising future resources.[21] According to FAO, approx-

---

18 FAO, IFAD, UNICEF, WFP and WHO, *The State of Food Security and Nutrition in the World 2019. Safeguarding against economic slowdowns and downturns* (Rome 2019), 25 ff.

19 Difficulties are also encountered at the regional level, although in these contexts it has been possible to obtain more precise results. Within the EU, for example, Member States are required to measure food waste production data in accordance with the European Commission Delegated Decision (EU) 2019/1597 of 3 May 2019, supplementing Directive 2008/98/EC of the European Parliament and of the Council as regards a common methodology and minimum quality requirements for the uniform measurement of levels of food waste. Against this background, according to Eurostat, data concerning food waste estimates at the EU level 'are considered stable and several countries have improved the measurement methodology': Eurostat, 'Food Waste and Food Waste Prevention—Estimates' <https://ec.europa.eu/eurostat/statistics-explained/index.php?title=Food_waste_and_food_waste_prevention_-_estimates> accessed 24 July 2025.

20 See eg Jenny Gustavsson and others, *The Methodology of the FAO Study: 'Global Food Losses and Food Waste—Extent, Causes and Prevention'* (SIK 2013), 3.

21 See, *ex multis*, Renzo Akkerman and Frans Cruijssen, 'Food Loss, Food Waste, and Sustainability in Food Supply Chains' in Yann Bouchery, Charles J Corbett, Jan C Fransoo and Tarkan Tan (eds), *Sustainable Supply Chains: A Research-Based Textbook on Operations*

imately 14% of global food production is lost post-harvest,[22] and, according to the UN Environment Programme (UNEP), 17% is wasted at the retail and consumer levels,[23] suggesting that nearly one-third of all food produced is lost or wasted annually. The environmental and economic costs of FLW are substantial, wasting water, land, and energy resources. FAO estimates, for instance, that 28% of global arable land is used to produce food that is never consumed.[24] Moreover, FLW is responsible for 8–10% of global greenhouse gas (GHG) emissions,[25] while contributing to widespread food insecurity[26] in a world where over 700 million people suffer from hunger and more than 2 billion lack regular access to adequate food.[27]

In the face of such serious consequences, numerous solutions have been identified to prevent and reduce the occurrence of FLW, one of which is the essential role played by technological innovation.[28]

---

and Strategy (Springer 2024), 219. For a definition of sustainable food systems, see FAO, *Sustainable Food Systems: Concept and Framework* (Rome 2018), 2: 'food systems that deliver food security and nutrition for all in such a way that the economic, social and environmental bases to generate food security and nutrition for future generations are not compromised'.

22 See the food loss index, elaborated and periodically updated by FAO <https://www.fao.org/sustainable-development-goals-data-portal/data/indicators/1231-global-food-losses/en> accessed 24 July 2025.

23 See UNEP, *Food Waste Index Report 2024* (Nairobi 2024), 3.

24 FAO, *Food Wastage Footprint. Impacts on Natural Resources. Summary Report* (Rome 2013), 41.

25 Cheick Mbow and others, 'Food Security' in Priyadarshi R Shulka and others (eds), *Climate Change and Land: An IPCC Special Report on Climate Change, Desertification, Land Degradation, Sustainable Land Management, Food Security, and Greenhouse Gas Fluxes in Terrestrial Ecosystems* (IPCC 2019), 440 <https://www.ipcc.ch/site/assets/uploads/2019/11/SRCCL-Full-Report-Compiled-191128.pdf> accessed 24 July 2025.

26 Daniel Durán-Sandoval, Gemma Durán-Romero and Francesca Uleri, 'How Much Food Loss and Waste Do Countries with Problems with Food Security Generate?' (2023) 13 (3) Agriculture 1.

27 FAO, IFAD, UNICEF, WFP and WHO, *The State of Food Security and Nutrition in the World 2024—Financing to End Hunger, Food Insecurity and Malnutrition in all its Forms* (Rome 2024), 7.

28 Addisalem A Benyam, Tammara Soma and Evan Fraser, 'Digital Agricultural Technologies for Food Loss and Waste Prevention and Reduction: Global Trends, Adoption Opportunities and Barriers' (2021) 323 Journal of Cleaner Production 1; Federica Ciccullo and others, 'Implementing the Circular Economy Paradigm in the Agri-Food Supply Chain: The Role of Food Waste Prevention Technologies' (2021) 164 Resources, Conservation & Recycling 1.

2.2 *Implementing Technological Innovation as a Solution to Food Loss and Waste: Opportunities and Limitations*

First, it must be stressed that technological innovation is only one of the possible solutions to address FLW. Other solutions, for instance those related to consumer awareness and education towards waste reduction, or regulatory interventions to redirect food surpluses into food solidarity initiatives, may also contribute to this end. While this chapter focuses on technological innovation, it is assumed that this should be accompanied by other interventions in the food supply chain to prevent and reduce FLW.[29]

Several advanced technologies have been identified as effective tools to support FLW prevention and reduction efforts.[30] A number of these have also been studied by research partners under the auspices of the ON Foods project[31] and present significant examples of technological implementation on this topic. Some of these studies cover the development of technological solutions to prevent FLW along certain supply chains, such as new storage facilities to reduce FLW in the coffee chain[32] or new digital systems for the management of food and packaging waste in catering services.[33] Other studies focus on technologies to reduce FLW once it has already occurred, eg a method to extract valuable bioactive compounds (such as proteins, amino acids, and antimicrobial agents) from agrifood waste through fermentation.[34] Finally, a few studies look at technologies for both FLW prevention and reduction, for instance a method to analyse, categorise,[35] and extract useful bio-compounds from food waste

29 UN General Assembly, (n 1) Preamble, fourteenth recital.

30 For a general overview, see Oznur Oztuna Taner, 'Sustainable Food and Agriculture Production: Reducing Food Waste through Technological Advancements and Assessing Its Economic Impact' (2024) 5 (3) Research on World Agricultural Economy 144.

31 See supra (n 5).

32 ON Foods, 'New Technologies and Strategies to Preserve Roasted Coffee Beans and Reduce Food Waste' <https://onfoods.it/research-projects/new-technologies-and-strategies-preserve-roasted-coffee-beans-and-reduce-food> accessed 24 July 2025.

33 ON Foods, 'Digital and Cyber Physical Twins Framework for Food and Packaging Supply Chain Waste Control and Optimization', <https://onfoods.it/research-projects/digital-and-cyber-physical-twins-framework-food-and-packaging-supply-chain-waste> accessed 24 July 2025.

34 ON Foods, 'Fermentation of Agri-Food by Product/Waste to Obtain Bioactive Compounds Enriched Foods', <https://onfoods.it/research-projects/fermentation-agri-food-product waste-obtain-bioactive-compounds-enriched-foods> accessed 24 July 2025.

35 ON Foods, 'Comprehensive Characterization of Bioactive Compounds and/or Macromolecules from Food By-products and Wastes', <https://onfoods.it/research-projects/comprehensive-characterization-bioactive-compounds-andor-macromolecules-food> accessed 24 July 2025.

that can be reutilised to help create 'active packaging',[36] ie packaging that extends food shelf-life and, thus, contributes to food waste prevention.[37] All of these inventions, which represent only a small sample of the many technological solutions that are being developed and can be applied to the problem of FLW, are evidence of the considerable potential of technological innovation in this area.[38] Despite their level of sophistication, many of the technologies mentioned above are already in use in some form. However, to fully understand their potential benefits, and, more importantly, conceptualise their implementation at scale, these types of solutions require an in-depth investigation. As is often the case, the main barrier to achieving this is cost, which highlights the need for investment in this area.

The degree of complexity of FLW technologies varies depending on the context in which it is to be implemented. For instance, simpler technological innovations can be useful in the prevention of food loss that occurs in the early stages of the food chain, ie during the harvesting, storage, and transport phases. This is a problem that, as mentioned, particularly affects small-scale food producers in developing countries and often does not require technologically complex inventions in order to be addressed, but rather practical and economically accessible solutions (eg the use of low-temperature storage systems in fishing practices[39] or the installation of metal containers for harvested grain storage[40]). The identification of such solutions can lead to significant achievements in FLW prevention, significantly contributing to reducing its negative nutritional and environmental effects.[41]

36 For more information, see Vilásia Guimarães Martins and others, 'Innovative Packaging that Saves Food' in Charis M Galanakis (ed), *Saving Food: Production, Supply Chain, Food Waste and Food Consumption* (Academic Press 2019), 171.

37 ON Foods, 'Extraction of Bioactive Compounds and/or Macromolecules from Food By-products and Wastes' and ON Foods, 'New Solutions for Sustainable Bio-Based Food Packaging', <https://onfoods.it/research-projects/extraction-bioactive-compounds-andor-macromolecules-food-products-and-wastes> accessed 24 July 2025.

38 For an overview of current trends and key advances in technologies regarding agrifood systems, including for FLW reduction, see the Report of the UN Secretary General, *Agriculture Technology for Sustainable Development: Leaving No One Behind*, UN Doc. A/78/228 of 28 August 2023.

39 See WWF-UK, *Driven to Waste: The Global Impact of Food Loss and Waste on Farms. Woking* (WWF-UK 2021), 7 <https://files.worldwildlife.org/wwfcmsprod/files/Publication/file/6yoepbekgh_wwf_uk__driven_to_waste___the_global_impact_of_food_loss_and_waste_on_farms.pdf> accessed 24 July 2025.

40 FAO, *Household Metal Silos. Key Allies in FAO's Fight against Hunger* (Rome 2008), 1.

41 FAO, *Achieving SDG 2 without breaching the 1.5 °C threshold: A global roadmap, Part 1—How agrifood systems transformation through accelerated climate actions will help achieving food security and nutrition, today and tomorrow* (Rome 2023), 7.

Although these new technologies offer important benefits, their implementation is not without challenges. In contexts where they are most needed, such as in the case of small food producers, their use may be hindered by a lack of adequate funding and/or appropriate technical expertise.[42] Moreover, in some cases, promising solutions are not adequately embraced because of the farmers' cultural traditions. This highlights not only the need for funding to ensure economic access to such technologies,[43] but also for such funding to be appropriate in the regional and cultural context in which it is implemented and come with adequate technical support. In this regard, States have a central role in promoting FLW reduction through innovation, while concurrently ensuring that diverse interests and potential externalities are taken into consideration.

3 Technological Innovation for Food Loss and Waste Reduction: International Legally-Binding Instruments

The international legal framework lacks legally-binding instruments specifically targeting FLW. Nonetheless, there are legal instruments that provide a foundation for promoting technological innovations aimed at its prevention. Multilateral environmental agreements (MEAs) and human rights treaties, in particular, may indirectly support technological advancements that reduce FLW by addressing topics like climate change, biodiversity loss, and the right to food.[44]

As a particularly relevant example, the UN Framework Convention on Climate Change (UNFCCC; New York, 9 May 1992),[45] while not explicitly mentioning FLW, promotes international cooperation in developing technologies that reduce GHG emissions, including those from agriculture. Article 4, para 1, lett c) of the UNFCCC encourages the development and diffusion of technologies in sectors like agriculture and waste management that can be linked to FLW reduction. It can be argued, in this regard, that reducing FLW contributes to mitigating GHG emissions, aligning with the UNFCCC's broader

42 Luciana Delgado, Monica Schuster and Maximo Torero, 'Food Losses in Agrifood Systems: What We Know' (2023) 15 Annual Review of Resource Economics 41.

43 FAO, *Transforming Food and Agriculture to achieve the SDGs: 20 Interconnected Actions to Guide Decision-Makers* (Rome 2018), 35.

44 Kateřina Mitkidis and Adriana Šefčíková, 'Ensure Sustainable Consumption and Production Patterns (SDG 12)' in Ilias Bantekas and Francesco Seatzu (eds), *The UN Sustainable Development Goals: A Commentary* (Oxford University Press 2023), 888.

45 Entered into force on 21 March 1994, <https://unfccc.int/resource/docs/convkp/conveng.pdf> accessed 24 July 2025.

purpose. States Parties to this Convention are, therefore, encouraged, albeit not expressly requested, to integrate technological solutions for FLW into their national commitments on climate change. Remarkably, in 2023, at the 28th Conference of the Parties (COP) to the UNFCCC, the relevance of this topic was underscored through the adoption of the COP28 Leaders Declaration on Sustainable Agriculture, Resilient Food Systems, and Climate Action.[46] In this Declaration, 159 States and the European Union expressed their commitment to transitioning from GHG-emitting practices to more sustainable food production and consumption models, explicitly referring to the reduction of FLW as a key element to doing so. To this end, they pledged to strengthen their individual and shared efforts by 2025 to 'accelerate and scale science and evidence-based innovations' to increase sustainable productivity and production in agriculture and related domains.[47]

Another relevant MEA is the Convention on Biological Diversity (CBD; Rio De Janeiro, 5 June 1992),[48] which, again, while not explicitly addressing FLW, highlights the role of technological development and diffusion in the sustainable use of components of biological diversity. In particular, Article 16 of the CBD emphasises that access to and transfer of technologies are 'essential elements' for the conservation and sustainable use of biological diversity. This could be interpreted as indirectly supporting FLW reduction through sustainable agricultural practices. Also in this regard, decisions adopted by the COP to the CBD contain more explicit references to the FLW issue. In particular, the Kunming-Montreal Global Biodiversity Framework, adopted by COP 15 in 2022 as a strategic plan for the implementation of the Convention by 2050,[49] highlights both FLW reduction and technological innovation as part of its 23 targets for achieving the CBD's objectives. In doing so, first, it calls for urgent action by 2030 to 'reduce the global footprint of consumption in an equitable manner,

46 The text of the Declaration is available at <https://www.cop28.com/en/food-and-agriculture> accessed 24 July 2025.

47 Ibid para 4.

48 Entered into force on 29 December 1993, <https://www.cbd.int/doc/legal/cbd-en.pdf> accessed 24 July 2025.

49 Decision 15/4, *Kunming-Montreal Global Biodiversity Framework*, UN Doc. CBD/COP/DEC/15/4 of 19 December 2022, Annex. As outlined in para 3 therein, the Kunming-Montreal Global Biodiversity Framework sets out 'an ambitious plan to implement broad based action to bring about a transformation in our societies' relationship with biodiversity by 2030, in line with the 2030 Agenda for Sustainable Development ... and ensure that, by 2050, the shared vision of living in harmony with nature is fulfilled'. On its relevance as a soft-law instrument adopted in the context of the CBD, see Francesco Seatzu and Paolo Vargiu, 'The Legal Dimension of the Kunming-Montreal Framework in International Law' (2025) 41 Anuario Español de Derecho Internacional 531.

including through halving global food waste'.[50] Second, it stresses the need to 'strengthen capacity-building and development, access to and transfer of technology', particularly in developing countries, through the promotion of joint technological development and collaborative scientific research programmes for the conservation and sustainable use of biodiversity.[51]

With regard to international human rights law, FLW reduction is interconnected with the right to food, as enshrined in several international instruments, in particular the International Covenant on Economic, Social and Cultural Rights (ICESCR; New York, 16 December 1966).[52] Article 1, para 2, of the ICESCR, specifically, contains a list of detailed measures that States Parties to the Covenant shall take 'individually and through international co-operation' in recognition of the 'fundamental right of everyone to be free from hunger'. These include measures needed 'to improve methods of production, conservation and distribution of food ... in such a way as to achieve the most efficient development and utilization of natural resources'. An interconnection between this provision and the need to reduce FLW, including through the promotion of technological innovation, can be inferred even if it is not explicitly stated.[53]

Although the above-mentioned provisions can be linked to the need to promote technological innovation for FLW reduction, they lack specific commitments in this regard. Their formulation, while fostering dialogue, does not seem to fully provide for the appropriate instruments to achieve meaningful technological progress, particularly in terms of ensuring technology transfer to disadvantaged States.

In the context of MEAs, for example, the lack of a specific focus on FLW is part of a broader issue, related to the difficulties that developing States face in obtaining the technological and financial support needed to effectively implement these agreements. A notable example is the Global Environmental Facility (GEF), a multilateral environmental fund established in the aftermath of the 1992 UN Conference on Environment and Development (Rio De Janeiro, 3–14 June 1992) to finance projects addressing major environmental

50 Ibid target 16, 11.

51 Ibid target 20, 12.

52 Entered into force on 3 January 1976, <https://www.ohchr.org/sites/default/files/cescr.pdf> accessed 24 July 2025.

53 On the connection between FLW and the right to food, Anastasia Telesetsky, 'Waste Not, Want Not: The Right to Food, Food Waste and the Sustainable Development Goals' (2014) 42 Denver Journal of International Law and Policy 484; Laura Costantino (n 7), 39. See also FAO, *Food Loss and Waste and the Right to Adequate Food: Making the Connection* (Rome 2018), 17 ff.

challenges, including climate change and biodiversity loss. Although the GEF is an essential mechanism for the implementation of MEAs, it suffers from inadequate funding and administrative barriers, which may hamper effective access for many developing countries to these resources.[54] Furthermore, the allocation of available funds concerns multiple areas—such as energy transition and decarbonisation—that may take precedence on the international environmental agenda over technological innovation aimed at FLW reduction.

4 Soft-Law Rules on Technological Innovation and Food Loss and Waste

While explicit references to technological innovation for FLW are largely absent from international legally-binding instruments, there are several non-legally-binding instruments that could prove particularly relevant in this regard. A number of UN documents, in particular, emphasise the importance of general technological progress for the achievement of sustainable development. Recent examples include the UN's internal strategies for new technologies[55] and the 2024 Global Digital Compact.[56] Although not centred on FLW, these documents provide useful guidance on how States should approach technological innovation in this area.

Additionally, a number of States have focused their attention directly on the adverse effects of FLW and the actions needed to mitigate it. As a consequence, various soft-law instruments exist—such as resolutions, declarations, guidelines, and recommendations—that, despite their non-binding nature, play a significant role towards understanding States' views on FLW and the role of technological innovation in its reduction. A notable example is the call to promote 'investment and innovations based on traditional and scientific knowledge to reduce FLW' contained in the 2014 Policy Recommendations on Food Losses and Waste in the Context of Sustainable Food Systems, adopted

54 See, for instance, Ellis Kalaidjian, Stacy-ann Robinson, 'Reviewing the Nature and Pitfalls of Multilateral Adaptation Finance for Small Island Developing States' (2022) 36 Climate Risk Management 1.

55 See the 2018 Strategy on New Technologies, developed by the UN Secretary General to shape the UN's approach to the use of new technologies for the achievement of the 2030 Agenda for Sustainable Development, and the subsequent 2020 Road Map for Digital Cooperation <https://www.un.org/en/newtechnologies/images/pdf/SGs-Strategy-on-New-Technologies.pdf> accessed 24 July 2025.

56 Unanimously adopted by the UN General Assembly as an outcome document of the 2024 Summit of the Future, UN Doc. A/RES/79/1 of 22 September 2024, Annex I.

by the Committee on World Food Security (CFS), a UN intergovernmental body mandated to promote policy convergence on long-term food security and sustainability.[57] Another relevant example is UN General Assembly resolution 78/144 of 2023, focused on agricultural technology for sustainable development, which specifically stresses the need to reduce FLW through a series of measures, including 'improved production planning, the promotion of resource-efficient production and processing practices, improved processing, preservation and packing technologies, [and] improved transportation and logistics management …'.[58]

Against this background, one particularly relevant document is the Voluntary Code of Conduct for Reducing Food Waste and Losses (Code of Conduct), developed by FAO in June 2021.[59] This Code consists of a set of internationally and regionally recognised standards and principles that outline responsible practices for reducing FLW and promoting inclusive and sustainable food systems. It contains several references to technological innovation as a vital tool to address the direct and, especially, systemic causes of FLW, while also providing guidance on how such innovation should be pursued.

The FAO Code of Conduct highlights the responsibility of governments, private operators, international organisations, and civil society, including academia, to invest in research and development and promote innovation aimed at reducing FLW.[60] It also underscores the importance of ensuring that technological innovations take into consideration the needs of vulnerable groups and small-scale supply chain actors, such as indigenous peoples, through participatory processes.[61] This is particularly relevant, as it reflects a recognition by FAO Member States of the need to balance the goal of reducing FLW—crucial for the sustainable transformation of food systems—with the imperative to protect disadvantaged individuals and communities. This balance aligns with

57 CFS, *Report of the 41st Session of the Committee on World Food Security (Rome, 13–18 October 2014)*, 4 ff. <https://www.fao.org/fileadmin/templates/cfs/Docs1314/CFS41/FinalReport/CFS41_Final_Report_EN.pdf> accessed 24 July 2025.

58 UN General Assembly, *Agricultural technology for sustainable development*, UN Doc. A/RES/78/144 of 19 December 2023, para 11. This is the latest in a series of resolutions cyclically adopted by the General Assembly on the topic of agricultural technology for development, dating back to 2007. Specific references to FLW have been included since 2011.

59 Following a request from the FAO Committee on Agriculture in 2018, the Code of Conduct was developed by FAO through an inclusive process and subsequently endorsed by the 42nd Session of the FAO Conference on 14–18 June 2021: FAO, *Voluntary Code of Conduct for Food Loss and Waste Reduction* (Rome 2022).

60 Ibid paras 4.9 ff.

61 Ibid para 4.9.1.

the broader protection recognised in international law for the rights of peasants and indigenous peoples, particularly the right to preserve their traditional knowledge,[62] which is often threatened by modern agricultural and food production approaches and technologies. The 2007 UN Declaration on the Rights of Indigenous Peoples[63] and the 2018 UN Declaration on the Rights of Peasants and Other People Working in Rural Areas[64] provide specific examples of these safeguards.[65]

The FAO Code of Conduct further outlines the key measures States should adopt to foster innovation in FLW prevention, tailored to local needs and contexts. These include establishing adequate institutional and regulatory frameworks to facilitate knowledge exchange; creating platforms to bring together relevant stakeholders; and fostering public-private partnerships as a means of driving innovation.[66] Moreover, the Code identifies specific challenges related to FLW that require targeted innovation efforts, including the effects of climate change, conflicts, human migration, pandemics, and the needs of small-scale producers and other vulnerable groups.[67]

The importance of promoting technological innovation for reducing FLW is further emphasised by the UN Environment Assembly (UNEA), the plenary body of UNEP, in resolutions adopted in 2016[68] and 2019.[69]

UNEA Resolution 4/2 of 2019, titled 'Promoting Sustainable Practices and Innovative Solutions for Curbing Food Loss and Waste', merits particular attention. This resolution highlights the significant environmental impact of FLW

62 In this regard, see Simone Vezzani, 'The Protection of Traditional Knowledge of Agricultural Interest in International Law', in Antonietta Di Blase and Valentina Vadi (eds), *The Inherent Rights of Indigenous Peoples in International Law* (Roma TrE-Press 2020), 279.

63 UN General Assembly, *United Nations Declaration on the Rights of Indigenous Peoples*, UN Doc. A/RES/61/295 of 13 September 2007.

64 UN General Assembly, *United Nations Declaration on the Rights of Peasants and Other People Working in Rural Areas*, UN Doc. A/RES/73/165 of 17 December 2018.

65 For a more in-depth examination of these declarations, which cannot be covered here, see Simone Vezzani, 'Il Progetto di Dichiarazione sui diritti degli agricoltori: nuovi diritti germogliano?' (2013) 7 Diritti umani e diritto internazionale 211; Priscilla Claeys and Marc Edelman, 'The United Nations Declaration on the Rights of Peasants and Other People Working in Rural Areas' (2020) 47 The Journal of Peasant Studies 1; Federico Lenzerini, 'Declaration on the Rights of Indigenous Peoples (UNDRIP)' in Christina Binder and others (eds), *Elgar Encyclopedia of Human Rights* (Edward Elgar Publishing 2022) vol 1, 452.

66 FAO Code of Conduct paras 4.9.3.1–4.9.3.3.

67 Ibid para 4.9.4.4.

68 UNEA, *Resolution 2/9, Prevention, Reduction and Reuse of Food Waste*, UN Doc. UNEP/EA.2/Res.9 of 27 May 2016.

69 UNEA, *Resolution 4/2, Promoting Sustainable Practices and Innovative Solutions for Curbing Food Loss and Waste*, UN Doc. EA.4/Res.2 of 15 March 2019.

and the critical role that national governments, international organisations, technology providers, and end-users can play in introducing innovations that promote sustainable practices and reduce FLW. The resolution calls on UNEP Member States to take a range of actions to this end, including establishing mechanisms to monitor FLW, supporting the development and dissemination of best practices in cold food storage chains, promoting applied research on the impact of climate change on FLW generation, and redirecting excess food. However, while the UNEA resolution demonstrates a strong belief in the potential of technological innovation to reduce FLW, it gives less attention to the potential risks associated with such innovations.

Of particular interest in Resolution 4/2 is the encouragement it provides to UNEP Member States to foster dialogue between public and private stakeholders across the food chain and to enhance regional and global cooperation on strategies to reduce FLW.[70] States have already undertaken various initiatives in this regard, not only at a regional level,[71] but also at the universal one. For example, partnerships and coalitions have been specifically established to address FLW, such as the 'Food is Never Waste' initiative, formed during the 2021 UN Food Systems Summit, and the 'Champions 12.3' coalition, dedicated to achieving Target 12.3 of the 2030 Agenda. In other cases, FLW reduction has been incorporated into broader initiatives, such as the Sustainable Food Systems Programme under the 10-Year Framework of Programmes on Sustainable Consumption and Production, and the Lowering Organic Waste Methane Initiative, part of the Global Methane Pledge to cut methane emissions by 30% by 2030. These initiatives demonstrate commendable efforts by some States to adopt a coordinated strategy for reducing FLW, fostering dialogue with various stakeholders, and promoting the development and exchange of technological innovations. However, participation in these actions remains voluntary, and the number of States involved is still relatively low, which limits their overall impact.

The proliferation of such partnerships and coalitions, alongside the adoption of numerous non-binding FLW instruments, highlights both the potential

70 Ibid paras 5 and 7(b).

71 Mention can be made, for instance, of the EU Platform on Food Losses and Food Waste, established by the European Commission's Directorate-General for Health and Food Safety in 2016 (and renewed in 2021 for a second term) as an expert group on FLW. To achieve its objective—to widely support EU action in exchanging information and defining appropriate measures to prevent FLW—the Platform places great emphasis on promoting partnerships between EU institutions, international organisations, and private sector actors.

and limitations of the soft-law approach taken by States.[72] On the one hand, soft-law instruments avoid the delays and challenges associated with negotiating legally-binding agreements. On the other hand, the absence of binding provisions gives States a wide margin of discretion in fulfilling their commitments, limiting the effectiveness of these instruments. This is particularly detrimental to developing States, which often can neither muster the technical and economic resources needed to develop and implement new technologies nor rely on sufficient guarantees of support from more developed countries.

Nonetheless, the adoption of soft-law declarations and resolutions does not necessarily indicate a lack of political will among States to eventually converge towards binding commitments. Especially when these instruments are adopted with broad participation and support, as in the case of UNEA resolutions or the FAO Code of Conduct, which could be viewed as important preliminary steps towards the future negotiation of international treaties. They might also reflect a growing *opinio juris* among States in the development of customary international rules on the subject.

It cannot be overlooked, however, that the current State practice in promoting, developing, and disseminating technological innovations to reduce FLW remains limited and inconsistent. As highlighted in the UNEP Executive Director's report on the implementation of Resolution 4/2,[73] critical gaps remain, including a significant number of States that still lack data on FLW and adequate measurement tools. Moreover, the low number of States—only 21 as of 2022—that have incorporated FLW reduction measures into their Nationally Determined Contributions under the Paris Agreement as part of their commitment to address climate change,[74] further underscores the inadequacy of the current international response to the growing problem of FLW.

5 Conclusions

Addressing FLW through technological innovation is a complex challenge requiring a comprehensive and coordinated approach under international law. While FLW reduction and prevention has gained increasing attention among

72 This approach is also widely adopted at the national level. See OECD, *Beyond Food Loss and Waste Reduction Targets: Translating Reduction Ambitions into Policy Outcomes* (Paris 2025), 32.

73 UNEP, *Progress in the Implementation of Resolution 4/2 on Promoting Sustainable Practices and Innovative Solutions for curbing Food Loss and Waste*, UN Doc. UNEP/EA.5/INF/23 of 29 November 2021, para 3.

74 UNEP, *Food Waste Index Report 2024* (n 23), 70.

States in recent years, there is still a lack of specific legally-binding commitments to drive substantive action towards it, including through the promotion and diffusion of technological innovations. The adoption of numerous soft-law instruments, such as voluntary guidelines and recommendations, demonstrates the existence of political will to tackle this pressing issue at the international level; it also highlights, however, the inherent limitations of non-binding measures in producing a meaningful and long-lasting change in States behaviour.

The environmental and humanitarian costs associated with FLW are substantial, with millions suffering from hunger and the ecological repercussions of inefficient food systems becoming increasingly apparent. The need for a more coordinated international response, therefore, is crucial. This response should not only foster technological innovation but also ensure equitable access to these new technologies, particularly for developing States that often lack the technical and financial resources to implement advanced solutions. Establishing robust mechanisms for technology transfer, investing in capacity-building initiatives, and promoting partnerships among diverse stakeholders are critical steps towards overcoming the barriers faced by less developed countries in addressing FLW.

Furthermore, the promotion of technological innovation must be supported by comprehensive policies that address the underlying causes of FLW, including infrastructural deficiencies, market inefficiencies, and socio-economic disparities. As international law continues to evolve, it is essential for States to recognise the need to make stronger commitments to achieve effective solutions to the FLW problem. By adopting a proactive stance that emphasises collaboration, inclusivity, and innovation, the international community can move towards a more sustainable and equitable food system that minimises waste and maximises the potential of food resources.

Bibliography

Akkerman R and Cruijssen F, 'Food Loss, Food Waste, and Sustainability in Food Supply Chains' in Bouchery Y, Corbett CJ, Fransoo JC and Tan T (eds), *Sustainable Supply Chains: A Research-Based Textbook on Operations and Strategy* (Springer 2024) 219.

Benyam AA, Soma T and Frase E, 'Digital Agricultural Technologies for Food Loss and Waste Prevention and Reduction: Global Trends, Adoption Opportunities and Barriers' (2021) 323 Journal of Cleaner Production 1.

Ciccullo F, Cagliano R, Bartezzaghi G and Perego A, 'Implementing the Circular Economy Paradigm in the Agri-Food Supply Chain: The Role of Food Waste Prevention Technologies' (2021) 164 Resources, Conservation & Recycling 1.

Claeys P and Edelman M, 'The United Nations Declaration on the Rights of Peasants and Other People Working in Rural Areas' (2020) 47 The Journal of Peasant Studies 1.

Conrad Z, Niles MT, Neher DA, Roy ED, Tichenor NE and Jahns L, 'Relationship Between Food Waste, Diet Quality and Environmental Sustainability' (2018) 13 (4) PLoS ONE 1.

Costantino L, *La problematica degli sprechi nella filiera agroalimentare. Profili introduttivi* (Cacucci editore 2018).

Delgado L, Schuster M and Torero M, 'Quantity and Quality Food Losses across the Value Chain: A Comparative Analysis' (2021) 98 Food Policy 1.

Delgado L, Schuster M and Torero M, 'Food Losses in Agrifood Systems: What We Know' (2023) 15 Annual Review of Resource Economics 41.

Delsignore M, Ramajoli M and Ricci C, 'Defining the Meaning of Food Waste as a Matter of Urgency' in Morone P, Papendiek F and Tartiu VE (eds), *Food Waste Reduction and Valorisation: Sustainability Assessment and Policy Analysis* (Springer 2017) 215.

Durán-Sandoval D, Durán-Romero G and Uleri F, 'How Much Food Loss and Waste Do Countries with Problems with Food Security Generate?' (2023) 966 (13) Agriculture 1.

Franco S, Barbanera M, Moscetti R, Cicatiello C, Secondi L and Massantini R, 'Overnutrition Is a Significant Component of Food Waste and Has a Large Environmental Impact' (2022) 12 Scientific Reports 1.

Galanakis MC (ed), *Saving Food: Production, Supply Chain, Food Waste and Food Consumption* (Academic Press 2019).

Garske B, Heyl K, Ekardt F, Weber LM, Gradzka W, 'Challenges of Food Waste Governance: An Assessment of European Legislation on Food Waste and Recommendations for Improvement by Economic Instruments' (2020) 9 (7) Land 1.

González Vaqué L, 'Food Loss and Waste in the European Union: A New Challenge for the Food Law?' (2015) 10 European Food & Feed Law Review 20.

Guimarães Martins V, Romani VP, Chavez Martins P and da Silva Filipini G, 'Innovative Packaging that Saves Food' in Galanakis CM (ed), *Saving Food: Production, Supply Chain, Food Waste and Food Consumption* (Academic Press 2019) 171.

Gustavsson J, Cederberg C, Sonesson U, Emanuelsson A, *The Methodology of the FAO Study: 'Global Food Losses and Food Waste—Extent, Causes and Prevention'* (SIK 2013).

Jeong S, Lee J, 'Effects of Cultural Background on Consumer Perception and Acceptability of Foods and Drinks: A Review of Latest Cross-Cultural Studies' (2021) 42 Current Opinion in Food Science 248.

Kalaidjian E and Robinson S, 'Reviewing the Nature and Pitfalls of Multilateral Adaptation Finance for Small Island Developing States' (2022) 36 Climate Risk Management 1.

Lenzerini F, 'Declaration on the Rights of Indigenous Peoples (UNDRIP)' in Binder C, Nowak M, Hofbauer JA and Janig P (eds), *Elgar Encyclopedia of Human Rights* (Edward Elgar Publishing 2022) vol 1, 452.

Lucifero N, 'Food Loss and Waste in the EU Law between Sustainability of Well-Being and the Implications on Food System and on the Environment' (2016) 8 Agriculture and Agricultural Science Procedia 282.

Mbow C, Rosenzweig C, Barioni LG, Benton TG, Herrero M, Krishnapillai M, Liwenga E, Pradhan P, Rivera-Ferre MG, Sapkota T, Tubiello FN, Xu Y, 'Food Security' in Shukla PR, Skea J, Calvo Buendia E, Masson-Delmotte V, Pörtner HO, Roberts DC, Zhai P, Slade R, Connors S, van Diemen R, Ferrat M, Haughey E, Luz S, Neogi S, Pathak M, Petzold J, Portugal Pereira J, Vyas P, Huntley E, Kissick K, Belkacemi M and Malley J (eds), *Climate Change and Land: An IPCC Special Report on Climate Change, Desertification, Land Degradation, Sustainable Land Management, Food Security, and Greenhouse Gas Fluxes in Terrestrial Ecosystems* (IPCC 2019) 437.

Mitkidis K and Šefčíková A, 'Ensure Sustainable Consumption and Production Patterns (SDG 12)' in Bantekas I and Seatzu F (eds), *The UN Sustainable Development Goals: A Commentary* (Oxford University Press 2023) 859.

Oztuna Taner O, 'Sustainable Food and Agriculture Production: Reducing Food Waste through Technological Advancements and Assessing Its Economic Impact' (2024) 5 (3) Research on World Agricultural Economy 144.

Röttgen D and Allocco F, 'Food Waste in EU Food Law' in Caporale C, Pavone IR and Ragionieri MP (eds), *International Food Law: How Food Law Can Balance Health, Environment and Animal Welfare* (Wolters Kluwer 2021) 305.

Seatzu F and Vargiu P, 'The Legal Dimension of the Kunming-Montreal Framework in International Law' (2025) 41 Anuario Español de Derecho Internacional 531.

Telesetsky A, 'Waste Not, Want Not: The Right to Food, Food Waste and the Sustainable Development Goals' (2014) 42 Denver Journal of International Law and Policy 479.

Vezzani S, 'The Protection of Traditional Knowledge of Agricultural Interest in International Law', in Di Blase A and Vadi V (eds), *The Inherent Rights of Indigenous Peoples in International Law* (Roma TrE-Press 2020) 279.

Vezzani S, 'Il Progetto di Dichiarazione sui diritti degli agricoltori: nuovi diritti germogliano?' (2013) 7 Diritti umani e diritto internazionale 211.

CHAPTER 10

The Role of Innovation in the Fight against Food Waste and Food Poverty: Experimental Regulatory Solutions through the Lens of Comparative Law

Chiara Cerbone

Summary

1. Food Systems Issues: The 'Paradox of Scarcity within Abundance'. 2. Sustainability, Food Waste, and Food Poverty in the International Context. 3. The European Union's Action Against Food Waste and Food Poverty. 4. Some Comparative Cases: A Comparison Between France and Italy. 5. Experimental Measures: The Italian *Reddito Alimentare*. 6. Brief Concluding Notes.

1 Food Systems Issues: the 'Paradox of Scarcity Within Abundance'

Food waste and food poverty are deeply interrelated phenomena that have affected food systems for decades, significantly undermining their sustainability objectives.

According to estimates from The State of Food Security and Nutrition in the World Report, in 2023 between 713 and 757 million people suffered from hunger,[1] while approximately 2.33 billion experienced moderate or severe food insecurity.[2] These figures are inextricably linked to data on food waste. The latest Food Waste Index Report estimates that the global volume of wasted

1 FAO, IFAD, UNICEF, WFP, and WHO, *The State of Food Security and Nutrition in the World 2024—Financing to end hunger, food insecurity and malnutrition in all its forms*, (Rome, 2024) 3, where, in addition to data on the percentage of the population that experienced hunger in 2023, specific continental percentages are also provided, highlighting that Africa is the continent with the lowest access to food.

2 According to FAO, '[A] person is food insecure when they lack regular access to enough safe and nutritious food for normal growth and development and an active and healthy life. This may be due to unavailability of food and/or lack of resources to obtain food. Food insecurity can be experienced at different levels of severity.' For further details, see FAO, *Measuring hunger, food security and food consumption*, <https://www.fao.org/hunger/en> accessed 5 February 2025.

© 2026 THE AUTHOR(S) | HTTPS://DOI.ORG/10.1163/9789004740907-012

food amounts to approximately 931 million tons.[3] Notably, as highlighted in the report, this figure has remained stable between 2019 and 2022.[4]

A comparative analysis of food waste and food poverty data reveals a pervasive situation of food insecurity, which becomes particularly striking when examined through the lens of what has been aptly described as the 'paradox of scarcity within abundance'.[5] This paradox encapsulates the coexistence of food surplus and deprivation in developed countries: despite a total food production theoretically sufficient to meet the needs of the global population, significant segments of society remain unable to access adequate nutrition.

In response to these challenges, international organisations, supranational entities, and national governments have introduced innovative regulatory measures and policies aimed at simultaneously reducing food waste and strengthening the protection of the 'right to be free from hunger'.[6]

Legal innovation in the domain of agrifood law takes multiple forms, all of which are particularly relevant to the present study.

As has been observed in multiple studies,[7] legal innovation may manifest both as reaction and as action. In the first case, regulatory frameworks emerge in response to the challenges posed by scientific and technological advancements, striving to establish a legal architecture capable of addressing novel and complex issues. In the second case, legal innovation is a proactive instrument through which lawmakers—at both national and supranational levels—introduce new regulatory provisions in anticipation of market trends

---

3 United Nations Environment Programme (UNEP), *Food Waste Index Report 2024* (Nairobi, 2024) 46.

4 ibid 46.

5 Luigi Campiglio and Rovati Giancarlo, 'Il paradosso della scarsità dell'abbondanza: il caso della povertà alimentare' in Luigi Campiglio and Giancarlo Rovati (eds), *La povertà alimentare in Italia. Prima indagine quantitativa e qualitativa* (Edizioni Angelo Guerini e Associati 2009).

6 The expression 'the right to be free from hunger' was first used by the then-President of the Italian Constitutional Court, Francesco Casavola, during a press conference on June 15, 1994. While commenting on Constitutional Court ruling No. 240 of June 10, 1994, he emphasised that the foremost fundamental right of citizens is the right to be free from hunger, to be understood as a necessary foundation for a free and dignified life. This expression has been acknowledged by Lucia Scaffardi, 'La sicurezza alimentare ovvero come il "diritto a togliersi la fame" evolve in un mondo che cambia' (2023) 59 DPCE Online, 2167 <https://www.dpceonline.it/index.php/dpceonline/article/view/1965> accessed 5 February 2025; Francesco Alicino, 'Il diritto fondamentale "a togliersi la fame". Banco di prova per il costituzionalismo contemporaneo' in Marusca De Castris (ed), *Cibo e Società. Una relazione da esplorare* (RomaTrE-Press 2018) 90.

7 Ferdinando Albisinni, 'Innovazione-azione e innovazione-reazione nel diritto agrario e alimentare europeo: i nuovi scenari' [2013] (1–2) Agricoltura Istituzioni Mercati 225.

and evolving societal needs, occasionally foreseeing the potential impact of scientific progress on these interests.

These dimensions of legal innovation must be interpreted in close connection with scientific innovation, which represents a fundamental driver of agri-food law, as demonstrated by its pivotal role in shaping production processes. For instance, technological advancements have facilitated the widespread adoption of Agriculture 4.0[8] techniques across all stages of the agrifood supply chain—sometimes raising unprecedented legal questions—and have enabled, particularly in the fight against food waste, the deployment of artificial intelligence to manage food surpluses efficiently.[9]

Furthermore, innovation may also pertain to institutional policies that, due to their experimental nature, can be considered pioneering initiatives within this domain.

This study aims to assess the impact of various policy and legislative interventions designed to address food waste and food poverty, while also critically examining the role of legal and political innovation in this field.

To this end, the analysis will first explore the complex framework of international legal instruments designed to enhance food security by mitigating both food waste and food poverty. It will then examine the legal and policy frameworks adopted at the European level before analysing specific measures implemented in select EU Member States. Particular attention will be devoted to the Italian case, tracing the legislative and policy developments that led to the adoption of the experimental measure known as the *reddito alimentare*.[10]

Finally, the concluding section will seek to address the following overarching question: Can innovative legal solutions that systematically integrate the fight against food waste with policies aimed at mitigating food poverty bring about a meaningful and structural shift in addressing these challenges, or do

---

8 Santiago Santos Valle, Josef Kienzle, *Agriculture 4.0.—Agricultural Robotics and Automated Equipment for Sustainable Crop Production*, FAO Report, (Roma 2020) <https://openknowledge.fao.org/server/api/core/bitstreams/14fc8bf7-fdeb-4c7c-a2ed-b2d59118a70b/content> accessed 5 February 2025.

9 Francesca Ferretti, 'Spreco alimentare e sostenibilità ambientale: i profili giuridici del ruolo dell'AI' [2023] EJPLT Special Issues 116.

10 As defined in Article 3 of Ministerial Decree No. 78 of 26 May 2023, issued by the Italian Minister of Labour and Social Policies, the term '*reddito alimentare*' refers to: '... the free distribution, also through Third Sector organizations operating locally, of food packages made from unsold goods from the food retail sector, donated by commercial businesses that voluntarily participate in the trial, in favour of the beneficiaries referred to in Article 4' (author's translation). Italian Ministry of Labour and Social Policies, Ministerial Decree No. 78 of 26 May 2023 <https://www.lavoro.gov.it/documenti-e-norme/normativa/dm-78-26052023.pdf> accessed 30 June 2025.

strategies that place greater responsibility on stakeholders within the food supply chain prove more effective in practice?

2 Sustainability, Food Waste, and Food Poverty in the International Context

As previously mentioned, before delving into the analysis of regulatory solutions adopted at the supranational and national levels, it is necessary to establish a few conceptual and legal reference points to frame the phenomena of food waste and food poverty within the broader context of international law.

For decades, international organisations—foremost among them, the United Nations—have addressed issues related to food security, the right to food, and the sustainability of production and consumption systems.

Since 1992, the international community has increasingly focused on the regulation of production and consumption systems, an interest explicitly affirmed in Principle 8 of the Rio Declaration on Environment and Development, which states: 'To achieve sustainable development and a higher quality of life for all people, States should reduce and eliminate unsustainable patterns of production and consumption and promote appropriate demographic policies.'[11]

The reduction of hunger—a phenomenon closely related but not entirely synonymous with food poverty—and food waste were not initially included among specific sustainability objectives. It was only in the early 2000s that the fight against these challenges became more clearly defined within international commitments.

In the United Nations Millennium Declaration, signed in New York in September 2000, the first of the Millennium Development Goals (MDGs) was 'to eradicate extreme poverty and hunger worldwide'.[12] However, a true turning point occurred in 2015, when the United Nations unanimously adopted Resolution A/RES/70/1, Transforming Our World: the 2030 Agenda for Sustainable Development[13] (commonly referred to as Agenda 2030). This resolution explicitly addressed not only hunger but also food waste.

11 United Nation, *Report of the United Nations Conference on Environment and Development* (New York 1993) <https://documents.un.org/doc/undoc/gen/n92/836/55/pdf/n9283655.pdf> accessed 5 February 2025.

12 UNGA, *United Nation Millennium Declaration, General Assembly Resolution 55/2* (New York 2020), <https://www.ohchr.org/en/instruments-mechanisms/instruments/united-nations-millennium-declaration> accessed 5 February 2025.

13 UNGA, *Resolution A/RES/70/1 "Transforming our world: the 2030 Agenda for Sustainable Development"*, (New York 2015) <https://documents.un.org/doc/undoc/gen/n15/291/89/pdf/n1529189.pdf> accessed 5 February 2025.

Specifically, Sustainable Development Goal (SDG) 2 aims to achieve 'zero hunger', accompanied by a series of targets promoting food security, improved nutrition, and sustainable agriculture. Meanwhile, SDG 12 commits to 'halving per capita global food waste at the retail and consumer levels and reducing food losses along production and supply chains, including post-harvest losses, by 2030'.[14]

These goals are inherently interlinked, as noted by some researchers,[15] who have highlighted how food waste directly influences the persistence of hunger and malnutrition worldwide. Food that would otherwise be discarded could instead be repurposed to mitigate food insecurity.

Moreover, the close connection between these two sustainability goals underscores the essential role that both consumers and businesses play in their achievement. Consumers, for instance, act as 'active participants, playing a guiding role that should be supported by adequate education'.[16] Their individual choices—if sustainable—contribute directly to the realisation of these global objectives. Likewise, businesses are responsible for adopting production, processing, and storage models aligned with sustainability principles, even when these objectives may require balancing economic interests with environmental and social concerns. Additionally, the role of third-sector organisations is particularly significant in facilitating the redistribution of food surpluses to individuals experiencing food insecurity.

Beyond Agenda 2030, the United Nations has promoted various awareness campaigns,[17] including 'SAVE FOOD: Global Initiative on Food Loss and Waste Reduction'[18] and 'Think.Eat.Save. Reduce Your Foodprint'.[19] More recently, in

14 ibid 22.

15 Gioia Maccioni, 'Lo spreco alimentare' in Luigi Costato and Ferdinando Albisinni (eds) *Trattato breve di diritto agrario italiano e dell'Unione Europea* (4th ed Wolters Kluwer—CEDAM 2023).

16 Eleonora Sirsi, 'Il diritto all'educazione del consumatore di alimenti' [2011] (4) Rivista di Diritto Agrario 496.

17 FAO, *Global Initiative on Food Loss and Waste Reduction* (Rome 2015) <https://openknowledge.fao.org/server/api/core/bitstreams/57f76ed9-6f19-4872-98b4-6e1c3e796213/content> accessed 5 February 2025.

18 As stated on the official FAO webpage dedicated to the SAVE FOOD initiative: 'FAO and Messe Düsseldorf are collaborating with donors, bi- and multi-lateral agencies and financial institutions and private sector partners (the food packaging industry and others) to develop and implement the programme on food loss and waste reduction.' Further information is available at the following webpage <https://www.fao.org/save-food/en/> accessed 5 February 2025.

19 The 'Think.Eat.Save' initiative, promoted by UNEP, FAO, and various international partners, aims to combat food waste by raising awareness among consumers, retailers, and the hospitality sector. The project seeks to reduce global food waste by highlighting the economic, environmental, and ethical impacts of food loss. It engages

2020, the International Day of Awareness for Food Loss and Waste was established, complementing earlier initiatives such as World Food Day and the International Day for the Eradication of Poverty.

Alongside these efforts, the Food and Agriculture Organisation (FAO) has played a key role in establishing internationally harmonised definitions for food security and related concepts.

The first concept requiring a standardised definition was food security. From the early 1970s onward, its meaning evolved in response to shifting political perspectives. For decades, definitions focused selectively on only one of the four dimensions of food security. However, during the 1996 World Food Summit, FAO introduced a comprehensive definition, linking food security to the right to food while adopting a multidimensional approach encompassing food access, availability, utilisation, and stability.[20]

The FAO Report concluded that, '[f]ood security exists when all people, at all times, have physical and economic access to sufficient, safe, and nutritious food to meet their dietary needs and food preferences for an active and healthy life'.[21]

From this definition emerged the concept of food poverty, understood at the international level as the inability of individuals to access safe, nutritious, and sufficient food for a healthy and active life within their social and economic context. A useful reference is the UK Department of Health's definition, which describes food poverty as: 'the inability to afford, or to have access to, food to make up a healthy diet'.[22]

As for the definitions of food waste and food loss, the term food waste refers to food discarded in the final stages of the supply chain—retail and consumption—despite being suitable for consumption. This waste may occur for various reasons, including failure to purchase products before expiration (often due to excessive availability in stores), spoilage at home, or uneaten food ordered at restaurants.[23]

---

governments and expert organisations to encourage responsible behaviours through awareness campaigns and a global platform for sharing ongoing initiatives. Further information is available at: https://www.unep.org/news-and-stories/press-release/think-eat-save-unep-fao-and-partners-launch-global-campaign-change.

20 FAO, *Report of the World Food Summit*, 13–17 November 1996 (Rome 1996) <https://www.fao.org/4/w3548e/w3548e00.htm> accessed 5 February 2025.

21 ibid.

22 UK Department of Health, *Choosing a better diet: a food and health action plan* (London 2005).

23 FAO, *Global food losses and food waste—Extent, causes and prevention* (Rome 2011).

Conversely, food loss refers to food discarded in the earlier stages of the supply chain—production and distribution. It primarily affects food that, despite being of high quality, is discarded before reaching the market, often due to failure to meet commercial aesthetic standards.[24]

These definitions underscore the direct link between food sustainability objectives and the need for coordinated action. Reducing food waste and food poverty must be pursued jointly to ensure the long-term sustainability of global food systems.[25]

With these foundational concepts established, the analysis will now focus on the European, French, and Italian contexts.

3 The European Union's Action against Food Waste and Food Poverty

The initiatives undertaken by international organisations have undoubtedly influenced both supranational and national regulatory frameworks.

Within the European Union, various measures have been adopted to combat food waste and food poverty, providing a structured framework within which Member States have developed their own regulations and policies.

Before analysing these measures, it is useful to highlight some key data regarding food waste and food poverty in Europe. According to the latest Eurostat data, in 2022, approximately 19.7% of the European population could not afford a proper meal, while the average amount of food waste per European citizen was 132 kg.[26] These figures underscore the need for a coordinated response to tackle both phenomena.

The European Union has approached the issue of food waste from two distinct but complementary perspectives. First, in June 2016, the European Council adopted its 'Conclusions on Food Loss and Food Waste',[27] setting out four operational objectives that have since guided EU institutions and Member States in their subsequent actions. Specifically, the Conclusions called for improving food waste monitoring, raising public awareness on the

24 ibid 12.

25 Silvio Franco, 'Introduzione. Produrre di più o sprecare di meno?' in Luca Falascioni and Silvio Franco (eds) *Lo spreco alimentare in Italia. Riflessioni, dati e testimonianze* (Carocci Editore 2022).

26 EUROSTAT, *Food waste and food waste prevention—estimated, Statistics Explained,* European Union, 27 September 2024, <https://ec.europa.eu/eurostat/statistics-explained/SEPDF/cache/110448.pdf> accessed 5 February 2025.

27 Council, *Conclusions on Food Loss and Food Waste,* <https://www.consilium.europa.eu/media/34583/food-losses-food-waste-en.pdf> accessed 5 February 2025.

responsible use of food resources, enhancing consumer understanding and use of 'best before' and 'use by' labels, and facilitating the donation of unsold food to charitable organisations.

This initiative, launched as part of the European Green Deal,[28] led to the first progress monitoring exercise in 2018. The initial assessment was largely positive: most Member States committed to meeting SDG 12 by establishing national food waste management and prevention plans. Moreover, EU-supported tools, such as the EU Platform on Food Losses and Food Waste, saw significant participation from Member States. Additionally, several educational campaigns, particularly targeting children and adolescents, were introduced to promote food waste awareness.

Despite these positive developments, several critical issues persist, including the absence of a standardised measurement methodology, challenges in repurposing surplus food, and concerns regarding the reliability of collected data.

The second pillar of the EU's approach concerns the management and reduction of food waste. To address this, the European Parliament and the Council adopted the Waste Framework Directive[29] (Directive (EU) 2018/851) on May 30, 2018, amending Directive 2008/98/EC.[30] This directive provides a legal definition of 'food waste', thereby addressing a long-standing regulatory gap that had previously hindered effective food waste management.[31]

Bridging both the reduction of food waste and the fight against food poverty, the European Commission introduced the Guidelines on Food Donation[32] in 2017. These guidelines aimed primarily at facilitating compliance with food safety, hygiene, liability, and traceability regulations for food donations. A secondary objective was to ensure a harmonised interpretation of EU legal provisions by regulatory authorities across Member States regarding surplus food redistribution. Within this context, the guidelines serve not only as a procedural

---

28 Commission, *COM (2019) 640 final, Communication from the Commission to the European Parliament, the European Council, the Council, The European Economic and Social Committee and the Committee of the Regions—'The European Green Deal'*, Brussels, 11/12/2019, <https://eur-lex.europa.eu/resource.html?uri=cellar:b828d165-1c22-11ea-8c1f-01aa75ed71a1.0002.02/DOC_1&format=PDF> accessed 5 February 2025.

29 Directive (EU) 2018/851 of the European Parliament and of the Council of 30 May 2018 amending Directive 2008/98/EC on waste [2018] OJ L150.

30 Directive 2008/98/EC of the European Parliament and of the Council of 19 November 2008 on waste and repealing certain Directives [2008] OJ L312.

31 Daniele Camoni, 'La lotta contro lo spreco alimentare nel diritto comparato' [2023] (3) Rivista di diritto alimentare 5.

32 EU Guidelines on Food Donation, 2017/C 361/01, Official Journal of the European Union, 25.10.2017, C 361/1.

framework for food donations but also provide key definitions to assist policymakers in developing national legislation aligned with EU standards.

With a specific focus on food poverty, alongside broader strategies to combat poverty and social inequalities, the European Union has established dedicated financial instruments. In 2014, the EU introduced the Fund for European Aid to the Most Deprived (FEAD), governed by Regulation (EU) No. 223/2014 of March 11, 2014. Initially covering the period 2014–2020 and later extended until 2022, the FEAD provides financial support to Member State initiatives aimed at distributing food, clothing, and essential goods to those in need. Since its establishment, the FEAD has played a crucial role in food distribution across Europe, reaching approximately 12.2 million people in over ten EU countries.[33] In 2022, the FEAD was merged into the European Social Fund Plus (2021–2027), which integrates various EU social policies to support vulnerable groups.

4 Some Comparative Cases: a Comparison Between France and Italy

The legislative initiatives adopted by individual Member States, particularly by policymakers and legislators in France and Italy, align with the direction indicated by the European Union. Before examining the specific actions taken in these two countries, it is necessary to provide some data on the scale of food waste in their respective contexts.

According to the EUROSTAT estimates, France generated 9.4 million tons of food waste in 2022, of which approximately 4 million tons consisted of still-edible food that was ultimately discarded. Analysing this data, the research conducted by Centro Studi Divulga[34] on the occasion of the twelfth National Day Against Food Waste highlighted that France ranks as the second-largest food-wasting country in Europe, preceded by Germany, which generates around 10.8 million tons of food waste, and followed by Italy, which, as will be examined, produces approximately 8.2 million tons of food waste annually.

Faced with this widespread issue of food waste, France has implemented various legal and policy measures since 2013. The first initiative aimed at combating food waste was the adoption of a strategic policy document, the '*Pacte*

---

33 Commission, COM (2021) 494 *final, Report from the Commission to the Council and the European Parliament—Summary of the Annual Implementation Reports for the Operational Programs Co-financed by the Fund for European Aid to the Most Deprived in 2019*, Brussels, 30/08/2021, <https://ec.europa.eu/social/main.jsp?catId=1089&langId=it> accessed 5 February 2025.

34 Centro Studi Divulga, *Focus spreco e fame 2025* (Rome 2025) <https://www.divulgastudi.it/wp-content/uploads/2025/02/Focus-Spreco-Fame-2025.pdf> accessed 5 February 2025.

national de lutte contre le gaspillage alimentaire' ('National pact to combat food waste').[35] Initially introduced for the period 2013–2016 and subsequently renewed for 2017–2020, this agreement was signed by over 60 public and private partners with the goal of reducing food waste by 50% in the distribution and institutional catering sectors by 2025 and achieving the same objective across all sectors by 2030.

Initiatives such as the implementation of a comprehensive plan, which engages multiple stakeholders with diverse perspectives, are particularly effective in the French context, where the fight against food waste is regarded as a pressing public concern. These efforts contribute to raising public awareness while complementing the necessary legislative provisions on the matter. Indeed, legal measures remain indispensable, as both food waste and food poverty require institutional responses that, through binding obligations and sanctions for non-compliance, can lead to a significant reduction in food waste.

For these reasons, several legal provisions have been enacted since 2015, culminating in 2016 with the adoption of a law specifically dedicated to food waste reduction. The legislative measures introduced in 2015 laid the groundwork for further regulatory developments. The *LOI n ° 2015–992 du 17 août 2015 relative à la transition énergétique pour la croissance verte*[36] (Law No. 2015-992 of August 17, 2015 on energy transition for green growth) marked an initial step in the fight against food waste by imposing an obligation on public sector institutional catering operators to adopt an anti-waste approach.

However, the most decisive step came with the adoption of the *LOI n ° 2016–138 du 11 février 2016 relative à la lutte contre le gaspillage alimentaire*[37] (Law No. 2016-138 of February 11, 2016 on combating food waste), commonly known as the Loi Garot. This law represents the first European legislative instrument to comprehensively address food waste. Following a legislative technique frequently employed in France, the Loi Garot introduced amendments to the *Code de l'Environnement* (Environment Code), thereby establishing, for the first time in Europe, sanctions for food waste.

35 For an overview of the two reports on the *Pacte* published by the French Ministry of Agriculture, please refer to the Ministry's website, specifically the section dedicated to the fight against food waste, <https://agriculture.gouv.fr/lutte-contre-le-gaspillage-alimentaire-les-lois-francaises> accessed 5 February 2025.

36 *LOI n ° 2015-992 du 17 août 2015 relative à la transition énergétique pour la croissance* <https://www.legifrance.gouv.fr/loda/id/JORFTEXT000031044385> accessed 5 February 2025.

37 The text of *LOI n ° 2016-138 du 11 février 2016 relative à la lutte contre le gaspillage alimentaire* can be accessed on the official French legislative portal at the following link: https://www.legifrance.gouv.fr/jorf/id/JORFTEXT000032036289/ accessed 25 June 2025.

A brief examination of this law is warranted. First, its regulatory framework is characterised by a 'command and control'[38] approach whereby non-compliance with its provisions results in financial penalties for retailers and distributors in the food sector. Second, it establishes a clear hierarchy for the utilisation of unsold food, akin to the hierarchy set out in the European Council Circular. Under this hierarchy, unsold food must first be donated. If donation is not possible, the food should be repurposed for animal feed. If neither of these options is feasible, the food must be converted into compost for agricultural use or used to generate electricity through methanisation. This structured approach, which regulates the stages of an unsold food product's 'life cycle', not only aims to prevent waste but also seeks to educate all actors within the food supply chain, from producers to end consumers.

In addition to these regulatory measures, between 2018 and 2021, various laws not specifically dedicated to food waste prevention introduced additional provisions to curb food waste. Notable among these is the *LOI n ° 2018–938 du 30 octobre 2018 pour l'équilibre des relations commerciales dans le secteur agricole et alimentaire et une alimentation saine, durable et accessible à tous* (Law No. 2018-938 of October 30, 2018 on balanced commercial relations in the agricultural and food sector and healthy, sustainable and accessible food for all) (known as '*loi EGalim*'), which included a provision mandating restaurants to offer customers the option of a doggy bag to take home uneaten food. Further measures were introduced by the Ordinance of October 21, 2019, issued by the French Ministry of Agriculture, which obligates large-scale retailers with annual revenues exceeding 50 million EUR, as well as restaurants serving more than 3,000 meals per day to establish agreements with third-sector associations to donate unsold food.

France's extensive legal framework for combating food waste promotes a comprehensive and multidimensional approach, addressing the environmental, social, and economic consequences of food waste.[39] This framework seeks to reduce the number of people experiencing food insecurity, which, according to the latest estimates, affects approximately 8 million individuals in France, while also better supporting the 5.5 million people who receive food aid.

Turning to the Italian context, an analysis of total food waste—including inedible food waste—reveals that, based on Eurostat data processed by Centro

---

38 Pamela Lattanzi, 'Le leggi "antispreco" alimentare. Esperienze nazionali a confronto' in Francesco de Leonardis (ed), *Studi in tema di economia circolare* (EUM—Edizioni Università di Macerata 2019).

39 Luc Bodiguel, 'French Legal Scheme on Food Waste and Agri-food Chain' (2021) 7 Journal of Rural Law 12.

Studi Divulga,[40] Italy generates approximately 8.5 million tons of food waste per year. Mirroring developments in France, Italy also adopted an anti-food waste law in 2016: *Legge 19 agosto 2016, n. 166, Disposizioni concernenti la donazione e la distribuzione di prodotti alimentari e farmaceutici a fini di solidarietà sociale e per la limitazione degli sprechi* (Law No. 166 of August 19, 2016, Provisions concerning the donation and distribution of food and pharmaceutical products for social solidarity purposes and for the reduction of waste),[41] commonly referred to as the 'Legge Gadda' or the Gadda Law.

This law regulates, inter alia, the donation and distribution of food products, aiming to prevent waste by granting fiscal benefits to large-scale distributors that donate food, as well as to those who donate pharmaceutical products. This approach stands in marked contrast to the regulatory framework adopted in France.

The Gadda Law builds upon the foundations laid by *Legge n. 155 del 16 luglio 2003, Disciplina della Distribuzione dei prodotti alimentari a fini di solidarietà sociale* (Law No. 155 of 16 July 2003 (Regulation of the distribution of food products for social solidarity purposes), commonly known as the *Legge del Buon Samaritano* or the Good Samaritan Law, which was enacted to encourage food donation.

One of the defining characteristics of the Gadda Law—which gained momentum following the debates held during EXPO 2015 in Milan, an event dedicated to food-related issues[42]—is its voluntary, solidarity-based, social orientation. Additionally, it emphasises the importance of collaboration between public institutions and the third sector, aligning with the broader strategy of fostering multi-stakeholder cooperation to achieve sustainability goals.

A further distinctive feature of the Gadda Law is its pedagogical dimension, which entrusts the Ministry of Agriculture, Food Sovereignty, and Forestry with the task of promoting, 'national communication campaigns on food recovery and waste reduction, with the aim of raising awareness among the public and businesses about the negative consequences of food waste' (Article 9).

Finally, while implicit, the Gadda Law establishes a clear link between food waste reduction and the fight against food poverty, reinforcing the idea that

40 Centro Studi Divulga, *Focus spreco e fame 2025* (n 34).

41 Official Journal of the Italian Republic, *Legge 19 agosto 2016, n. 166, Disposizioni concernenti la donazione e la distribuzione di prodotti alimentari e farmaceutici a fini di solidarietà sociale e per la limitazione degli sprechi*, G.U. Serie Generale, n. 202 del 30/08/2016, <https://www.gazzettaufficiale.it/eli/id/2016/08/30/16G00179/sg> accessed 5 February 2025.

42 Diana Cerini, 'La legge Gadda di contrasto agli sprechi alimentari: la solidarietà tra food security e food safety' [2017] (3) Quaderni costituzionali 623.

tackling these two issues in an integrated manner is essential to achieving sustainable and equitable food systems.

5 Experimental Measures: the Italian *Reddito Alimentare*

The connection between food waste and food poverty, already established in the so-called Gadda Law, is made explicit in the measure introduced by Article 1, para 434, of the 2022 Budget Law, which created the so-called *reddito alimentare*. This initiative provides for the donation of food parcels sourced from large-scale retail distribution to individuals in need through projects developed on an urban scale.

The implementation of this measure has followed a long trajectory, worth analysing, which only reached its operational phase in September 2024. The act that marked the beginning of this phase was Decree 78 of May 26, 2023, issued by the Ministry of Labour. This decree was drafted following a series of consultations among the involved stakeholders, including the Ministry of Agriculture, Food Sovereignty, and Forestry, the Agency for Agricultural Payments (AGEA), and the National Association of Italian Municipalities (ANCI), as well as the Working Group on Food Waste and Food Assistance and partner organisations of the Fund for European Aid to the Most Deprived (FEAD). The Decree defined the objectives (Article 2), final beneficiaries (Article 4), procedures for municipalities selected for the pilot phase to submit their projects (Article 5), funding allocation and reimbursement of costs for packaging, storage, and transport (Articles 6 and 7), and finally, the monitoring mechanisms for the experimental phase (Article 8).

This decree has served as a guiding framework for all subsequent phases of the experimental project. Initially, in the framework of the State-Regions Unified Conference, four metropolitan cities were identified as pilot locations for the initiative: Genoa, Florence, Naples, and Palermo. This was followed by Directorate Decree No. 41/468, which allocated financial resources for the 2023–2025 triennium and approved a non-competitive public notice for the four selected cities.

Following the procedures initiated by the municipalities, in the summer of 2024, the four cities submitted their project proposals, which were formally approved by Decree No. 289 of September 13, 2024, issued by the Head of the Department of the Ministry of Labour and Social Policies. As of September 2024, the experimental phase of the *reddito alimentare* has officially commenced.

Although it is not yet possible to analyse the funded projects, as they had not been made publicly available at the time of the drafting of this report, two aspects are particularly noteworthy. First, the financial allocation is not uniform across municipalities but is instead calibrated based on the number of individuals in need within each territory. Second, the methods by which each municipality will identify the target group of beneficiaries represent a critical aspect, as selection criteria may have significant implications for both social inequalities and the overall effectiveness of the measure.

Regarding the funding distribution among municipalities, Florence has been allocated the smallest amount, approximately 534,000 EUR, followed by Genoa with 970,000 EUR, Naples with 1,420,000 EUR, and finally Palermo, which received the highest allocation, 2,169,000 EUR. These figures align with ISTAT's most recent report on poverty, which indicates that in Northern Italy, 8% of the population lives in absolute poverty,[43] whereas in Southern Italy and the islands, the percentage rises to 10%. These statistics reflect a slight decline from the 2022 data, when poverty levels stood at 7.5% in the North and 9% in the South and islands.[44]

The identification of beneficiaries represents another particularly delicate issue, as the criteria set out in the individual municipal projects could affect both social inequalities and the effectiveness of the initiative itself. The selection process, depending on the methodologies adopted, could either enhance or hinder the impact of the programme on those most in need.

The overarching goal of the *reddito alimentare* is twofold. On the one hand, it seeks to reduce food waste by repurposing unsold products that are approaching expiration or that do not meet market-imposed aesthetic standards. On the other hand, and most importantly, it aims to combat food poverty by supporting segments of the population experiencing socio-economic vulnerability.

This measure may contribute to overcoming the 'paradox of scarcity within abundance', previously discussed, by ensuring that food surpluses are effectively redistributed to those who need them most.

---

43 ISTAT, *Le statistiche dell'ISTAT sulla povertà | anno 2023. Stabile la povertà assoluta, 17 ottobre 2024*, <https://www.istat.it/wp-content/uploads/2024/10/REPORT_POVERTA_2023.pdf> accessed 30 June 2025. The report includes a glossary that defines absolute poverty within the Italian context, based on the methodology adopted by ISTAT. It states that 'households are classified as being in absolute poverty if their monthly expenditure is equal to or below the value of the absolute poverty threshold (which varies depending on the size and age composition of the household, as well as by region and type of municipality of residence)'. For additional definitions, see 9.

44 ISTAT, *Resta stabile la povertà assoluta, la spesa media cresce ma meno dell'inflazione, 25 marzo 2024*, <https://www.istat.it/wp-content/uploads/2024/03/STAT_TODAY_POVERTA-ASSOLUTA_2023_25.03.24.pdf> accessed 5 February 2025.

6 Brief Concluding Notes

Based on the data and policies analysed thus far, it is possible to argue that coordinated measures addressing both food waste and food poverty can lead to mutually beneficial solutions, such as the *reddito alimentare*. Repurposing food surpluses to alleviate food poverty is not merely a desirable course of action but an imperative one.

Moreover, the data on food waste in the examined contexts suggest that legislative initiatives have achieved a measurable degree of success. Studies assessing the impact of the Gadda Law in Italy indicate a reduction in food waste, primarily attributable to the dissemination of the values embodied in the law.[45]

However, returning to the research question, it is worth emphasising that, in addressing food poverty, policies—particularly those that are innovative and foster collaborative action—appear to be more effective. As some researchers have observed, individual actions, even when guided by policy frameworks, tend to have a greater impact than legislation alone. This is partly because one of the key obstacles to reducing food poverty is ensuring that aid reaches those in need. This challenge necessitates state intervention, often facilitated through local entities, to ensure the effective inclusion of vulnerable populations in the resulting programmes.

Bibliography

Albisinni F, 'Innovazione-azione e innovazione-reazione nel diritto agrario e alimentare europeo: i nuovi scenari' [2013] 1–2 Agricoltura Istituzioni 225.

Alicino F, 'Il diritto fondamentale "a togliersi la fame". Banco di prova per il costituzionalismo contemporaneo' in Marusca De Castris (ed), *Cibo e Società. Una relazione da esplorare* (RomaTrE-Press 2018) 90.

Bodiguel L, 'French Legal Scheme on Food Waste and Agri-food Chain' (2021) 7 Journal of Rural Law 12.

Camoni D, 'La lotta contro lo spreco alimentare nel diritto comparato' [2023] (3) Rivista di diritto alimentare 5.

45 Simone Pitto, 'Tutela ambientale e sostenibilità dei sistemi alimentari. Una comparazione tra possibili soluzioni normative' (2023) 58 DPCE online 723.

Campiglio L and Rovati G, 'Il paradosso della scarsità dell'abbondanza: il caso della povertà alimentare' in Campiglio L and Rovati G (eds), *La povertà alimentare in Italia. Prima indagine quantitativa e qualitativa* (Edizioni Angelo Guerini e Associati 2009).

Cerini D, 'La legge Gadda di contrasto agli sprechi alimentari: la solidarietà tra food security e food safety' [2017] (3) Quaderni costituzionali 623.

Ferretti F, 'Spreco alimentare e sostenibilità ambientale: i profili giuridici del ruolo dell'AI' [2023] EJPLT Special Issue 116.

Franco S, 'Introduzione. Produrre di più o sprecare di meno?' in Falascioni L and Franco S (eds), *Lo spreco alimentare in Italia. Riflessioni, dati e testimonianze* (Carocci Editore 2022).

Lattanzi P, 'Le leggi "antispreco" alimentare. Esperienze nazionali a confronto' in de Leonardis F, *Studi in tema di economia circolare* (EUM—Edizioni Università di Macerata 2019).

Maccioni G, 'Lo spreco alimentare' in Costato L and Albisinni F (eds) *Trattato breve di diritto agrario italiano e dell'Unione Europea* (4th ed Wolters Kluwer—CEDAM 2023).

Pitto S, 'Tutela ambientale e sostenibilità dei sistemi alimentari. Una comparazione tra possibili soluzioni normative' (2023) 58 DPCE Online 723.

Scaffardi L, 'La sicurezza alimentare ovvero come il "diritto a togliersi la fame" evolve in un mondo che cambia' (2023) 59 DPCE Online 2167.

Sirsi E, 'Il diritto all'educazione del consumatore di alimenti' [2011] (4) Rivista di Diritto Agrario 496.

CHAPTER 11

The Reuse of Food Industry Scraps through the Lens of Public Law: Critical Issues and the Potential of Italian Legal Regulations

Alessia Depietri

Chapter structure

1 Introduction: Food Sustainability within the Circular Economy Framework to Address the Complexity of a Polycrisis

Earth[1] is currently facing risks threatening its very habitability, with critical concerns such as human and animal health, soil preservation, climate change, biodiversity, and responsible management of resources.[2] Addressing these

1 Research activity funded under the National Recovery and Resilience Plan (NRRP), Mission 4 Component 1 Investment 3.4 and 4.1. Call for tender No. 351 of 09/04/2022 of Italian Ministry of University and Research funded by the European Union – NextGenerationEU CUP D92B22000500005.

2 This topic refers to the so-called Planetary Boundaries, as best described in Johan Rockström and others, 'A Safe Operating Space for Humanity' (2009) 461 Nature 472; See also Will Steffen and others, 'Sustainability. Planetary Boundaries: Guiding Human Development on a Changing Planet' (2015) 347 Science 736.

multi-scalar issues, with an eye to safeguarding the future, can be viewed from two key perspectives: complexity[3] and 'polycrisis'.[4]

Mankind studies and manipulates the environment, a system of systems through science, economics, and law.[5] When these areas interact effectively, they produce coordinated, functional results. But to be effective, human action must be guided by responsibility rather than entitlement.[6]

In this context, European strategies such as the Green Deal,[7] and international ones such as the United Nations' 2030 Agenda[8] call on today's generations to think ahead, with the aim of fostering fertile ground for the pursuit of its Sustainable Development Goals (SDGs).

---

3 On the issue of complexity, see Edgar Morin, *Introduction à la pensée complexe* (Points 2014). On this point, the French philosopher and sociologist developed a theory of complexity that critiques reductionist thinking and proposes a systemic and interdisciplinary approach. In his view, reality is characterised by interconnections, feedback loops, and non-linearity, making it impossible to fully understand it through separate and fragmented analyses.

4 The term highlights how global challenges are interconnected rather than isolated, requiring coordinated and multidisciplinary responses. This was coined in the context of the study of the philosophy of complexity. On this point, see Edgar Morin and Anne Brigitte Kern, *Homeland Earth: A Manifesto for the New Millennium* (Hampton Press 1999). The term has been widely used by the World Economic Forum (WEF) to describe the convergence and interconnectedness of global crises that reinforce each other, creating unprecedented complexity. In the Global Risks Report 2023, the WEF highlighted how simultaneous events, such as climate change, geopolitical instability, economic crises, and social tensions, can no longer be analysed separately but must be understood as an interconnected system. This perspective aligns with Edgar Morin's complexity thinking, emphasising the need for systemic and collaborative approaches to tackle global challenges. World Economic Forum, *Global Risks Report 2023* (Ginevra, 2023) <www.weforum.org/publications/global-risks-report-2023/> accessed 31 January 2025.

5 Italian legal doctrine applies Luhmann's theory to analyse interactions between systems with different semantics. See Fabrizio Fracchia, *Transizioni: il punto di vista del diritto amministrativo* (Editoriale Scientifica 2024). In this regard, for a basic understanding of Luhmann's theory, reference is made to Niklas Luhmann, *Rechtssoziologie 1* (Studium RoRORO 1972).

6 On the issue of the necessity of intergenerational duties refer to Fabrizio Fracchia, 'The Legal Definition of Environment: from Right to Duty' [2006] The ICFAI Journal of Environmental Law 17.

7 Commission, *Communication from the Commission to the European Parliament, the Council, the European Economic and Social Committee and the Committee of the Regions: The European Green Deal*, COM (2019) 640 final, 11 December 2019. Among the various doctrinal contributions on the subject, see Ann Pettifor, *The Case for the Green New Deal* (Verso Book 2019) and Dario Bevilacqua, *Il Green New Deal* (Giuffrè 2024).

8 United Nations, *Transforming Our World: The 2030 Agenda for Sustainable Development* (UNGA Res 70/1, 21 October 2015) <https://sdgs.un.org/2030agenda> accessed 25 January 2025.

A concrete example is the need for new development paradigms that balance both ecological and economic requirements. Along these lines, is the idea to review the role of the state as a driver of new market philosophies and tools, in which supply and demand curves are complemented by that of sustainability.[9]

In line with the principle of integration,[10] one of the main objectives of EU public policy is to encourage the industrial sector to shift as many production systems as possible towards a circular economy,[11] a development paradigm that contrasts with the traditional linear model, with biomimicry[12] serving as an essential constant within it.[13]

At its core, this approach is rooted in the awareness of the planet's finite natural resources and the necessity of devising production strategies where goods can act as resources across multiple successive cycles.[14]

---

9 On this topic, see Massimo Cafagno, *Principi e strumenti di tutela dell'ambiente come sistema complesso, adattativo, comune* (Giappichelli 2007).

10 The principle of integration, enshrined in Article 11 of the Treaty on the Functioning of the European Union, requires environmental protection to be incorporated into the definition and implementation of all EU policies, ensuring sustainability across sectors. Pål Wennerås, 'Towards an Ever-Greener Union? Competence in the Field of the Environment and Beyond' [2008] 45 Common Market Law Review 1645.

11 The issue is thoroughly discussed in Benedetta Celati, *L'intervento pubblico per la riconversione tecnologica dell'economia* (CEDAM 2021); see also Elisa Scotti, 'Poteri pubblici, sviluppo sostenibile ed economia circolare' (2019) 98 Il Diritto dell'Economia 493; Chiara Feliziani, 'Industria e ambiente. Il principio di integrazione dalla rivoluzione industriale all'economia circolare [2020] Diritto Amministrativo 843; Monica Cocconi, 'La nuova politica industriale europea verso un modello di crescita circolare e rigenerativo' in Monica Cocconi (ed), *Il mosaico dell'economia circolare. Regole, principi e modelli* (Franco Angeli 2023).

12 Biomimicry is an approach inspired by nature to create innovative, sustainable, and efficient solutions by imitating the forms, functions, or evolutionary strategies of living beings.

13 The most authoritative definition of circular economy is that developed by the Ellen MacArthur Foundation, an organisation that promotes the circular development paradigm worldwide: 'circular economy is an industrial economy that is conceptually regenerative and replicates nature by actively improving and optimising the systems through which it operates.' As is well known, the concept of circular economy has been a concern for economists for many years. The starting point is the Brundtland Report of 1983, which highlighted the unsustainability of the so-called linear system. However, what is particularly relevant today is the legal effort to regulate the circular economy, which, as will be seen, dates back to less than a decade ago. See, Monica Cocconi, *La regolazione dell'economia circolare* (Franco Angeli, 2020).

14 For the sake of synthesis, the initial key steps taken by the EU towards a circular economy can be summarised as: Commission, *Closing the Loop: An EU Action Plan for the Circular Economy* COM (2015) 614 final. This communication introduced the

The New European Industrial Strategy[15] clearly shows that the circular economy is not just an economic tool, but one closely linked with achieving climate neutrality and reducing the EU's dependence on raw materials from non-EU countries. This new industrial policy aims to position businesses as key players in the ecological transition, challenging the outdated notion that environmental protection and economic growth are inherently at odds.[16]

Within this framework, the circular economy is strongly linked to food sustainability goals,[17] underscoring that environmental and food law are not separate fields but rather increasingly integrated.[18] Indeed, the transition to a

---

Circular Economy Package, which aimed to transition the EU towards a more sustainable and resource-efficient economy by focusing on waste reduction, recycling, and innovation. Complementing this communication, the European Parliament passed Directive 2008/98/EC of the European Parliament and of the Council on waste, which outlines the key principles of waste management, including the promotion of recycling and reducing landfill use. In 2017, the European Parliament approved the *Second Circular Economy Package*, which includes Directive (EU) 2018/851 of the European Parliament and of the Council of 30 May 2018 amending Directive 2008/98/EC on waste, Directive (EU) 2018/852 of the European Parliament and of the Council of 30 May 2018 on packaging and packaging waste, Directive (EU) 2018/850 of the European Parliament and of the Council of 30 May 2018 on the landfill of waste, and Directive (EU) 2018/849 of the European Parliament and of the Council of 30 May 2018 amending Directive 94/62/EC on packaging waste. For a general dissertation on the legal regulation of the circular economy, see Francesco De Leonardis, 'Economia circolare: saggio sui suoi diversi aspetti giuridici. Verso uno Stato circolare' (2017) 25 Diritto Amministrativo 163.

15 Commission, *A New Industrial Strategy for Europe* COM (2020) 102 final.

16 The recent *Draghi Report 2024* highlights that inclusive and sustainable growth is key to addressing global challenges, with industry playing a central role in the EU's economic and technological sovereignty; see Mario Draghi, *The Draghi report: A competitiveness strategy for Europe* <www.commission.europa.eu/topics/eu-competitiveness/draghi-report_en#paragraph_47059> accessed 8 January 2025. This aligns with the EU's Competitiveness Compass, which emphasises strengthening industrial capabilities for a more resilient economy: Commission—Press release, *An EU Compass to regain competitiveness and secure sustainable prosperity* <www.https://ec.europa.eu/commission/presscorner/detail/en/ip_25_339> accessed 2 February 2025. For a doctrinal dissertation on the topic, reference can be made to Anna Maria Poggi and Federica Fabrizzi, *Il nuovo Whatever it takes. Il rapporto Draghi: ambizioni e difficoltà del futuro dell'Europa* [2024] (22) federalismi.it IV; see also Monica Cocconi, *L'Unione europea ad un bivio sul futuro del mercato unico e della competitività europea* [2025] (4) federalismi.it 144.

17 On this topic, see Maria Carlotta Rizzuto, 'La sostenibilità come chiave di sintesi dell'economia circolare: prospettive e criticità nella filiera agroalimentare' in Silia Gardini (ed), *Percorsi di circolarità tra diritto ed economia* (Mucchi editore 2023).

18 On this topic, please refer to Massimo Monteduro, 'Alimentazione e ambiente' in Giampaolo Rossi (ed), *Diritto dell'ambiente* (5th edn, Giappichelli 2021).

sustainable economy, as envisioned by the Green Deal, must also include the creation of sustainable food systems, addressing every stage of the food chain.

This is the foundation of the European Commission's Farm to Fork Strategy,[19] which represents a fundamental shift in how food systems are viewed: from major contributors to environmental and climate damage to potential solutions for achieving climate neutrality and boosting the economic competitiveness of EU countries.

The interplay between circular economy tools and food sustainability goals, therefore, deserves to be analysed in the context of industrial production methodologies, especially in the innovative context of 'upcycled food'. This concept, in its simplicity, could be a harbinger of revolutionary impacts: recovering ingredients that would otherwise be wasted and transforming them into other production cycles through safe and traceable processes. It is, therefore, an innovation that not only combats food waste, but also helps the environment by reducing CO_2 emissions and consumption of natural resources.

As will be discussed later, upcycling in the food sector can be considered to be not only a subset of the waste hierarchy,[20] but also a useful regenerative tool for natural assets such as soil.

And it is precisely within the scope of food upcycling where, at the intersection of law and technology, the implementation of circularity tools devoted to the development of resilient food systems becomes decisive in driving a more robust industrial production sector.

This paper explores the Italian legal system's approach to sustainability, focusing on the reuse of agro-food-industry scraps, in line with circular economy objectives.

It aims to evaluate the strengths and weaknesses of the legal framework, balancing ecological and economic needs, and ensuring that technology leads to practical, sustainable results.

---

19 In particular, see Commission, *Farm to Fork Strategy for a Fair, Healthy, and Environmentally-Friendly Food System* COM (2020) 381 final. On this topic, see Filippo Venturi, 'The farm to fork strategy. A comprehensive but cautious approach to "multidimensional" food sustainability' [2021] (1) Rivista Quadrimestrale di Diritto dell'Ambiente 70.

20 Specifically, this refers to a priority order of actions to be taken to reduce and manage waste, promoting prevention first and disposal only as a last resort. Specifically, the order of priority is prevention, reuse, recycling, energy recovery and, only if none of these steps are feasible, disposal.

2 Legal Categories Supporting the Circular Economy: Critical Issues and Potential of Italian Legal Regulations

2.1 *Context*

Before examining the Italian regulatory framework in detail, it is essential to understand the broader context in which this analysis takes place.

With the amendment of Articles 9 and 41, the Italian Constitution has become one of the first examples of a fourth-generation constitutional charter, aligning with the concept of 'Environmental Constitutionalism'.[21] Article 9 establishes environmental protection—particularly for future generations—as a fundamental principle of Italy's legal system.[22] Meanwhile, Article 41 redefines the relationship between the economy, health, and environmental sustainability, emphasising that these elements are not in opposition but should guide economic activities. The outdated notion that environmental protection and economic development are incompatible has been replaced by a vision of sustainable progress in line with evolving European models.[23]

Recognising that the ecological transition requires a collective effort from public institutions, businesses, and consumers, the Italian Legislature has adopted a proactive approach to directing and coordinating economic activities within ecological limits (the so-called blue economy). This shift is supported by post-pandemic recovery efforts and significant EU funding under the NextGenerationEU programme,[24] which aims to foster a green, digital transition centred on biodiversity protection, research, and sustainable production models.

One of the key initiatives within Italy's National Recovery and Resilience Plan, funded by the EU, is the National Strategy for the Circular Economy[25]

---

21 Italian Constitutional Law 1, 11 February 2022, Official Gazette 44 of 22 February 2022.

22 See Antonio D'Aloia, *La Costituzione e il dovere di pensare al futuro* [2022] (2) Biolaw Journal 1; Paola Lombardi, *Ambiente e generazioni future: la dimensione temporale della solidarietà* [2023] (1) federalismi.it 86.

23 For a comprehensive dissertation on the topic, reference can be made to Francesco De Leonardis, *Lo stato ecologico. Approccio sistemico, economia, poteri pubblici e mercato* (Giappichelli 2023).

24 Council Regulation (EU) 2020/2094 of 14 December 2020 establishing a European Union Recovery Instrument to support the recovery in the aftermath of the COVID-19 crisis [2020] OJ L433I/23.

25 Refer to Ministero dell'Ambiente e della Sicurezza Energetica <www.mase.gov.it/pagina/riforma-1-1-strategia-nazionale-l-economia-circolare> accessed 3 January 2025; On this point, see Alessia Depietri, 'Residui di produzione e bioeconomia: un'analisi dei principali driver dell'economia circolare' [2023] (6) federalismi.it 41.

which promotes sustainable production and consumption patterns, encouraging market dynamics that align with environmental goals.

In the food sector, key objectives of the Strategy include reducing food waste through improved distribution strategies and implementing an integrated nutrient management plan to enhance resource efficiency.

Agribusiness can be analysed through Ayres' concept of industrial metabolism, where industries, like living organisms, absorb resources, transform them, and produce waste.[26] Therefore, the shift from a business-as-usual model to a circular economy, where waste is seen as a resource, is crucial in addressing issues like food loss and waste.

Food industry scraps can be categorised as either surplus food that can be donated or production residues from industrial processes.

In Italy, the Good Samaritan Law[27] and the Gadda Law[28] regulate food recovery and donation, with the latter simplifying the system and offering incentives for businesses.[29]

The focus here is on production residues, which pose technical and legal challenges. Reintroducing these residues into agribusiness or pet food production aligns with the circular economy and upcycling principles.

This approach, governed by Italian law, follows EU waste management regulations on classifying and reintegrating production residues into the supply chain for sustainable agribusiness. The framework was created by Directive 2008/98/EC, amended by Directive 2018/851/EU, and transposed into Italian law via Legislative Decree 116/2020, integrated into the Environmental Code.[30]

2.2 *Waste, End of Waste, and By-Products in the Italian Legal System*

Article 183 of the Italian Environmental Code defines waste as any substance or object that is discarded, intended to be discarded, or required to be

26 Robert U. Ayres and others, *Industrial Metabolism, the Environment, and Application of Materials-balance Principles for Selected Chemicals* (International Institute for Applied Systems Analysis 1989).

27 Law 155 of 25 June 2003, *Regulation on the Distribution of Food Products for Social Solidarity Purposes* [2003] Official Gazette of the Italian Republic, General Series, 150.

28 Law 166 of 19 August 2016, *Provisions on the Donation and Distribution of Food and Pharmaceutical Products for Social Solidarity Purposes and the Reduction of Waste* [2016] Official Gazette of the Italian Republic, General Series, 202.

29 See Daniele Camoni, 'La lotta allo spreco alimentare nel diritto comparato' [2023] (3) Rivista di diritto alimentare 5.

30 Italian Environmental Code (Legislative Decree 152 of 3 April 2006) [2006] Official Gazette of the Italian Republic, General Series, 88.

discarded.[31] The legal framework allows certain materials to be reclassified as 'End of Waste' or 'by-products' under specific conditions, in line with the goal of fully implementing the waste hierarchy, which is primarily based on the principle of prevention.

'End of Waste'[32] (regulated by Article 184-ter of Environmental Code) applies to recovered waste for reuse, while by-products (under Article 184-bis) are not classified as waste if they meet specific conditions. However, this distinction is often unclear, creating a regulatory gray area that causes uncertainty for businesses and enforcement authorities.[33]

To understand the concept of by-product, it's essential to trace its origins back to case law.

After years of assuming that all production residues were waste, a significant shift occurred in the early 2000s. In the Palin Granit ruling,[34] the Court of Justice initially distinguished between waste and production residues, defining the latter as secondary substances that can be marketed and used. While early rulings required by-products to undergo no transformation before being reused in the same process, the concept has since evolved with more flexibility. This shift in case law has influenced both European and national legislation.

In Italian law, Article 184-bis, para 1 of the Environmental Code sets the specific conditions that production residues must meet to be classified as by-products.[35]

First, the residue must come from a production process whose primary aim is not to produce the by-product itself. Another key requirement is the certainty of reuse of the secondary substance, which must not undergo treatments

31 The European Court of Justice has broadly interpreted this definition to prioritise human health and environmental protection. See Joined cases C 418/97 and C 419/97—ARCO Chemie Nederland Ltd v Minister van Volkshuisvesting, Ruimtelijke Ordening en Milieubeheer (C 418/97), Vereniging Dorpsbelang Hees et al v Directeur van de dienst Milieu en Water van de provincie Gelderland (C 419/97) [2000] ECR I-04475, paras 43–97.

32 For a dissertation on this topic in the Italian legal system see Giovanni Barozzi Reggiani, 'Ambiente, rifiuti, principio di legalità: obiettivo End of Waste' [2018] (4) federalismi.it 2.

33 On this point, the interpretative difficulties of these categories can be inferred from several rulings by the Court of Justice of the European Union. See joined cases C 206/88 and C 207/88—Criminal proceedings v G. Vessoso and G. Zanetti [1990] ECR I-0146, paras 11–13 and joined cases C 304/94, C 330/94, C 342/94 and C 224/95—Criminal proceedings against E. Tombesi and A. Tombesi (C 304/94), R. Santella (C 330/94), G. Muzi and others (C 342/94) and A. Savini (C 224/95) [1997] ECR I-03561, paras 19–54.

34 C 9/00—Palin Granit Oy and Vehmassalon kansanterveystyön kuntayhtymän hallitus [2002] ECR I-03533, paras 3–51.

35 Stefano Palmisano and Vito Rubino, 'I sottoprodotti: senso, potenzialità e incertezze applicative di un elemento fondamentale del diritto dell'economia circolare' in Monica Cocconi (ed), *Il mosaico dell'economia circolare* (n 11).

beyond those that are part of standard industrial practice. Second, the use of the by-product must be legal, meaning it must meet all technical, health, and environmental standards required for creating a new product. If any of these conditions are not met, the production residue falls back into the waste category, requiring compliance with 'End of Waste' regulations that are characterised by a stringent authorisation process for recovery.[36]

What distinguishes by-product regulations from waste management ones is that the use of by-products is not subject to an authorisation regime. Entrepreneurs must prove that the residue they classify as a by-product meets the requirements of Article 184-bis of the Environmental Code and relevant product-specific regulations.

2.3 *The Legal and Operational Challenges of the By-Product Category*

As particular as it may seem to regulate such a focused category, by-product has uncertain boundaries that, at least partially, sought clarification in Ministerial Decree 246/16,[37] which was followed by an additional operational circular.[38]

Prominent among the main innovations of the Ministerial Decree in question is the introduction of a Supply and Demand Exchange Platform[39] for the purpose of knowledge sharing and facilitation of by-product exchanges between producers. Its strengths include easy access through free, voluntary registration, and transparency via a searchable public list. The tool helps optimise resources and simplify inter-firm exchanges, but its effectiveness relies on widespread adoption by companies. This adherence largely depends on resolving legal issues that affect its practical implementation.

---

36 Giacomo Biasutti, 'Autorizzazioni ambientali ed End of Waste. Tra procedimenti amministrativi sui generis e garanzie in favore del privato' [2020] (29) federalismi.it 17.

37 *Ministerial Decree 246/2016, Regulation on the Implementation of Provisions Concerning the Separate Waste Collection* (Minister for the Environment and Protection of Land and Sea, 6 April 2016) [2016] Official Gazette of the Italian Republic, General Series, 95.

38 See the Circular of May 30, 2017, Prot. No. 7619 of the Ministry of the Environment and Protection of Land and Sea, which begins as follows: 'In response to numerous inquiries, the Ministry finds it useful to provide clarifications to ensure uniform application and clear interpretation of the provision. Given the complexity of both domestic and European regulations on by-product use and the lack of established interpretative practices, these clarifications, along with a technical-legal appendix, are provided as an integral part of the circular' (free translation).

39 In accordance with Art 10, para 1, of Ministerial Decree 264/2016, to facilitate the exchange of supply and demand for by-products, 'the competent Chambers of Commerce establish a dedicated list where producers and users of by-products are registered, at no cost' (free translation). Registration on this platform is not mandatory but encourages the expansion of a marketplace for the commercialisation of by-products.

With reference to the by-product category and the requirements of Article 184-bis of the Environmental Code, the critical issues that emerge are as follows:

- the difficulty of defining whether or not a production residue has been treated according to normal industrial practice (in other words, what does normal industrial practice consist of?);
- placing the burden of proof on the producer to prove the provision of certainty of the nature of by-product,
- the risk of instrumentalisation of the by-product category for illegal or criminal purposes.

The concept of normal industrial practice has caused practical uncertainties, as distinguishing between normal and non-normal practices can be difficult across industries. To clarify this, the Italian Supreme Court, in 2012, defined normal industrial practice as excluding activities that radically transform the material or alter its original nature, as well as interventions that differ from typical actions in the production process. Scholars have interpreted this definition as fundamentally misleading and contradictory, as it fails to recognise the lack of an automatic connection between radical transformations and their non-ordinary nature. According to this interpretation, normal industrial practice would only encompass minimal interventions, thus significantly limiting opportunities for reusing production waste.[40]

Only a year later, Italian judges proposed a more flexible definition, suggesting that normal industrial practice should be understood as the series of operations that a company routinely performs on the raw material, that the by-product is intended to replace, thereby excluding any manipulative interventions on the residue that differ from those typically executed in the production process in which it is utilised.[41]

The issue was addressed in Ministerial Decree 264/2016, which provides guidelines for determining whether production residues should be classified as by-products or waste.[42] The decree defines normal industrial practice as any

40 Cass. pen. 17 April 2012, 17453; For a detailed commentary, see Alberto Muratori, 'Sottoprodotti: la Suprema Corte in difesa del sistema Tolemaico? (nota a Cass. n. 17453/2012)' [2012] Ambiente e sviluppo 605 and Stefano Maglia, 'Normale pratica industriale: la contraddittoria e "pericolosa" interpretazione della Cassazione (nota a Cass. n. 17453/2012)' [2012] Ambiente e sviluppo 611.

41 Cass. pen. 15 May 2013, 20886.

42 In particular Art 5, para 1, of Ministerial Decree 264/2016 states that processes required to make a substance or object suitable for specific use, ensuring environmental and health protection, do not constitute normal industrial practice unless performed within the same production cycle. Paragraph 2 adds that activities forming an integral part of

treatment necessary to make a residue suitable for its specific use, in full compliance with health and environmental standards, while being an integral part of the main production process.

Even if regulation seeks to balance preventing improper handling of waste with promoting the circular economy—recognising that by-products, like raw materials, may require some processing before use—this definition still leaves room for interpretation.[43]

To provide certainty of a by-product's status, the entrepreneur must demonstrate that the residue, classified as a by-product, meets the requirements of Article 184-bis of the Environmental Code and the relevant regulations. For example, the certainty of the by-product's reuse can be demonstrated through contracts or sales invoices transferring the by-product to a user; documentation confirming its role in the intended production process; and/or data sheets detailing its characteristics, storage, and handling procedures.[44]

In any case, the absence of an integrated, well-established administrative practice on the matter and the divergent definitions of jurisprudential matrix that have followed over the years, still leave room for error for the operator who, in the event that he or she fails to provide adequate documentation or evidence to justify that a material is a by-product and not a waste product, could incur administrative or criminal penalties for illegal waste management. This implies a legal risk for entrepreneurs and an additional burden of liability, which could lead to greater caution in day-to-day operations.

While the category of by-products doesn't require administrative authorisation, it could be exploited for illegal waste trade and transport, especially through new practices being employed by organised environmental crime. This concern, often overlooked, requires careful attention from authorities to ensure the circular economy does not inadvertently foster illegal activities. Achieving a balance remains complex.[45]

---

the production cycle to adapt environmental or health characteristics to meet relevant requirements are considered normal industrial practice, even if designed specifically to meet those requirements without negative environmental impacts.

43 Alberto Muratori, 'D.M. n. 264/2016: criteri realmente "indicativi" per riconoscere i sottoprodotti' [2017] Ambiente e Sviluppo 251.

44 This aspect, outlined in art 5 of Ministerial Decree 246/2017, is further explained in point 4 of the explanatory circular. It aims to provide a more detailed description of the requirements for contractual documentation and technical sheets necessary to meet the burden of proof. This clarification helps ensure compliance with legal and environmental standards when demonstrating that a product or substance meets the necessary criteria for use without negative impacts.

45 On this point, see Annachiara Nicoli, 'Economia circolare e contrasto alla criminalità ambientale nel ciclo di rifiuti. Un approccio integrato' [2023] (7) federalismi.it 129.

2.4 *Some Observations on a Missing Link in the Regulation of By-Products*

In addition to difficulties applying the legal framework mentioned above, this paper aims to point out that, at present, the Italian Environmental Code does not devote any space to the category of 'second degree by-product'.

This term, which does not belong to any official classification, can be interpreted as a category that identifies materials derived from a first cycle of by-product recovery, thus no longer directly related to the original production process, but which could still be valuable to other sectors. In other words, these are materials or substances that, while already derived from a value-extracting process (eg the transformation of a primary by-product), could be further reused in other production contexts, nullifying their classification as waste.

The use of second degree by-products maximises resource efficiency by reducing the amount of wasted materials, creates new business opportunities, decreases environmental impact by avoiding the landfilling or incineration of materials that can still be used, and fosters industrial symbiosis by enabling collaboration between different productive sectors.

The regulatory silence on this point could be resolved through a reinterpretation of Article 184-bis, paragraph 1, letter a) which outlines the conditions under which a material can be categorised as a by-product and not waste. Sub-letter a) states 'the substance or object originates from a production process, of which it constitutes an integral part, and whose primary purpose is not the production of that substance or object'.

In these terms, it would be necessary to start with the idea that the by-product, from the moment it is reused, is considered a product tout court, resetting the steps in the production chain and its need to meet all the requirements of Article 184-bis.

But given already the operational difficulties associated with the category of first-degree by-products, it would perhaps be useful to introduce an explicit legal definition of second-degree by-product, clearly distinguishing it from waste and primary by-products and making a reasonable assessment of the requirements that the latter must have in order for them to be safely and legally reused in other production cycles.

3 Focusing on the Potential of the By-Products Category in the Agrifood Industry: the Role of Food Upcycling

As stated earlier, a particularly interesting topic exists at the intersection between the circular economy and food sustainability: the reuse of organic industrial scraps, with the food industry being the primary contributor.

The reuse of food industry scraps, in fact, has an important operational scope, in between 'inorganic' and 'organic' circular economy.[46]

These definitions, undoubtedly borrowed from chemistry, are intended to subdivide two fundamental areas of action of the circular economy.

While the inorganic circular economy relates to the actions that must be undertaken to implement the steps in the waste hierarchy, the organic circular economy mainly touches on the need to rebalance the regeneration cycles of resources from the soil and the sea and to transform organic waste into compost.[47]

What is special about the food sector, with a particular focus on the issue of food upcycling,[48] is that it is able to incorporate both.

In the Italian legal system, the regulatory tools exist to reuse food surpluses, and these tools can also be applied to the category of by-products.

It is worth mentioning that when production scraps can be easily classified as by-products, there are numerous opportunities for circular reuse of food industry scraps.[49] A prime example is the reuse of coffee silverskins, the outer layer of coffee beans discarded during roasting. This scrap is widely recognised as a by-product under specific regulations and is increasingly utilised in various sectors, including animal feed, food ingredients, health supplements, natural packaging materials, and cosmetics. Another segment of the food industry where waste is well-established as a by-product is tomato processing. For instance, tomato peels can be repurposed not only in the food sector but also in beauty products and even paint manufacturing. Or consider the peels from oranges that are discarded during juice production—these can be effectively repurposed in the textile industry.

From these examples, several insights emerge:

- First, it is clear that the scientific community, spanning fields like green chemistry and engineering, is making significant strides in optimising the circular reuse of production food scraps. The role of the hard sciences is to not only find opportunities to upcycle this waste but to also subject these processes to repeated lifecycle assessments (LCA) to quantify the intervention's impact on the process's environmental footprint, from cradle to grave.

---

46 See Francesco De Leonardis, *Lo stato ecologico*, 111.

47 ibid, 115.

48 For a discussion on the concept of food upcycling, see the paper by the Upcycled Foods Definition Task Force (2020) <www.upcycledfood.org/upcycled-food> accessed 20 February 2025. The Upcycled Foods Definition Task Force established a standardised definition of upcycled food to enhance clarity and sustainability. Upcycled foods are made from ingredients that would otherwise go to waste, sourced through verifiable supply chains, and contribute positively to the environment.

49 Refer to Alessia Depietri, Residui di produzione e bioeconomia (n 22), 60.

- Second, it should be remembered that the reuse of waste in the agribusiness sector should always be linked back to food safety requirements.
- Third, where waste is reused in a non-agrifood context, the impact of the by-product's use on the overall environmental performance of the product should be disclosed in line with recent eco-design requirements promoted by the EU.[50]

Where it is impossible to recover the food scraps for upcycling—or reuse in a higher value product—the waste falls into the category of organic waste[51] and may well be treated and returned to the environment—also known as down-cycling, or reuse in a lower value product—contributing to regenerative action (ie soil compost).

On this point, it should be noted that the organic circular economy is a decisive driver for the bioeconomy, an economic model primarily based on the use of biomass to replace fossil-based materials, promoting a circular and low-carbon economy.[52]

The hierarchy of food upcycling synthesises these two different souls of the circular economy—inorganic and organic—and demonstrates how the food sector presents a unique opportunity to address all three dimensions of sustainability, as characterised by the well-known triple bottom line framework of people, planet, and profit.

---

50 Regulation (EU) 2024/1781 of the European Parliament and of the Council of 13 July 2024 establishing a framework for setting ecodesign requirements for sustainable products.

51 With reference to this last point, it should be noted that with Directive 2018/815/EU, food waste has been classified as organic waste, defined as any substance or product intended for human consumption that has become waste because its holder has disposed of it or has been ordered to do so. On this aspect, see Monica Delsignore, 'Sulla necessità di una definizione armonizzata del rifiuto alimentare per la concreta realizzazione dell'economia circolare' (2018) 96 Il Diritto dell'Economia 329.

52 The bioeconomy integrates biological industries with circular waste management and sustainable product design. It uses organic waste for biofuels, fertilisers, and textiles to support sustainability. The EU's bioeconomy strategy (2012, updated in 2018) focuses on food security, resource efficiency, climate mitigation, and economic competitiveness, aiming to strengthen bio-based sectors and national strategies while respecting ecological limits. See Commission, Directorate-General for Research and Innovation, *A Sustainable Bioeconomy for Europe: Strengthening the Connection Between Economy, Society and the Environment—Updated Bioeconomy Strategy* (Publications Office 2018). See also Robert Costanza (ed), *Ecological economics. The Science and Management of Sustainability* (Columbia University Press 2002) and Francesco De Leonardis, 'The ecosystem services provided by soil and the importance of its protection: the essential role of organic waste' [2022] (1) Rivista Quadrimestrale di Diritto dell'Ambiente 400.

4 Conclusions: Final Food for Thought on Enhancing the Current State of the Issue

The challenges of the agro-industrial sector represent one of the many pieces of the mosaic underlying the European ecological transition process, which still needs more attention from public authorities. From this framework emerges the need for an ecologically oriented state figure, capable of understanding the context in which it operates through a dialogue with science and whose political choices-thanks to the legal instrument-can generate the purposes within which to promote technological innovation; added to this is the role of business-an entity considered among the largest holders of environmental responsibility-that needs to have its own profit using that of the blue economy as a key.

In this context, the circular economy is the only development paradigm that can dictate the rules of the game.[53]

The circular economy is a constantly evolving model, and within its context, food upcycling offers a new impetus for analysis. The reuse of production scraps in the food industry straddles the organic and inorganic circular economies, between traditional recycling and bioeconomic approaches, between social needs and innovation.

In light of these observations, it could therefore be argued that the reuse of food scraps represents the crux of the circular food economy, a specific evolution and subcategory of the traditional circular model in which economic, nutritional, innovation, and biological regeneration needs intersect.

This category focuses on maximum utilisation of food resources, reducing waste throughout the supply chain and enhancing the value of food in all its forms. The goal is to preserve the nutritive value of food and reintegrate it back into the system, rather than that value being lost.

If its first purpose is the prevention of waste throughout the supply chain through improved production practices (think, for example, of innovative technologies such as smart packaging to optimise product shelf-life) and the redistribution of surpluses, then the valuing of food scraps becomes the most strategic step in drawing the line between food waste and reusable input. But even when food recovery is not feasible, closing the biological loop (through composting practices) or biomass production remain sustainable solutions.

---

53 On this point, some scholars have begun to introduce conditions for the existence of a true circularity principle to guide public action in its chase to avoid the much-feared point of no return; on this specific aspect, see Scilla Vernile, *Dall'economia circolare al principio di circolarità. Una lettura giuridica nel solco dell'Art. 9 Cost.* (Giappichelli 2024).

If, with reference, to the Italian legal system, the dynamics of food waste are and are becoming increasingly clear and defined (both on the producer side and on the consumer side), the issue of legal categories related to the valuing of industrial production scraps is still marked by gray areas.

These are characterised, above all, by the uncertainty faced by entrepreneurs in identifying by-products due to the regulatory imprecision and unstable jurisprudential approach applied to its definition. Almost ten years after the entry into force of Ministerial Decree 246/2016, the productive world tends to fear defining production waste in clear terms, unless they are cases in which repeated practice over time makes up for regulatory uncertainty. This has a negative impact on the potential for collaboration and exchange in the by-product market and the encouragement of the use of such waste through platforms created specifically for this purpose.

What is lacking, then, in the Italian regulations is a classification of second-degree by-products. The formalisation of this category, together with a clarification of the requirements stated in Article 184-bis of the Environmental Code, may be grounds for reflection as part of a recodification of environmental law in Italy. This process should take into account the apparent differences of opinion and confrontational positions that have occurred between the political and academic worlds regarding this topic.

An improvement in regulatory dynamics would lay the groundwork for new spaces for public intervention in the agribusiness market. In addition to providing fiscal interventions (ie pay-as-you-throw systems) and tax relief (ie in exchange for donating surpluses),[54] it could prove fruitful to drive public interest in the green procurement (in this case, food procurement)[55] system by promoting the purchase of goods and services that use upcycled food, through public contracting. Related to this is the idea of introducing at the European level specific environmental certifications[56] for food obtained through upcycling processes, which already exist in the United States.

As Mark Victor Hansen put it, 'garbage is a great resource in the wrong place that lacks someone's imagination for it to be recycled for the benefit of all'.

---

54 On these two points see Benedetta Celati, *L'intervento pubblico per la riconversione tecnologica dell'economia* (n 11), 48.

55 On the topic of Green Public Procurement as a tool to steer businesses towards sustainability, among other contributions, reference is made to Sara Valaguzza, *Governing by Contract: Procuring for Value. Creating Value through Public Contracts* (Editoriale Scientifica 2021); ibid *Sustainable Development in Public Contracts: An Example of Strategic Regulation* (Editoriale Scientifica 2016); Mark Stein and others (eds), *Sustainable Food Procurement: Legal, Social and Organisational Challenges* (Routledge 2024).

56 For a general overview on the topic, see Auretta Benedetti, *Certezza pubblica e 'certezze' private* (Giuffrè 2010).

Only by bridging the gap between science and law, can imagination turn food upcycling into a mainstream paradigm, shaping a more sustainable future for society.

Bibliography

Ayres R, Norberg-Bohm V, Prince J, Stigliani WM, Yanowitz J, *Industrial Metabolism, the Environment, and Application of Materials-balance Principles for Selected Chemicals* (International Institute for Applied Systems Analysis 1989).

Barozzi Reggiani G, *Ambiente, rifiuti, principio di legalità: obiettivo end of waste* [2018] (4) federalismi.it 2.

Benedetti A, *Certezza pubblica e 'certezze' private* (Giuffrè 2010).

Bevilacqua D, *Il Green New Deal.* (Giuffré 2023).

Biasutti G, *Autorizzazioni ambientali ed End of Waste. Tra procedimenti amministrativi sui generis e garanzie in favore del privato* [2020] (29) federalismi.it 17.

Cafagno M, *Principi e strumenti di tutela dell'ambiente come sistema complesso, adattativo, comune* (Giappichelli 2007).

Camoni D, *La lotta allo spreco alimentare nel diritto comparato* [2023] (3) Rivista di Diritto Alimentare 5.

Celati B, *L'intervento pubblico per la riconversione ecologica dell'economia. Modelli, strumenti e prospettive giuridiche* (CEDAM 2021).

Cocconi M, *La regolazione dell'economia circolare* (FrancoAngeli 2020).

Cocconi M, 'La nuova politica industriale europea verso un modello di crescita circolare e rigenerativo' in Cocconi M (ed), *Il mosaico dell'economia circolare. Regole, principi, modelli* (Franco Angeli 2023).

Cocconi M, *L'Unione europea ad un bivio sul futuro del mercato unico e della competitività europea* [2025] (4) federalismi.it 144.

D'Aloia A, *La Costituzione e il dovere di pensare al futuro* [2022] (2) BioLaw Journal 1.

De Leonardis F, *Economia circolare: saggio sui suoi diversi aspetti giuridici. Verso uno Stato circolare* (2017) 25 Diritto Amministrativo 163.

De Leonardis F, *Lo stato ecologico. Approccio sistemico, economia, poteri pubblici e mercato* (Giappichelli 2024).

De Leonardis F, 'The ecosystem services provided by soil and the importance of its protection: the essential role of organic waste' [2022] (1) Rivista Quadrimestrale di Diritto dell'Ambiente 400.

Delsignore M, 'Sulla necessità di una definizione armonizzata del rifiuto alimentare per la concreta realizzazione dell'economia circolare' (2018) 96 Il Diritto dell'Economia 329.

Depietri A, 'Residui di produzione e bioeconomia: un'analisi dei principali driver dell'economia circolare' [2023] (6) federalismi.it 41.

Feliziani C, 'Industria e ambiente. Il principio di integrazione dalla rivoluzione industriale all'economia circolare' (2020) (4) Diritto Amministrativo 843.

Fracchia F, *Transizioni: il punto di vista del diritto amministrativo* (Editoriale Scientifica 2024).

Fracchia F, 'The Legal Definition of Environment: from Right to Duty' [2006] The ICFAI Journal of Environmental Law (IJEL) 17.

Lombardi P, *Ambiente e generazioni future: la dimensione temporale della solidarietà* [2023] (1) federalismi.it 86.

Luhmann N, *Rechtssoziologie 1* (Studium RoRORO 1972).

Maglia S, 'Normale pratica industriale: la contraddittoria e "pericolosa" interpretazione della Cassazione (nota a Cass. n. 17453/2012)' [2012] (7) Ambiente e sviluppo 611.

Monteduro M, 'Alimentazione e ambiente' in Rossi G. (ed), *Diritto dell'ambiente.* (Giappichelli 2023) 352.

Morin E and Brigitte Kern A, *Homeland Earth: A Manifesto for the New Millennium* (Hampton Press 1999).

Morin E and Brigitte Kern A, *Introduction à la pensée complexe* (Points 2014).

Muratori A, 'Sottoprodotti: la Suprema Corte in difesa del sistema Tolemaico? (nota a Cass. n. 17453/2012)' (2012) (7) Ambiente & Sviluppo 251.

Muratori A, 'D.M. n. 264/2016: criteri realmente "indicativi" per riconoscere i sottoprodotti' [2017] Ambiente e Sviluppo 605.

Nicoli A, 'Economia circolare e contrasto alla criminalità ambientale nel ciclo di rifiuti' [2023] (7) Federalismi 129.

Palmisano S and Rubino V, 'I sottoprodotti: senso, potenzialità e incertezze applicative di un elemento fondamentale del diritto dell'economia circolare' in Cocconi M (ed), *Il mosaico dell'economia circolare. Regole, principi e modelli* (FrancoAngeli 2023) 173.

Poggi AM and Federica Fabrizzi F, *Il nuovo Whatever it takes. Il rapporto Draghi: ambizioni e difficoltà del futuro dell'Europa* [2024] (22) Federalismi 4.

Pettifor A, *The case for the Green New Deal* (Verso Book 2019).

Rizzuto MC, 'La sostenibilità come chiave di sintesi dell'economia circolare' in Gardini S (ed), *Percorsi di circolarità tra diritto ed economia* (Mucchi Editore 2023).

Rockström J, Steffen W, Noone K, Persson Å, Stuart Chapin III F, Lambin EF, Lenton TM, Scheffer M, Folke C, Schellnhuber HJ, Nykvist B, de Wit CA, Hughes T, van der Leeuw S, Rodhe H, Sörlin S, Snyder PK, Costanza R, Svedin U, Falkenmark M, Karlberg L, Corell RW, Fabry VJ, Hansen J and Foley JA, *A Safe Operating Space for Humanity* (2009) 461 Nature 472.

Scotti E, 'Poteri pubblici, sviluppo sostenibile ed economia circolare' (2019) 98 Il diritto dell'economia 493.

Stein M, Mariani M, Caranta R and Polychronakis Y (eds), *Sustainable Food Procurement: Legal, Social and Organisational Challenges* (Routledge 2024)

Steffen W, Richardson K, Rockström J, Cornell SE, Fetzer I, Bennett EM, Biggs R, Carpenter SR, De Vries W, De Wit CA, Folke C, Gerten D, Heinke J, Mace GM, Persson LM, Ramanathan V, Reyers B and Sörlin S, 'Sustainability. Planetary Boundaries: Guiding Human Development on a Changing Planet' (2015) 347 Science 736.

Valaguzza S, *Governing by Contract: Procuring for Value. Creating Value through Public Contracts* (Editoriale Scientifica 2021).

Valaguzza S, *Sustainable Development in Public Contracts: An Example of Strategic Regulation* (Editoriale Scientifica 2016).

Venturi F, 'The farm to fork strategy. A comprehensive but cautious approach to "multidimensional" food sustainability' [2021] (1) Rivista Quadrimestrale di Diritto dell'Ambiente 70.

Vernile S, *Dall'economia circolare al principio di circolarità* (Giappichelli 2024).

Wennerås P, *Towards an ever-greener Union? Competence in the field of the environment and beyond* [2008] 45 Common market law review 1645.

CHAPTER 12

Regulatory and Market-Based Incentives for Combating Food Waste: the Italian Example

Laura Costantino

Summary

1 Food Waste or Surplus Production?

The current political climate, in which the achievement of sustainability-related objectives has been placed at the centre of public planning, represents a crucial turning point in the implementation of measures that are completely different from the past, not only from a substantive point of view but also from an implementation standpoint.

With the European Agricultural Policy, a new model is emerging for the implementation and monitoring of measures for the agricultural sector based on performance. The overarching strategy will be defined at the European level, but it will be the Member States that devise roadmaps for achieving these objectives in National Strategic Plans that will be tailored to the needs of agricultural systems in their territories and identify key performance indicators to monitor progress.[1]

At the national level, the model is general enough for each State to be able to adapt the strategies it will use to achieve the Policy's stringent sustainability objectives (social, environmental, and economic) to its own territory.

---

1 Stefano Masini and Vito Rubino (eds), *La sostenibilità in agricoltura e la riforma della* PAC (Cacucci 2021); Ferdinando Albisinni, 'La nuova PAC e le competenze degli Stati membri tra riforme annunciate e scelte praticate' [2020] (1) Rivista di Diritto Agrario 43; Stefano Masini, 'Pianificazione nazionale e ruolo di Stato e Regioni nell'ottica della nuova PAC' in Stefano Masini, Vito Rubino (eds) (n 1), 39.

In other words, governance is shifted from a top-down approach to a more local approach.[2] This clarification is not negligible, when you consider the normative objectives of the Common Agricultural Policy (CAP) contained in Article 39 of the Treaty on the Functioning of the European Union (TFEU). From the outset, agriculture has been assigned a significant place within the structure of European public policy as a productive activity of essential goods for the economic autonomy of Member States. The objectives of the CAP consist in both ensuring that the single market can guarantee internal food supply and that citizens have guaranteed access to food at a reasonable price. To guarantee adequate production in quantitative terms, and ensure market stability, the CAP further specifies adequate income for agricultural entrepreneurs and all agricultural workers.

The first approach to implementing the CAP, considering the political and economic context of the post-war period, promoted and incentivised production quantity. And, indeed, this objective was clearly expressed in several sectors.

The CAP's initial version, aimed at encouraging quantity, had a dual nature: the presence of a structural productive surplus and its management through a series of instruments that were implemented and diversified according to the product. The management of agricultural surpluses has always represented a central issue of European agricultural policy.[3] However, within the governance system of agrifood production that focused on protecting the European market, the CAP rules resulted in the production of surpluses without any specific regulation to limit them.

Over the last thirty years, the CAP has evolved by decoupling the provision of aid from production quantity, instead structuring targeted aid interventions and agricultural support. While structural overproduction has, as a result,

---

2 Laura Costantino, *Profili giuridici dei sistemi produttivi agroalimentari locali nell'era della sostenibilità* (Giappichelli 2024).

3 Francis G Snyder, *Diritto agrario della Comunità Europea* (Lefebvre Giuffré 1990); Antonio Iannarelli, 'Il diritto agrario comunitario alla fine degli anni Ottanta' in ibid, 171; Luigi Costato, 'Il 2 ° piano Mansholt e la legislazione agraria italiana' [1972] (1) Rivista di Diritto Agrario 219; Ferdinando Albisinni and Luigi Costato (eds), *Trattato breve di diritto agrario italiano e comunitario* (4th ed Wolters Kluwer—CEDAM 2023); Paolo De Caterini, 'Politiche comunitarie, I) Politica agricola', *Enciclopedia Giuridica* (1998); Emilio Cappelli and Sergio Ventura, 'Problemi giuridici dell'agricoltura comunitaria' [1964] III Rivista di Diritto Agrario 4; Joseph A McMahon, *EU Agricultural Law* (OUP 2008); Danièle Bianchi, *La politique agricole commune (PAC). Toute la PAC, rien d'autre que la PAC!* (Bruylant 2006); Giancarlo Olmi, 'Agricoltura in diritto comunitario', *Digesto delle Discipline pubblicistiche* (1987) 118; ibid, 'Common organisation of agricultural markets at the stage of the single market' (1967) 5 Common market law review 359.

decreased, cyclical surpluses due to various production and market variables nonetheless continue to plague the agrifood sector.

The disruptive emergence of the phenomenon of food waste is therefore a likely driver behind the EU's more recent economic policy choices aimed at gradually shifting regulatory interventions in the agrifood production system away from the interventionist measures that characterised the initial period of the CAP. In an economic system where there are no longer interventions on price setting or on the trends of agrifood production, the sustainability of value chains is instead left to the free market. In this scenario, food waste is inevitable when one considers the peculiarities and specificities of the agrifood sector compared to other market sectors. These include production dynamics linked to the variability of agricultural supply and the rigidity of demand for agrifood products, which generate food surpluses that, if not otherwise utilised, risk becoming waste.

The CAP adopts various techniques for managing productive surpluses, relating both to supply control and demand management. In the current governance system, surplus management tools, such as the withdrawal of products from the market, are not considered first-line approaches and are typically only used for the prevention and management of crises as a safety net in specific cases.

Thus, managing food waste has become a decisive issue, particularly in lieu of the changed structure of interventions in agricultural policy. The first text specifically addressing the issue of waste in the agrifood chain, the European Declaration Against Food Waste[4] dating to October 28, 2010, was followed by

4 Specific attention to the issue of food waste within European policies is found in the 'European Parliament Resolution of 19 January 2012 on how to avoid food wastage: strategies for a more efficient food chain in the EU' (2011/2175(INI)) and the 'European Parliament Resolution of 16 May 2017 on initiative on resource efficiency: reducing food waste, improving food safety'. It is further affirmed as a target for future European policy actions (2016/2223(INI)), as stated in the Conclusions of the EU Council, 10730/16 of 28 June 2016, 'Food Losses and Food Waste', where it is explicitly recognised that the cross-cutting nature of the issue necessitates action throughout the entire agrifood chain. The recent acknowledgement by European institutions of the need to address food waste challenges is situated within the broader context of European measures related to the circular economy, including: the Commission Communication to the European Parliament, the Council, the European Economic and Social Committee, and the Committee of the Regions, 'Roadmap to a Resource Efficient Europe', COM(2011)571 final, dated 20 September 2011; the Commission Communication to the European Parliament, the Council, the European Economic and Social Committee, and the Committee of the Regions, 'Towards a Circular Economy: A Zero Waste Programme for Europe', COM(2014)398 final, dated 2 July 2014; and Decision No. 1386/2013/EU of the European Parliament and of the Council of 20 November 2013 on a General Union Environment Action Programme to 2020, 'Living Well, Within the Limits of Our Planet'. Upon closer examination, the pursuit of

much consultation, study, and research aimed at adopting ad hoc measures, including legislative ones.

The Declaration first denounces the presence in the EU of 122 million citizens at risk of poverty, urging the Commission 'to encourage Member States to take action against food waste at all levels of the food supply chain, from production to consumption.'

The generation of food waste has significant ethical and economic consequences,[5] as well as health and environmental impacts, with food waste contributing considerably to global warming. In fact, the impact of food waste is so significant that it has been described as a 'parallel sector to the productive one', generating a considerable number of negative externalities.[6] From an economic perspective, food waste represents a financial loss to farmers and increased costs to consumers. From an environmental standpoint, the inefficient use of water and land results in a serious depletion of natural resources, as well as the release of greenhouse gases (GHGs) into the atmosphere. The Declaration states that for each ton of food waste avoided, the equivalent of 4.2 tons of CO_2 could be saved.

The analysis of different product types highlights that food loss varies by type of supply chain. For example, the production of fruits and vegetables is generally characterised by product losses during production (eg mechanical damage during harvesting operations) and storage (eg the short shelf life of fresh fruit and vegetables).

Considering the significant negative effects, briefly outlined above, of inefficiency in the supply chain and ambitious European goals to develop a circular

greater efficiency along the agrifood chain—from the standpoint of both agricultural enterprise profitability and the long-term stability of food prices for the final consumer—has long been the subject of study by European institutions. However, the absence of a comprehensive vision encompassing the various, specific challenges of the supply chain has led to the adoption of sectoral measures which, while successful in focusing attention on the most vulnerable aspects of the chain, suffer from a lack of overall coherence. Indicatively, on the same day—19 January 2012—two separate European Parliament Resolutions were adopted: the first, as mentioned, on strategies to prevent food waste, and the second on imbalances in the food distribution chain (following the Commission Communication on the better functioning of the food supply chain in Europe, COM(2009)591), with no cross-reference between the two documents. The quest for greater efficiency in the agrifood chain cannot disregard the efficient management of natural resources, fair remuneration of agricultural producers, and balanced contractual relationships along the chain, all within a global perspective. For a more detailed analysis, Laura Costantino, *La problematica degli sprechi nella filiera agroalimentare* (Cacucci 2008).

5 FAO, *Food wastege footprint. Impacts on natural resources. Summary report* (Rome 2013).

6 Luis Gonzàlez Vaqué, 'Food loss and waste in the European Union: a new challenge for the Food law?' [2015] 10 European Food and Feed Law Review 20.

economy, the fight against food waste fits squarely within the broader objectives of the 2030 Agenda and the goal of building a sustainable food system.[7] The Communication on the Green Deal and the Farm to Fork Strategy contemplate combating food waste both from the perspective of seeking greater supply chain sustainability and to reduce waste.

In this context, this chapter focuses on analysing the national regulatory framework on food waste, with an eye towards the rules to prevent and/or manage its generation, both during agricultural production and in the subsequent processing, distribution, and sales phases.

Multiple factors lead to the creation of food waste: climatic events damaging harvests, the need to comply with aesthetic and quality standards, the economic disadvantage of harvesting agricultural products due to excessively low prices, and consumer behaviour. Alongside these aspects, others peculiar to the agrifood supply chain come into play, namely the structural dependence of supply on the concentration of purchasing demand and the strong market power of large-scale retail distribution (GDO).

An impact on the possible creation of food waste is also linked to the development of European legislation on food safety, insofar as it raises the quality and safety standards of agrifood products, leading to products that fall short being removed from the market. Consider, for example, non-compliant labels or unsold foods that have passed their maximum shelf life.

Thus, the transversal nature of the issue is evident, as is the need to investigate not only the regulations specifically aimed at combating the phenomenon but also the legal instruments that functionally affect the reduction of inefficiencies in the supply chain.

2 Preventive Instruments to Properly Manage Agrifood Production

Within the framework of European legal instruments introduced by the new CAP aimed at rationalising agricultural production, it is interesting to focus

7 Irene Canfora, 'Agenda 2030, agricoltura e alimentazione' in Paolo Borghi and others (eds), *Trattato di diritto alimentare italiano e dell'Unione europea* (Giuffrè 2024) 25; Pamela Lattanzi, 'La transizione verso un sistema alimentare sostenibile nel Green Deal' in Paolo Borghi and others (eds), *Trattato di diritto alimentare italiano e dell'Unione europea* (Giuffrè 2024) 29. With specific reference to the topic, see Gioia Maccioni, 'La legislazione sugli sprechi alimentari' in Paolo Borghi and others (eds), *Trattato di diritto alimentare italiano e dell'Unione europea* (Giuffrè 2024) 888. More general, Christian Reynolds and others, 'Halving Food Loss and Waste in the EU by 2030: the major steps needed to accelerate progress' (WWF-WRAP 2020).

on the role assigned to market actors, from the perspective of preventing the creation of waste or productive surpluses.

Agricultural cooperatives have always played a central role in the management of productive surpluses and the various interventions aimed at recovering products not placed on the market. Producer Organisations (POs) linking production and the market represent the instrument entrusted by the EU, and supported by EU law, with balancing the agricultural and purchasing enterprises. This was initially regulated through the pricing system and later through tools to discourage production, since the 1970s especially for the functioning of the fruit and vegetable sector.

POs seek to establish market balance and stability through their assigned regulatory and operational powers. This includes functions related to market rationalisation, through the concentration of supply and production planning, and even the withdrawal of products from the market and the qualitative diversification of production, via production and marketing rules set by the PO. Therefore, POs play a central role in preventing the creation of surpluses, insofar as they are called upon to optimise production by using production planning tools in both qualitative and quantitative terms, relative to demand.

Moreover, POs perform other key functions related to sustainability, such as promoting the use of sustainable production methods, innovative practices, economic competitiveness, and the management and valorisation of by-products.

From a different perspective, within the framework of supply chain management, interbranch organisations, composed by farmers and processors or traders in the supply chain, also play a significant role. Among the tasks assigned to interbranch organisations, Article 157 of EU Regulation No. 1308/2013[8] also specifies encouraging healthy and responsible consumption, enhancing the marketability of by-products, and reducing and managing waste. Interbranch agreements, therefore, also stipulate these as objectives in line with European policies aimed, ultimately, at establishing a circular economy.

National legislation, implementing the provisions of Regulation (EU) 1308/2013, as amended by Regulation (EU) No. 2117/2021, establishes the rules

8 Regulation (EU) 1308/2013 of European Parliament and of the Council of 17 December 2013 establishing a common organisation of the markets in agricultural products and repealing Council Regulations (EEC) No 922/72, (EEC) No 234/79, (EC) No 1037/2001 and (EC) No 1234/2007 (EEC) 922/72, (EEC) 234/79, (EC) 1037/2001 <1234/2007, https://eur-lex.europa.eu/legal-content/IT/TXT/PDF/?uri=CELEX:32013R1308&qid=1750872222899> accessed 24 June 2025.

regarding the recognition of POs, most recently through the Ministerial Decree of September 29, 2022.

The decree specifically defines the activities that POs should carry out, in line with the objectives set out in the current CAP regulations. Among these, provisions concerning the destination of products withdrawn from the market are noteworthy. POs may allocate such products to free food distribution, biomass production for energy purposes, animal feed, non-food industrial processing—including alcohol distillation—or, if these destinations are not feasible, biodegradation or composting.

Financial aid from the European Union covers all expenses incurred by the PO to withdraw products from the market and redirect them to free distribution, as long as such products are delivered to '[c]haritable entities recognised under national and regional legislation in the matter, accredited by paying agencies according to criteria established by AGEA and registered in the national list maintained by the same Agency' (Article 23).

This provision is nothing more than the implementation of what is set forth in Article 52 of Regulation (EU) No. 2115/2021 regarding financial aid for fruit and vegetable products.[9]

Therefore, European legislation encourages the use of free food distribution in cases of market withdrawals by POs by fully financing the related operations. This measure is particularly important considering the issues that will be discussed later concerning the role of recipient entities in Italy. Indeed, when fruit and vegetable POs are engaged in the recovery of food products during the marketing phase, they receive specific aid to cover the expenses incurred. This aid should support them in choosing to move towards a system of redistribution of unsold products rather than disposing of them.

Structuring the agricultural production system around recognised aggregative entities within POs establishes a proper market structure. This supports not only the profitability of all the operators involved, but also significantly contributes to achieving sustainability and circularity objectives in production.

---

9 Regulation (EU) 2021/2115 of the European Parliament and of the Council of 2 December 2021 establishing rules on support for strategic plans to be drawn up by Member States under the Common Agricultural Policy (CAP Strategic Plans) and financed by the European Agricultural Guarantee Fund (EAGF) and by the European Agricultural Fund for Rural Development (EAFRD), repealing Regulations (EU) No 1305/2013 and (EU) No 1307/2013 <https://eur-lex.europa.eu/legal-content/EN/TXT/PDF/?uri=CELEX:32021R2115&qid=1750873584465> accessed 24 June 2025.

3 The Italian Legal Framework for Combating Food Waste

Italy and France are credited with being the first countries in Europe to adopt specific laws aimed at limiting food waste, prioritising the free distribution of all foodstuffs that, for various reasons, do not reach the final consumer.

The search for a regulatory response to counter the phenomenon of food waste was accelerated by the approval of the Milan Charter, the final document of Expo 2015, an event that acted as a megaphone for the theme of 'food'. The document focuses on the right to food and the equitable distribution of resources at the global level and examines the role various actors—namely consumers, members of civil society, and businesses—could play in helping feed the world population while respecting the environment and future development.

The Charter calls on national and international institutions to adopt legal rules that make food accessible, simplify existing food safety regulations, and adopt measures to combat food waste. It places significant emphasis on cooperation and supply chain agreements to improve the forecasting of food demand and on the need to improve production, storage, and logistics in the agrifood supply chain to minimise food waste.

3.1 *The Gadda Law*

On August 19, 2016, Law No. 166 titled '*Disposizioni concernenti la donazione e la distribuzione di prodotti alimentari e farmaceutici a fini di solidarietà sociale e per la limitazione degli sprechi*' or 'Provisions concerning the donation and distribution of food and pharmaceutical products for social solidarity purposes and to limit waste' (also known as the Gadda Law) came into force.[10] The law aims to reduce waste across the full product lifecycle: production, processing, distribution, and administration of food, pharmaceutical, and other products through the recovery and donation of food surpluses for social solidarity purposes, prioritising their use for human consumption.

It falls within the scope of interventions aimed at limiting negative impacts on the environment and natural resources by reducing waste production and promoting reuse and recycling to extend the lifecycle of products. Finally, it is consistent with the general objectives established by the National Waste Prevention Program and the National Plan for the Prevention of Food Waste.

10 Legge 19 agosto 2016, n. 166, Disposizioni concernenti la donazione e la distribuzione di prodotti alimentari e farmaceutici a fi ni di solidarietà sociale e per la limitazione degli sprechi, Gazzetta ufficiale n. 202 del 30 agosto 2016 <https://www.gazzettaufficiale.it/eli/gu/2016/08/30/202/sg/pdf> accessed 24 June 2025.

The Gadda Law defines the goods subject to regulation, the entities called upon to act against food waste, and the methods of use of the indicated goods. Article 2 sets out certain definitions which mainly pertain to the agrifood supply chain and the scope of application of which appears to be limited to the enforcement of the law itself. Definitions are provided for food sector operators, recipient entities, food surpluses, food waste, donation, minimum conservation periods, and expiration dates.[11] It is worth noting that the definitional scope does not distinguish between production surpluses in the field and industrial production waste, which are the result of different causes and subject to specific regulations. The definitions proposed by the Italian legislator, instead, find their usefulness exclusively within the logic of donation for social utility purposes.

Legally, donation is defined in Article 2, letter e) as the transfer of goods free of charge, and the provisions of Title V of Book II of the Civil Code related to validity do not apply.

The legal act consists in the completion of the transfer of goods wherein the moment in which responsibility for maintaining hygienic and sanitary requirements (Article 5) passes from donor to recipient.

Field collection of agricultural products is a different story: to comply with hygiene and food safety regulations (Article 3, para 5), the free transfer may take place directly in the field, but the harvesting and collection of agricultural products must be carried out directly by and under the responsibility of the recipient entities.

Articles 3, 4, and 5 of the Gadda Law represent the core of the regulation, as they specify the methods of free transfer of food and the priority order of its use. Food sector operators may transfer food surpluses free of charge to recipient entities who may collect them directly or through third parties. Once the food is received, the recipients are required to allocate it to the needy. Article 3 specifies the priority order for the use of food surpluses: human consumption or, alternatively and exclusively for those foods unfit for human consumption, animal feed and composting.

Food sector operators may also transfer surpluses free of charge beyond the minimum conservation period, provided that the integrity of the primary packaging and appropriate storage conditions are guaranteed. Unsold finished

---

11 For a detailed analysis of the legislative text, see Anna I Trapè, 'Lo spreco alimentare e la legge italiana n.166 del 2016' [2017] 2 Rivista di Diritto Agrario 263; Laura Costantino, 'Proposta di legge contro gli sprechi alimentari: analisi e inquadramento sistematico' [2016] 2 Diritto Agroalimentare 401; Laura Costantino, *La problematica degli sprechi nella filiera agroalimentare* (Cacucci 2018) chapter 3, part II.

bakery products may be donated by retailers, large-scale distribution, producers, and the catering sector within 24 hours after production.

Article 5 establishes that food sector operators who carry out transfers must adopt practices that ensure the hygienic and sanitary safety of the food. Pursuant to Law no. 155 of July 16, 2003,[12] which equates recipient entities with consumers, food sector operators are responsible for the food until the moment of delivery to the recipients; they must also adopt necessary measures to prevent risks of mixing or interchanging products intended for different uses as provided by the law.

An incentive measure is contained in Article 17, which provides that municipalities may apply a proportional reduction coefficient on waste tariffs (when duly certified), based on the quantity of goods and products withdrawn from sale and donated, aiming at tax relief for those who donate food surpluses free of charge.

Eight years after the entry into force of the Gadda law, it is useful to propose some analytical observations, considering the—albeit few—data available. As previously mentioned, the regulatory approach is focused on avoiding food becoming waste and negatively impacting the environment, rather than being used for social utility purposes.

If, therefore, the tool identified by the law is donation, it is necessary to investigate the role of the involved parties. On one side are companies operating along the agrifood chain which will need to organise or reorganise their production activities to distinguish among the foods not placed or removed from the market, those suitable for free transfer. A shift towards reorganising activities is called for, though approaches will vary greatly depending on the product, whether perishable or potentially storable for a certain period. Considering the cost of internal reorganisation for companies, fiscal incentives could be further enhanced to encourage them to transition to donation.

As noted earlier, full coverage of expenses incurred for the recovery of unsold, fresh fruit and vegetables is provided if the operations are carried out by POs. This underscores the importance of a well-structured market and the achievement of the broader objectives of the current CAP, which includes the reduction of food waste using the aggregative tools provided by European legislation. Indeed, if best practices in managing unsold fresh produce were widespread among POs, the entire redistribution chain would benefit, with greater impact and effectiveness in meeting sustainability goals.

---

12 Legge 25 giugno 2003, n. 155, Disciplina della distribuzione dei prodotti alimentari a fini di solidarietà sociale, Gazzetta ufficiale n. 150 del 1 luglio 2003, <https://www.gazzettaufficiale.it/eli/gu/2003/07/01/150/sg/pdf> accessed 24 June 2025.

Public administrations, in drafting food policies or structuring regional policies to implement broader national objectives, should focus on raising awareness of the available legal tools as well as encouraging virtuous behaviours, while respecting their specific roles.

Another significant element regarding the capacity of recipient entities to intervene concerns the size of the companies involved: among Italian food processing companies, 85% of large enterprises operating in sectors such as fresh products (meat, fish, fruits and vegetables, dairy), oils, pasta, and baked goods make food donations annually, donating an average of about 332 tons of surpluses to organisations that recover them for social purposes.[13] The percentage drops to 60% for medium-sized companies and falls to 52% for small processing companies.

Also interesting is the internal assignment of responsibilities related to food donations, which in most cases is jointly assigned to multiple roles (production manager, quality and food safety manager, logistics, supply chain management), while the management of surpluses by sustainability and corporate social responsibility functions appears to be much less common.

Looking ahead, the role of the third sector could be strengthened, without which the entire regulatory framework would be completely ineffective. Increasing donations without enhancing the capacity and resources of the associations involved in redistribution risks overburdening these organisations, which will only be able to collect part of the donated food, most likely the easiest to recover.[14]

3.2 *Other Supporting Regulations*

Useful regulatory tools to combat food waste are also present in other laws, which have broader systemic objectives but align with the purpose analysed here.

First among these is the National Strategy for Sustainable Development,[15] approved by the Interministerial Committee for Ecological Transition on September 18, 2023. The Strategy has been updated in line with the

13 Paola Garrone and others, *Indagine sulle eccedenze e sullo spreco alimentare in Italia: l'industria della trasformazione alimentare*, (Fondazione Banco Alimentare 2023).

14 A valuable comparative perspective on the various experiences in combating food waste is offered in Simone Busetti and Noemi Pace (eds), *Food Loss and Waste Policy: From Theory to Practice* (Routledge 2023); Daniele Camoni, 'La lotta contro lo spreco alimentare nel diritto comparato' [2023] 2 Rivista di diritto alimentare 5.

15 The strategy constitutes the national reference framework for environmental and territorial planning, programming, and assessment processes. It implements Article 34 of Legislative Decree No. 152/2006.

objectives of the National Recovery and Resilience Plan (PNRR), particularly Mission 2—Green Revolution and Ecological Transition—and its component 'sustainable agriculture and circular economy'. Objective 4 of the Strategy, 'sustainable production and consumption models', considers systemic food waste to be an indicator of waste production, thereby linking the goal of combating food waste with the goal of reducing overall waste within the framework of the circular economy model.

The National Strategic Plan, which identifies national tools for achieving CAP objectives, also includes combating food waste within its section on strategies aimed at more efficient resource use and the reuse of by-products, framed within the objectives of the circular economy, such as measures related to winemaking by-products which target the reuse of agricultural outputs.

Another central objective of the Plan is to strengthen communication about the value of sustainability for food production and certification, which are seen as fundamental to stimulating a radical change in consumer eating habits. Within this scope, the Plan foresees information campaigns targeted at operators and consumers to prevent and reduce waste.

Finally, an important tool linked to the creation of waste is the regulation of below-cost sales, defined by Article 1 of Presidential Decree No. 218 of April 6, 2001[16] as the:

> [S]ale to the public of one or more products at a price lower than that resulting from purchase invoices increased by value-added tax and any other tax or duty related to the nature of the product and decreased by any discounts or contributions attributable to the same product.

Selling products below production cost negatively affects the market, for reasons related both to competition protection and the stability of the markets themselves. In the agrifood sector, below-cost sales pose an additional problem because they directly impact the balance of contractual relations along the supply chain and the profitability of agricultural businesses.

However, the legislator allows below-cost sales in the case of fresh and perishable food products, food products near their expiration date, and holiday- or festivity-specific products after the date or occasion of their celebration has passed (Article 2, Presidential Decree No. 2018/2001).

---

16 Decreto del Presidente della Repubblica 6 aprile 2001, n. 218, Regolamento recante disciplina delle vendite sottocosto, a norma dell'articolo 15, comma 8, del decreto legislativo 31 marzo 1998, n. 114, in GU n.134 del 12-06-2001, <https://www.gazzettaufficiale.it/eli/gu/2001/06/12/134/sg/pdf> accessed 24 June 2025.

The same regulation related to contracts for the transfer of agricultural and food products—implementing EU Directive 2019/633 on unfair trading practices along the agrifood supply chain[17]—permits below-cost sales of fresh and perishable agricultural and food products that remain unsold and are at risk of spoiling (Article 7, Legislative Decree No. 198/2021).[18]

Although these regulations belong to market regulation frameworks, the rules on below-cost sales help combat food waste in retail sales, representing a useful tool both for consumers, who benefit from lower prices, and for supply chain businesses, which avoid having to dispose of unsold products.

4 Food Waste at the Intersection of Citizens' Rights and Public Administration Obligations

The fight against food waste is today framed within a broader regulatory context, which at the European level aims at building a sustainable 'food system'. Recently, legal rules have been developed that, starting from the objectives of the 2030 Agenda, seek to impact the entire agrifood supply chain, introducing provisions concerning production, commercial relations among operators within the chain, and consumer information.

Actors in the agrifood supply chain are therefore responsible for complying with sustainability rules in order to steer the agrifood system towards the model the European Union has committed to implementing within the framework of international objectives.

At the same time, the role of public administrations regains central importance, especially considering the relative retreat of public guidance during the years of market globalisation. Enterprises must thus adapt their market conduct in compliance with rules increasingly affecting both their internal and external organisation, even when operating outside the EU.

---

17 Directive (EU) 2019/633 of the European Parliament and of the Council of 17 April 2019 on unfair trading practices in business-to-business relationships in the agricultural and food supply chain <https://eur-lex.europa.eu/legal-content/EN/TXT/PDF/?uri=CELEX:32019L0633&qid=1750874431811> accessed 24 June 2025.

18 Decreto Legislativo 8 novembre 2021, n. 198, Attuazione della direttiva (UE) 2019/633 del Parlamento europeo e del Consiglio, del 17 aprile 2019, in materia di pratiche commerciali sleali nei rapporti tra imprese nella filiera agricola e alimentare nonché dell'articolo 7 della legge 22 aprile 2021, n. 53, in materia di commercializzazione dei prodotti agricoli e alimentari, in GU n.285 del 30-11-2021—Suppl. Ordinario n. 41, <https://www.gazzettaufficiale.it/eli/gu/2021/11/30/285/so/41/sg/pdf> accessed 24 June 2025.

From this perspective, the fight against food waste takes on a forward-looking dimension: in the absence of rules imposing a direct obligation on enterprises to act (as in the French regulatory framework, for example), the reduction of food waste will be an effect of compliance with rules aimed at structuring a sustainable food system. This outcome is further facilitated by the introduction of incentives, which, through tax relief, offer enterprises an alternative route to dispose of unsold products.

However, when framing the issue with reference to the nature of the goods involved, the fight against food waste assumes a different dimension, as it is necessarily linked to the protection of rights.

It is evident that public institutions bear responsibility for ensuring the right to food, from a dual perspective: first, with regard to the structuring of social policies aimed at safeguarding the rights of citizens; and second, with regard to the proper management of territorial policies, ranging from the protection and enhancement of rural areas to the implementation of instruments designed to intervene in local food distribution processes. Consider, for example, the proliferation of local food policies, recently translated into programmatic and regulatory documents adopted at the municipal level, which seek to support the construction of sustainable food systems based on territorial analysis. Such food policies invariably include measures to combat food waste, often grounded in the free redistribution of food.

Nevertheless, these two levels remain complementary: Member States are obligated to respect the right to food, as prescribed by the well-known Article 11 of the International Covenant on Economic, Social, and Cultural Rights. However, free redistribution as a tool to combat food waste cannot exhaust the array of measures implementable within the legal system, unless one accepts the paradox of a food system that must create waste to meet the social needs of indigent citizens. The protection of individual rights, rather, is far broader and can generate positive externalities and guide food systems towards a reasonable balance between territorial productive capacity and food consumption.

Bibliography

Albisinni F, 'La nuova PAC e le competenze degli Stati membri tra riforme annunciate e scelte praticate' [2020] (1) Rivista di Diritto Agrario 43.

Albisinni F and Costato L (eds), *Trattato breve di diritto agrario italiano e comunitario* (Wolters Kluwer CEDAM 2023).

Bianchi D, *La politique agricole commune* (PAC). *Toute la PAC, rien d'autre que la PAC!* (Bruylant 2006).

Busetti S, Pace N (eds), *Food Loss and Waste Policy: From Theory to Practice* (Routledge 2023).

Camoni D., *La lotta contro lo spreco alimentare nel diritto comparato* [2023] (2) Rivista di diritto alimentare 5.

Canfora I, 'Agenda 2030, agricoltura e alimentazione' in Borghi P, Canfora I, Di Lauro A, Russo L (eds), *Trattato di diritto alimentare italiano e dell'Unione europea* (Giuffrè 2024) 25.

Cappelli E and Ventura S, 'Problemi giuridici dell'agricoltura comunitaria' [1964] III Rivista di Diritto Agrario 4.

Costantino L, 'La proposta di legge contro gli sprechi alimentari: analisi ed inquadramento sistematico' in [2016] 2 Dir. Agroalimentare 401 ff.

Costantino L, *La problematica degli sprechi nella filiera agroalimentare* (Cacucci 2018).

Costantino L, *Profili giuridici dei sistemi produttivi agroalimentari locali nell'era della sostenibilità* (Giappichelli 2024).

Costato L, 'Il 2 ° piano Mansholt e la legislazione agraria italiana' [1972] I Rivista di Diritto Agrario 219.

De Caterini P, 'Politiche comunitarie, I) Politica agricola', *Enciclopedia Giuridica* (1998).

González Vaqué L, 'Food loss and waste in the European Union: a new challenge for the Food law?' [2015] 1 European Food and Feed Law Review 20.

Iannarelli A, 'Il diritto agrario comunitario alla fine degli anni ottanta' in Snyder FG, Diritto agrario della Comunità Europea (Lefebvre Giuffré 1990) 171.

Lattanzi P, 'La transizione verso un sistema alimentare sostenibile nel Green Deal' in Borghi P, Canfora I, Di Lauro A, Russo L (eds), *Trattato di diritto alimentare italiano e dell'Unione europea* (Giuffrè 2024).

Maccioni G, 'La legislazione sugli sprechi alimentari' in Borghi P, Canfora I, Di Lauro A, Russo L (eds), *Trattato di diritto alimentare italiano e dell'Unione europea* (Giuffrè 2024) 888.

Masini S and Rubino V (eds), *La sostenibilità in agricoltura e la riforma della* PAC (Cacucci 2021).

McMahon JA, *EU Agricultural Law* (OUP 2008).

Olmi G, 'Agricoltura in diritto comunitario', *Digesto delle Discipline pubblicistiche* (1987) 118.

Olmi G, 'Common organization of agricultural markets at the stage of the single market (1967) 5 Common market law review 359.

Garrone P, Randellini N, Scotti G, Valentini G, *Indagine sulle eccedenze e sullo spreco alimentare in Italia: l'industria della trasformazione alimentare*, (Fondazione Banco Alimentare 2023).

Reynolds C, Boulding A, Pollock H, Sweet OBEN, Ruiz J, Draeger de Teran T, *Halving Food Loss and Waste in the EU by 2030: the major steps needed to accelerate progress* (WWF-WRAP 2020).
Snyder FG, *Diritto agrario della Comunità Europea* (Lefebvre Giuffré 1990).
Trapè I, 'Lo spreco alimentare e la legge italiana n.166 del 2016' [2017] 2 Rivista di Diritto Agrario 263.

Conclusions

Providing concluding remarks to research so rich in suggestions and perspectives is no small task. The chapters in this volume not only cut cross the legal sphere but bravely go beyond the scope of the law, highlighting the need for engagement with different scientific fields, perspectives, and ever-evolving paradigms.

This volume's title, 'Food innovation and legal challenges' is instructive: the latter is clearly shaped and influenced by the former. We often view the law as slow-moving and unilateral. What this volume reminds us is that the law, at its most effective, is both dynamic and reciprocal, at times responding to new scientific developments and, at others, anticipating them. The law is called upon to navigate uncharted territory, whereas science simultaneously provides warnings about pressing global issues (such as the climate crisis and the importance of the environment as a complex ecosystem), and offers solutions or remedies (even if incomplete) to these issues.

This dance between law and science finds an extraordinary new stage with sustainability.

A new word (and, perhaps, a new world), that promises a new future, sustainability provides a reprieve from the concern that what we are doing (our model of development, our individual and collective behaviors) has an impact that the planet may not be able to bear.

In this complex relationship, the food system—the chain (production and consumption) of food—can play a significant role, a concept highlighted early on by the author Jonathan Safran Foer in his popular book on the climate crisis[1].

Firstly, two methodological reflections.

As a constitutional scholar, and, at the same time, a scholar of the complex world of interests, conflicts, anxieties, and hopes that define the fields of bioethics and biolaw, I feel a constant tension to expand the boundaries of my scientific and disciplinary field of reference. This principle also applies to the legal realm, more generally, as it is pushed to rapidly adapt to new problems and transitions (especially the ecological transition and the AI revolution) that characterise our time.

The ecological transition is, in a sense, the symbol of a modernity marked by unprecedented, even unthinkable crises, which give to the law a mission

1 Jonathan Safran Foer, *We are the Weather: Saving the Planet Begins at Breakfast* (Hamish Hamilton, 2019).

that perhaps, in these terms, it has never had: to guarantee the survival of the human community over time. This goes well beyond simply facilitating social coexistence—it is looking to the future not as scenery to be reconfigured or improved compared to the present but rather as a foundational structure to be urgently salvaged, preserving conditions before they further deteriorate from today's. Faced with the unprecedented nature of certain challenges and the confusion they cause, the law responds with new terms that convey new narratives, seemingly alluding to the need for a global renewal of social, economic and political organisational models. In this way, the word sustainability expresses a holistic scope, transversally touching every segment of individual and collective life.

Rightly, Lorenza Violini, in her introductory notes, speaks of sustainability not only as 'a crucial third dimension to the relationship between law and science' but also a concept that goes beyond the scientific or legal to take on a 'deeply political' imprint, 'reflecting the global discourse of the 2020s'. Sustainable development is a kind of summarizing principle for the great issues of modernity. When we talk about it, then, we think of a 'comprehensive model of development that considers environmental health, economic stability, and social equity'.

Indeed, the relationship between science, technology, and law is the main and most controversial theme through which modernity can be understood. Science and law meet and interact in almost all areas of the law, through different modalities and variables.

As noted, this is not a one-way relationship. It does not proceed in a single direction, from science as the source of truth and certainty, to law and politics as intrinsically biased and imperfect.

Instead, most of the time, it is a relationship between two uncertainties.

Science is also uncertain and imperfect. In fact, errors (and sometimes unexpected discoveries) are simply the normal condition of scientific knowledge, the very premise for the continuous updates that mark scientific research and its practical applications.

Thus, the relationship between law and science is defined by two dimensions of discretionality, meaning that every decision carries a condition of provisionality; it holds as long as the scientific parameter remain assured.

This applies to science as equally as it does to the law.

For the law, the inadequacy of its cognitive mechanisms is exacerbated by the difficulty of mediating between scientific advancements, social claims, and ethical, religious, and cultural norms. Nevertheless, even for the law, uncertainty can have positive effects—it means dynamism, and attention to and awareness of the plurality of ideas and values, as well as the ability to adapt to new developments in the scientific, social, and cultural fields.

The Constitution (my original field of study), with its open-ended and indeterminate clauses (life, dignity, personal identity, equality, health, environment, and today—after the 2022 constitutional reform—biodiversity and ecosystems), best represents a normative universe capable of keeping pace with the changes in social structures induced by new scientific and technological possibilities, without abandoning the task of filtering them through constitutional principles and guiding them, rather than simply adapting to them.

Scientific 'facts' can thus penetrate constitutional clauses, reworking their meanings and potential applications. In fact, in many cases, the law must take scientific facts into account if it wants to maintain its legitimacy (as many rulings of our Constitutional Court outline, in particular 282/2002 and 151/2009).

From this, new possibilities and unforeseen options arise that, connected to the values of dignity, full personal development, and equality, aspire to become (and often succeed in becoming) rights, no less fundamental than the values from which they find nourishment and justification.

The constitutional 'container' is shaken. Specialised public functions to manage scientifically sensitive sectors are needed. Just think of the proliferation of independent Authorities to manage sectors where the need for scientific and technical expertise is particularly relevant, such as privacy, communications, antitrust requirements, energy, and indeed food.

Yet, the adaptive capacity of law does not mean that it functions merely as a sounding board for the transformations produced by scientific and technological development. The impact of science on the constitutional structure is not one-way; even science must maintain its 'measure', its balance with the fundamental values of society as identified in the Constitution and its principles. Constitutional law is full of stratifications, experiences, and principles; it is open towards new meanings but, at the same time, does not give up its guiding power, which has a central priority, an irreplaceable compass: human value and dignity. As Antonio Ruggeri writes, 'The Constitution is at the same time scientifically conditioned and conditioning, feeding partly from science but also orienting its developments and halting its expressions that harm human dignity'. It is a complex balance, far from obvious, but, as Ruggeri adds, 'the maintenance of this balance is the great bet of the constitutional State'[2].

2 Antonio Ruggeri, 'Mutamenti di contesto politico-istituzionale, progresso scientifico e tecnologico, Teoria della Costituzione' (2020) 1 Consulta online, 157.

Within the complex and multidimensional landscape of sustainability, it is becoming clear that the agrifood sector is an increasingly intriguing and complicated intersection between law and science.

This volume highlights many of these connection points.

Some are now 'classic' topics in biolaw, and particularly food law, such as the precautionary principle and the regulation of GMOs; the latter being a theme that today is enriched and altered via new technological possibilities posed by gene editing (as Maria Chiara Errigo's contribution highlights).

Alongside these, new issues and points of connection emerge between scientific and technological possibilities, sustainability needs, and legal and social regulation.

Let us think, especially, about the use of insects as edible resources. Insect farming, as Grilli explains very well in her chapter, can have a significant impact on environmental sustainability indicators of the global food system, reducing demand for and consumption of water, land, and energy.

This topic touches a raw nerve in the climate and ecological crisis. The problem is not only represented by the 'bad' oil companies and transport sector.

Grilli shows how 'livestock farming is one of the most environmentally impactful sectors ... Key contributors to the high environmental impact of livestock farming include enteric fermentation in ruminants, manure management emissions, and the inefficiency in feed conversion typical of conventional farming practices, in addition to extensive water and land use. In contrast, insects require significantly less feed than traditional livestock to produce an equivalent amount of protein'[3] (see also S. Pitto's chapter[4]).

Jonathan Safran Foer is right, then. We can (and must) save the planet *beginning at breakfast*: 'We are the flood, we are the Ark'. But 'we' includes all of us, with our consumption choices, our lifestyles, and our development model. And 'saving the planet' requires a profound restructuring of eating habits globally, considering the estimated growth of the world population in the next 20–30 years.

Among the new innovations of food sustainability, vertical farming technology could play an important role, which raises, in Pitto's analysis, 'diverse and multidisciplinary'[5] legal issues, starting with the qualification of the technique as an agricultural activity which would bring with it a whole host of consequences and implications, and even before that, almost 'ancestral' premises related to the relationship between agriculture and land.

3 See Grilli in this Volume, xx.
4 See Pitto in this Volume, xx.
5 See Pitto in this Volume, xx.

The law shows its ability to circumvent 'natural' obstacles here as well, adapting its definitions to new things advancing in the scientific and technological fields. As Pitto recalls, the Italian Court of Cassation also affirmed that agricultural activities need only a functional connection to land and not necessarily a strict physical one (See Court of Cassation, 07/03/2018, no. 5391).

Meanwhile, some regions, such as Lombardy, are beginning to regulate this new agricultural model, defining it. Lombardy Regional Law no. 21/2021 identifies 'vertical farming' as a 'cultivation system in closed growth chambers with full environmental control, without soil, or even without natural light, using vertical modules and techniques such as aquaponics, hydroponics, or aeroponics'.

Thus, these first regulations attest to the agricultural nature of vertical farming, but above all, they place it among the tools for mitigation or adaptation to the climate crisis[6].

As a constitutional scholar, I can say that this pioneering role of the regional authorities is important, as it shows the capacity for them to function as laboratories for innovative solutions that can anticipate and prepare national-level regulation. Regionalism is often talked about as being hard to find meaning in, with complaints about the repetitive nature of regional legislation, also due to the constraints imposed by European law and the broad interpretation that the Constitutional Court has given over the years to clauses regarding the exclusive and transverse legislative powers of the State (such as competition, essential levels of service, civil order, and environmental and ecosystem protection).

In these cases, however, the regions position themselves as experimental players, capable of reading and 'guiding' the novelties that come from scientific and technological development to meet emerging social and economic needs, while the state legislator may continue to rigidly adhere to traditionalism (as in the case of the 'strange' law, 172/2023, on 'cultured meat' or 'cell-based meat').

Finally, with the theme of Food Loss and Waste (FLW)—which Romano identifies as 'a real 'wicked problem''[7], intersecting with food security, environmental sustainability, and economic development —sustainability expresses its complex, multifaceted face, both environmentally and socio-economically.

Food waste produces absolutely unacceptable human and social costs. For this emergency, the law is called on to accomplish an important task: promoting technological innovations and social behaviours that can lower FLW levels, doing something meaningful to both combat climate change and protect the right to food.

6 Ibid xx.

7 See Romano this Volume, xx.

How the law will move, with rules that are either promotional or incentive-based, or with mandatory, prohibitive rules—and how binding those rules are—will be one of the main issues in bioethics in the 21st century.

Antonio D'Aloia

Bibliography

Ruggeri A, 'Mutamenti di contesto politico-istituzionale, progresso scientifico e tecnologico, Teoria della Costituzione' (2020) 1 Consulta online.

Safran Foer J, *We are the Weather: Saving the Planet Begins at Breakfast* (Hamish Hamilton 2019).

Index